Deleuze's Wake

SUNY series in Contemporary Continental Philosophy
Dennis J. Schmidt, editor

Deleuze's Wake

Tributes and Tributaries

Ronald Bogue

State University of New York Press

Published by
State University of New York Press, Albany

© 2004 State University of New York

All rights reserved

Printed in the United States of America

No part of this book may be used or reproduced in any manner whatsoever without written permission. No part of this book may be stored in a retrieval system or transmitted in any form or by any means including electronic, electrostatic, magnetic tape, mechanical, photocopying, recording, or otherwise without the prior permission in writing of the publisher.

For information, address State University of New York Press,
90 State Street, Suite 700, Albany, NY 12207

Production by Judith Block
Marketing by Jennifer Giovani

Bogue, Ronald, 1948–
    Deleuze's wake : tributes and tributaries / Ronald Bogue.
        p. cm. — (SUNY series in contemporary continental philosophy)
    Includes bibliographical references and index.
    ISBN 0-7914-6017-7 (hc : alk. paper) — ISBN 0-7914-6018-5 (pbk. : alk. paper)
    1. Deleuze, Gilles. I. Title. II. Series.

B2430.D454B64 2004
194—dc22
                                                              2003058125

10 9 8 7 6 5 4 3 2 1

For my mother,
Joanne Bogue

Contents

Acknowledgments		ix
Abbreviations		xi
Introduction		1

Tributes

1	Deleuze's Style	9
2	Is Deleuze a Postmodern Philosopher?	27
3	Deleuze, Foucault, and the Playful Fold of the Self	43

Tributaries

4	Minor Writing and Minor Literature	63
5	Becoming Metal, Becoming Death . . .	83
6	Word, Image, and Sound: Deleuze and Semiosis	109
7	Deleuze and the Invention of Images: From Beckett's Television Plays to Noh Drama	127
8	The Betrayal of God	143
Notes		161
Works Cited		177
Index		185

Acknowledgments

"Deleuze's Style" originally appeared in *Man and World* 29, no. 3 (July 1996): 251–268, © Kluwer Academic Publishers, reprinted with kind permission of Kluwer Academic Publishers.

"Is Deleuze a Postmodern Philosopher?" originally appeared under the title "Gilles Deleuze: Postmodern Philosopher?" in *Criticism* 32, no. 4 (fall 1990), 401–418, © Wayne State University Press, reprinted with kind permission.

"Deleuze, Foucault and the Playful Fold of the Self" originally appeared under the title "Foucault, Deleuze, and the Playful Fold of the Self" in *The Play of the Self*, ed. Ronald Bogue and Mihai Spariosu (Albany: State University of New York Press, 1994), 3–21.

"Minor Writing and Minor Literature" originally appeared in *Symploke* 5, no. 5. 1–2 (1997): 99–118, © *Symploke*, reprinted with kind permission.

"Word, Image, and Sound: Deleuze and Semiosis" originally appeared under the title "Word, Image and Sound: The Non-Representational Semiotics of Gilles Deleuze" in *Mimesis, Semiosis and Power*, ed. Ronald Bogue (Amsterdam and Philadelphia: John Benjamins Press, 1991), 77–97, © John Benjamins Press, reprinted with kind permission.

"Deleuze and the Invention of Images: From Beckett's Television Plays to Noh Drama" originally appeared in *The Comparatist* 26 (2002): 37–52, © *The Comparatist*, reprinted with kind permission.

"The Betrayal of God," originally appeared in *Deleuze and Religion*, ed. Mary Bryden (London: Routledge, 2001), 9–29, © Routledge, reprinted with kind permission.

Abbreviations

All translations from Deleuze, Guattari, and Deleuze-Guattari are my own. For works that have appeared in English translation, citations include page numbers of the original French edition followed by the page numbers of the corresponding passages in the English translation.

AO   Deleuze, Gilles, and Félix Guattari. *L'Anti-Oedipe: Capitalisme et schizophrénie I*. Paris: Minuit, 1972. *Anti-Oedipus*. Trans. Robert Hurley, Mark Seem, and Helen R. Lane. Minneapolis: University of Minnesota Press, 1977.

CC   Deleuze, Gilles. *Critique et clinique*. Paris: Minuit, 1993. *Essays Critical and Clinical*. Trans. Daniel W. Smith and Michael A. Greco. Minneapolis: University of Minnesota Press, 1997.

D   Deleuze, Gilles and Claire Parnet. *Dialogues*. Paris: Flammarion, 1977. *Dialogues*. Trans. Hugh Tomlinson and Barbara Habberjam. New York: Columbia University Press, 1987.

DR   Deleuze, Gilles. *Différence et répétition*. Paris: Presses Universitaires de France, 1968. *Difference and Repetition*. Trans. Paul Patton. New York: Columbia University Press, 1994.

E   Deleuze, Gilles. *L'Épuisé* (published with Samuel Beckett's *Quad*). Paris: Minuit, 1992. "The Exhausted." In *Essays Critical and Clinical,* trans. Daniel W. Smith and Michael A. Greco, 152–174. Minneapolis: University of Minnesota Press, 1997.

FB	Deleuze, Gilles. *Francis Bacon: Logique de la sensation*. Vol 1. Paris: Éditions de la différence, 1981.
IM	Deleuze, Gilles. *Cinéma 1: L'image-mouvement*. Paris: Minuit, 1983. *Cinema 1: The Movement-Image*. Trans. Hugh Tomlinson and Barbara Habberjam. Minneapolis: University of Minnesota Press, 1986.
IT	Deleuze, Gilles. *Cinéma 2: L'image-temps*. Paris, Minuit, 1985. *Cinema 2: The Time-Image*. Trans. Hugh Tomlinson and Robert Galeta. Minneapolis: University of Minnesota Press, 1989.
K	Deleuze, Gilles and Félix Guattari. *Kafka: Pour une littérature mineure*. Paris: Minuit, 1975. *Kafka: Toward a Minor Literature*. Trans. Dana Polan. Minneapolis: University of Minnesota Press, 1986.
LP	Deleuze, Gilles. *Le pli: Leibniz et la baroque*. Paris: Minuit, 1988. *The Fold: Leibniz and the Baroque*. Trans. Tom Conley. Minneapolis: University of Minnesota Press, 1993.
LS	Deleuze, Gilles. *Logique du sens*. Paris: Minuit, 1969. *The Logic of Sense*. Trans. Mark Lester, with Charles Stivale, ed. Constantin V. Boundas. New York: Columbia University Press, 1990.
MP	Deleuze, Gilles and Félix Guattari. *Mille plateaux: Capitalisme et schizophrénie, II*. Paris: Minuit, 1980. *A Thousand Plateaus*. Trans. Brian Massumi. Minneapolis: University of Minnesota Press, 1987.
N	Deleuze, Gilles. *Nietzsche*. Paris: Presses Universitaires de France, 1965.
NP	Deleuze, Gilles. *Nietzsche et la philosophie*. Paris: Presses Universitaires de France, 1962. *Nietzsche and Philosophy*. Trans. Hugh Tomlinson. Minneapolis: University of Minnesota Press, 1983.
PP	Deleuze, Gilles. *Pourparlers*. Paris: Minuit, 1990. *Negotiations*. Trans. Martin Joughin. New York: Columbia University Press, 1995.
PS	Deleuze, Gilles. *Proust et les signes*. 3rd ed. Paris: Presses Universitaires de France, 1976. *Proust and Signs: The Complete Edition*. Trans.

Richard Howard. Minneapolis: University of Minnesota Press, 2000.

QP   Deleuze, Gilles and Félix Guattari. *Qu'est-ce que la philosophie?* Paris: Minuit, 1991. *What Is Philosophy?* Trans. Hugh Tomlinson and Graham Burchell. New York: Columbia University Press, 1994.

S   Deleuze, Gilles. *Spinoza: philosophie pratique.* 2nd ed. Paris: Minuit, 1981. *Spinoza: Practical Philosophy.* Trans. Robert Hurley. San Francisco: City Lights, 1988.

SM   Deleuze, Gilles. *Présentation de Sacher-Masoch.* Paris: Minuit, 1967. *Masochism: An Interpretation of Coldness and Cruelty.* Trans. Jean McNeil. New York: G. Braziller, 1971.

Introduction

These chapters were all written in Gilles Deleuze's wake, the swells and ripples of which continue to expand in the years following his death November 4, 1995. Some are tributes to his thought offered in the long wake that still goes on, as special issues, commemorative volumes, and retrospective assessments follow one upon another (a recent instance being the special February 2002 issue of *Magazine littéraire*, "L'effet Deleuze"). Others address specific problems in Deleuze's writings, or attempt to tease out the implications of a few of his more cryptic remarks and extend them to domains beyond their original application. But all are conceived of as tributaries to the flows that issue from his works, efforts to speed the dispersion of his concepts.

This volume is by no means a philosophical *Finnegans Wake*, but a Joycean allusion is in order when reading Deleuze, given the importance of art in his thought and the fact that the artwork for him is "a chaosmos, as Joyce says, a composed chaos, neither foreseen nor preconceived" (QP 192/204). My focus throughout these chapters is on the aesthetic dimension of Deleuze's work, whether it be manifested in his analyses of various arts, in his own style, or in his treatment of extra-aesthetic topics in aesthetic terms. Deleuze consistently insists on the specificity of philosophical activity and the distinction between philosophical concepts and aesthetic sensations, but he also views philosophy as a mode of creation with close ties to the arts. "Philosophy," he says, "always consists of the invention of concepts" (PP 186/136). As a painter creates with lines and colors, so a philosopher creates with concepts. The arts make use of what Deleuze calls "percepts" and "affects," which may be distinguished from concepts, yet in certain regards the three are inextricable. "The concept does not move solely within itself (philosophical comprehension), it also moves in things and in us: it inspires in us new *percepts* and new *affects*, which constitute the non-philosophical comprehension of philosophy itself. And philosophy needs non-philosophical comprehension as much as philosophical comprehension" (PP 223/164). In this regard, "the affect, the percept and the concept are three inseparable powers; they go from art to philosophy and from philosophy to art" (PP 187/137). Thus for Deleuze the arts are neither within nor without philosophy. Rather, they form its membranous outer surface, its proper outside, and much of Deleuze's work may be viewed as an articulation of the passage of affects, percepts, and concepts across that permeable divide.

Perhaps no tribute to Deleuze is more fitting than an examination of his style. Deleuze is a philosopher, but he is also a writer, and the style of his thought reinforces the style of his prose. For Deleuze, style is a matter of stuttering, of fashioning a foreign language within one's own tongue. The object in writing is to instill movement in words, to engender a "becoming-other" of language. Deleuze sees philosophical style as preeminently syntactic, as an instigation of movement in concepts. The shape of thought, the line of its development, entails a style, and the unfolding of a line of thought echoes, resonates with, and plays through the elements of linguistic style. Deleuze's ideal, he says, is to create a page that is neatly closed in upon itself, like an egg, but such that the egg at the same time "leaks from all sides" (PP 25/14). The style of his thought is that of the leaking egg, a systematizing rigor in the invention of concepts that nevertheless engenders open movements in all directions. In "Deleuze's Style," I consider both his style of thought and the properly linguistic style of his writing, suggesting that the interacting rhythms, tone, and form of the two styles give rise to the peculiarly abstract, apersonal sensuality that informs much of his work.

Deleuze's styles of thought and writing are distinct and idiosyncratic, and many have regarded him as an anomalous outsider in modern French philosophy. Deleuze frequently calls for a thought that is "untimely," in the sense that Nietzsche gave the term: "untimely—that is to say, acting counter to our time and thereby acting on our time and, let us hope, for the benefit of a time to come" (*Untimely Meditations* 60). And indeed, Deleuze often pays little attention to the controversies and debates of his day. Yet at the same time, many have found in his thought an efficacy that is very much of the moment, a capacity to counter our time "for the benefit of a time to come." In an effort to situate Deleuze within our time, I consider in the second chapter the proposition that Deleuze might be deemed a "postmodern" philosopher. A list of the characteristics most frequently associated with postmodernism reads like a compendium of Deleuzian motifs, but his approach to those motifs gives them an unexpected verve and freshness. His thought is antifoundational, but without any anxiety about the death of philosophy or overcoming metaphysics. His historical analyses stress late capitalism's culture of simulation, surfaces, and schizophrenic disjunction, yet without privileging the present as the site of unique modes of social formation. And his treatments of literature, painting, and cinema, while often focusing on monuments of high modernism, suggest means of engaging both modern and postmodern artworks in a single configuration that opens them to forces at once formal and political. Whether Deleuze should be labeled "postmodern" or not is finally of little importance, since no doubt our age will eventually be called something else entirely (indeed, both "modernism" and "postmodernism" strike me as terribly temperocentric terms that future ages will find amusingly self-congratulatory). What is important is that his untimeliness be situated within our own time, and that his ability to transform tired notions into vital concepts be exploited.

The third tribute of this volume is double—a tribute to the summary chapter of Deleuze's own tribute to Foucault, in which Deleuze details Foucault's ethics of self-formation. Deleuze is much taken with Foucault's conception of one's life as a work of art, and he argues that Foucault's model for the creation of the self is that of the fold. The fold is an invagination of forces, something like an alveolus of the lungs or a coastal cove, that allows the outside to come within while permitting as well a communication between the inside and the outside. A creative formation of the self entails an internalization of chaos, a "pure Outside" that defies ready assimilation or comprehension. The self's engagement with the Outside causes a rupture in ordinary experience and reveals the "pure and empty form of time," a split in time that is "between-time." This "between-time" is the time of the Event, a floating, nonpulsed time that allows the emergence of something new. In Deleuze's analysis, Foucault's aim throughout his writings is to think and live differently, and his concern with the self in his late works is simply the logical result of this search for new possibilities of thinking and living. Such an ethics of self-creation, I believe, is finally as much Deleuzian as Foucauldian, and perhaps nowhere more than in this analysis does Deleuze articulate his own sense of how one's life might be shaped as a work of art.

In "Minor Writing and Minor Literature," I try once again to situate Deleuze, in relation not to postmodernism in this instance, but to cultural studies, which some have seen as the discipline of choice in a "posttheory" age. Deleuze's concept of "minor literature" has appealed to many in cultural studies, but I find that this complex concept most often is only partially appropriated. Minor literature for Deleuze is a category that includes within it elements of secondary literature (the literature of minor as opposed to major writers), marginal literature (the literature of minorities), and experimental literature (literature that involves what Deleuze calls a "minor usage" of a major language). And the notion of minor writing as a linguistic practice is inextricably bound with several related concepts—those of stuttering in one's own tongue, becoming-other, inventing a people-to-come, and creating nonlinguistic "Visions and Auditions" within language. There is no harm in one's selectively using the concept of minor literature, but in so doing one should be aware that the concept is no longer Deleuze's. Minor literature is very much a theoretical, philosophical concept, and hence no symptom of a posttheory age. It is instead, I believe, a rich concept that has not yet been thoroughly exploited, and one that, if fully developed, could revitalize cultural studies as well as the supposedly dead field of literary theory.

Becoming-other is a crucial feature of minor literature, and in *A Thousand Plateaus* becoming-other is identified as a pervasive aspect of all artistic creation. In that work as well it is said that all becoming-other necessarily passes through a "becoming-woman." I test this hypothesis in "Becoming Metal, Becoming Death . . ." by examining death metal music, an aggressive, extreme form of heavy metal played almost exclusively by males for a largely male audience. Death metal, I find, does engender a strictly musical process of becoming-other, though its lyrics in general remain decidedly unenlightened. Its varied tempos, modal harmonies, deep timbres, and sheer volume aspire to an ascetic, stripped-down music of pure speed and intensity, and in this regard it provides an apt illustration of what a musical becoming-other might be (something Deleuze himself does not specify in detail). But for the most part death metal's becoming-other does not pass through a becoming-woman, I conclude, primarily because music is an underdetermined art form capable of appropriation for any number of ends.

Death metal's disjunction between lyrics and music poses the larger question of how one should understand the relationship between linguistic and nonlinguistic signs, a question that also comes up in Deleuze's notion of minor writing as the linguistic production of nonlinguistic Visions and Auditions. In "Word, Image, and Sound: Deleuze and Semiosis," I address this question by outlining Deleuze's conception of language within his larger theory of signs. Language is action for Deleuze, a pragmatic dimension within which discursive and nondiscursive practices shape words and things. Linguistic signs perform "incorporeal transformations" by "intervening" in things, but in no way do they represent them. In his analysis of Foucault's *Discipline and Punish*, Deleuze shows that the Panopticon of the modern prison is constituted through the interplay of linguistic and nonlinguistic signs, which interact with one another while remaining separate. Certain power relations generate a discourse of delinquency; others generate nondiscursive ways of seeing (the prison's surveillance mode of "seeing without being seen"); and the panoptic prison is a composite of linguistic statements and nonlinguistic "visibilities" intervening in one another. In his books on cinema, Deleuze extends this analysis of linguistic and nonlinguistic signs, showing how the visual image is affected by the word first in silent film and then in the classic sound cinema. In the modern cinema, he argues, film becomes truly audiovisual, the dimension of sound constituting an autonomous sonic continuum of speech acts, noises, and musical signs, the dimension of sight forming a separate continuum of visual images. What the modern cinema reveals, finally, are the interrelated yet incommensurable semiotic processes that produce the words, sounds, and images through which our world is structured.

One of the primary aims of the modern cinema, in Deleuze's analysis, is to create "opsigns," visual images devoid of conventional narrative, linguistic, and semiotic coordinates. Deleuze finds this same pursuit of "pure images" in Beckett's television plays, and it is this quest I consider in "Deleuze and the Invention of Images: From Beckett's Television Plays to Noh Drama." Deleuze sees in Beckett a lifelong impatience with language, one that leads him constantly to "bore holes" in words so that the "something or nothing" beneath may emerge. Deleuze argues that Beckett in his television plays takes this impatience with language to its logical conclusion, exhausting words of their possibilities, halting the babble of incessant voices, stripping space of all specific demarcations, and allowing detached, evanescent visual and sonic images to come into appearance. Deleuze regards television as a medium especially well suited for the invention of pure images, and in Beckett Deleuze discovers a master in the exploitation of that medium. Curiously, Deleuze also implies that there is an affinity between Beckett's television plays and traditional Noh drama, one mediated by Yeats's conscious imitation of Noh in his own theater. The common element Deleuze discerns in Noh drama, Yeats's theater, and Beckett's television plays, I conclude, is an ascetic devotion to the invention of pure images that transcend words.

In "The Betrayal of God," I examine Deleuze's concept of betrayal, a central element of what he calls the "postsignifying regime of signs," "the regime of betrayal, universal betrayal, in which the true man never ceases to betray God just as God betrays man, in a wrath of God that defines the new positivity" (MP 154–55/123). What Deleuze means by "betrayal" emerges first in his reading of the book of Jonah, which Deleuze takes to be a model of Jewish prophetism. God and prophet define their relationship to one another through their mutual betrayal, constantly renewing their covenant as each turns away from the other. This mutual betrayal Deleuze links to the crisis Hölderlin discerns in *Oedipus the King* and *Oedipus at Colonus*, tragedies in which the gods turn away from humans and humans are forced to define their relation to the divine by likewise turning away from the gods. In this Sophoclean crisis of mutual turning away, Hölderlin sees the dilemma of the modern self and its experience of justice and time (a dilemma whose philosophical articulation Hölderlin phrases in decidedly Kantian terms). When the gods turn from humans, the self is split while justice and time are suffered as pure and empty forms. For Hölderlin, the modern self is condemned to perpetual misery as it endures the blank judgment of the absent gods, but for Deleuze the crisis Hölderlin delineates is the harbinger of a new conception of the self and a new experience of time, a new dispensation in which the self and time are no longer subject to the judgment of the gods but open to the play of chaos and the free-floating time of the Event.

The self Deleuze discerns in this moment of betrayal, in short, is the self as fold, an inner enfolding of a pure Outside. For Deleuze, the chaos of the Outside is not a mere threat to coherence but the generative source of new possibilities. It is the material from which we may fashion a chaosmos, be it in the form of an artwork, a self, or a body of thought. The chaotic Outside always intervenes as an "in-between," a "between-time" and a "between-space" in which commonsense orientations collapse and uncharted dimensions unfold. The in-between of the Outside puts thought in motion and makes possible the invention of new concepts. In the arts, it engenders various processes of becoming-other, each specific to a given art. In some arts, the in-between involves multiple modalities—lyrics and music in death metal; speech acts, sounds, music, and images in film and television. Each art exploits the generative chaos immanent within signs, setting images, sounds, shapes, or words in unpredictable motion, each art doing so in its own way. But in all creative activities, the goal is to instigate movement, to make something happen. Whether it be a philosophy, an artwork, or a self, that which is shaped engages a passage from chaos to chaosmos, a mutative form-in-formation that inaugurates something new. Deleuze's thought is one such chaosmos, I believe, and in saying that I offer what I regard as the highest tribute he may be paid.

Tributes

❖ 1

Deleuze's Style

For over twenty years I have spent a good deal of my time reading books by Gilles Deleuze. They have often brought me great joy, and they continue to do so, even (or especially) after numerous rereadings. Where does this joy come from? It has something to do with what Deleuze calls style and the power of nonorganic life. In a 1988 interview Deleuze says:

> Signs imply ways of living, possibilities of existence, they are the symptoms of an overflowing *{jaillissante}* or exhausted *{épuisée}* life. But an artist cannot be content with an exhausted life, nor with a personal life. One does not write with one's ego, one's memory, and one's illnesses. In the act of writing there's an attempt to make life something more than personal, to liberate life from what imprisons it.... There is a profound link between signs, the event, life, and vitalism. It is the power of nonorganic life, that which can be found in a line of a drawing, a line of writing, a line of music. It is organisms that die, not life. There is no work of art that does not indicate an opening for life, a path between the cracks. Everything I have written has been vitalistic, at least I hope so, and constitutes a theory of signs and the event. (PP 195–96/143)

An organism has died but a life endures. A way of writing, a way of thinking, a way of living—a style. What is that style? What is the nature, shape and movement of that unfolding line of signs and events? Deleuze remarks, "My ideal, when I write about an author, would be to write nothing that could fill him with sadness, or if he is dead, that would make him weep in his grave: think *about* the author on whom you are writing. Think about him so hard that he can no longer be an object, and likewise so that you cannot identify with him. Avoid the double shame of the scholar and the familiar. Return to an author a little of that joy, that energy, that amorous and political life that he knew how to give and invent" (D 142/119). This is a tribute in the present tense to the joy, the energy, and the life of the event that continues to take place in those works that bear the name Deleuze.

The Imperceptible

Clément Rosset relates that a reader of *Difference and Repetition* once remarked to him, "I have the impression of eating a cracker that lacks butter. It's excellent, but it's dry" (89). This dryness *{sécheresse}* Rosset finds in all of Deleuze's early work (through *The Logic of Sense* and *Difference and Repetition*), a dryness that initially suffocates but eventually seduces readers through what it spares them: "Here, no tears, no emotion, no metaphysical shudders. . . . What characterizes Deleuze above all is a beautiful lack of enthusiasm" (Rosset 89). Rosset speaks of a "coldness" in Deleuze, an "'objectivity' quite indifferent to the content it examines" (89). When analyzing others' thought, says Rosset, Deleuze disregards the motives and goals that inspire the work and considers only whether the system of concepts coheres: "Deleuze tries to be indifferent to such affective 'significations,' like an anatomist concerned only about the articulations of the corpse he dissects" (90). Dryness, coldness, objectivity, indifference, the detached, clinical gaze of the forensic surgeon.

What Rosset astutely isolates here is the impersonality of Deleuze's style, the analytic rigor and ascetic sobriety of his thought. Deleuze himself, of course, values sobriety in other writers. To those who experiment with language through accretion, elaboration, and enrichment, Deleuze prefers Kafka, who accepts "the German language of Prague as it is, in its very poverty," and who goes "always further in deterritorialization . . . to the point of sobriety," making an "arid *{desséché}*" language "vibrate with a new intensity," or Beckett, who "proceeds through dryness *{sécheresse}* and sobriety, a willed poverty, pushing deterritorialization to the point that nothing remains but intensities" (K 34-35/19). Sobriety itself is not the goal, but only the means to a liberated intensity, a purification through elimination (how often Deleuze speaks of pure intensities, pure events, pure affects, pure images, and so on), an extraction of an abstract, vital line: "We are trying to extract from love all possession, all identification, to become capable of loving. We are trying to extract from madness the life it contains, while hating the madmen who ceaselessly bring death to that life, turn it against itself. We are trying to extract from alcohol the life which it contains, without drinking: the great scene of drunkenness on pure water in Henry Miller. To do without alcohol, drugs and madness—that is becoming, becoming-sober, for a richer and richer life" (D 67/53).

What Deleuze eliminates in his writing is the personal—the anecdotal, memory-laden, intentional subject. The goal of writing, says Deleuze, is becoming-imperceptible: "The end, the finality of writing? Well beyond a becoming-woman, a becoming-black, -animal, etc., beyond a becoming-minoritarian, there is the final enterprise of becoming-imperceptible" (D 56/45). To be imperceptible "means many things . . . the (anorganic) imperceptible, the (asignifying) indiscernible and the (asubjective) impersonal," and one aspect of becoming imperceptible is "to be like everybody else *{tout le monde}*" (MP 342/279), which in writing might mean to adopt an anonymous, conventional style. There are indeed many passages in Deleuze that seem to be indistinguishable at the level of form from the standard expository prose of academic philosophy, such as this brief excerpt randomly selected from *Difference and Repetition* (similar examples could be found in any of Deleuze's books): "Problems and their symbolic areas stand in a relationship with signs. It is the signs that 'cause problems' and are developed in a symbolic field. The paradoxical usage of the faculties—including, first of all, sensibility within the sign—thus refers to Ideas, which run through all the faculties and awaken them each in turn" (DR 213/164).

But such mimicry is a ruse, a means of divesting oneself of personality in order to instigate a nonpersonal individuation, an event that has the identity of a season, a battle, or a disease: an "effect," the "Doppler effect," the "Kelvin effect," the "Kafka effect." Deleuze's style often seems conventional, but a "Deleuze effect" plays through everything he writes, even when he writes with someone else. The nonpersonal individuation of events proceeds *between* things, and in his work with Guattari the Deleuze effect arises between the two writers, who combine "like two streams, two rivers. . . . Félix and I, and many others like us, do not feel that we are exactly persons. Rather, we have an individuality of events" (PP 193/141).[1] Far from being anomalous creations, Deleuze's collaborative projects only make patent the interactive nature of all his works, in which something passes between Deleuze and the various writers with whom he thinks: "It suffices that something passes through, a current that alone has a proper name. Even when you think you're writing by yourself, it's happening with someone else who can't always be named" (PP 194/141). The Deleuze effect is metamorphic, mutative, constantly altered through the interactions that produce it, yet possessed of a nonpersonal identity that unfolds in its complexity as it is generated.

What is the source of the Deleuze effect, that nonpersonal style which plays through his works? One obvious element of this style is vocabulary, the collection of idiosyncratic terms that populate the Deleuzian discursive universe. Here one finds traces of the coldness and austerity Rosset identifies in Deleuze, for few of these terms possess sensual, concrete specificity. Several have a mathematical provenance, the geometric figures of point *(aleatory point, singular point),* line *(line of continuous variation, line of flight, line of supple segmentation),* and plane *(plane of immanence, plane of consistency)* or surface, as well as such concepts as *series, axiomatic, singularity, numbering number, n dimensions, qualitative multiplicity, distribution,* and so on. Others are borrowed from various sciences *(rhizome, black hole)* and many, of course, from philosophy. Most are abstract: *difference/repetition, expression, explication/implication/perplication, individuation, quasi-cause, extra-being, univocity, affect, percept, functive, prospect, problem, movement, speed, event, modulation, redundancy, resonance, subjectification, the virtual.* Some, such as *diagram* and *map,* are themselves names for abstractions. Greek and Latin words appear from time to time—*Aion/Chronos, compars/dispars, haecceities, nomos/logos, spatium/extensum/extensio*—and lend a similar distanced, disembodied (incorporeal) aura to the writing. Even when a possibly tangible referent is invoked, it is often dematerialized through a problematic combination of terms—an *abstract* machine, a *desiring* machine, a machinic *assemblage,* a body *without organs,* a *melodic* landscape, a *rhythmic* character (although one might say as well, and possibly with greater justice, that the abstract is made sensible through these combinations—palpable, sensual, *real*). But perhaps it is finally the strangeness of the lexicon *(crowned anarchy, schiz-flow, becoming-animal),* the heterogeneity of the abstract terms and their sheer number that are most striking about Deleuze's diction: an abstract, incorporeal, alien vocabulary for a new foreign language.

The Leaking Egg

But words do not take us very far toward an understanding of Deleuze's style. As Deleuze notes, "[W]hile vocabulary in philosophy is one aspect of a style, since it entails now the invocation of new words, now the uncommon valorization of ordinary words, style is always a matter of syntax"

(PP 223/164). By "syntax" Deleuze means not simply sentence structure but also the general dispensation of the materials of thought, the trajectory of a line of argumentation or a sequence of ideas.[2] This, I believe, is the sense of his remark, "Style in philosophy is the movement of the concept" (PP 192/140). For Deleuze, the movement of the concept is both internal and external, as we know from *What Is Philosophy?* Each concept refers to other concepts, "not only in its history but in its becoming or its present connections" (QP 24/19). And each concept is itself in motion, consisting as it does of inseparable elements traversed by a conceptual point: "The concept is in a state of *overflight {survol}* in relation to its components, ceaselessly traversing them according to an order without distance. It is immediately co-present in all its components or variations, at no distance from them, passing back and forth throughout them" (WP 26/20-1).

Consider, for example, *insomnia,* a relatively modest concept that Deleuze develops in *L'Épuisé*, his 1992 study of four of Beckett's dramas for television.[3] The concept's components are generated from four basic elements: the posture of a character (the Dreamer) in Beckett's *Nacht und Träume;* an image of disembodied female hands interacting with the head of the immobile seated Dreamer; Blanchot's notion that sleep betrays the night; and the description from Kafka's "Wedding Preparations in the Country" of a bifurcated dreamer who sends his body to the country while remaining in bed. Deleuze establishes "the *consistency* of the concept, its endoconsistency" (QP 25/19) by first pointing out that in the Dreamer's rigid posture we see the figure of a waking dream. Then Deleuze extracts from Blanchot's fragment on sleep, night, and dreams in *L'Espace littéraire* the opposition of sleep to night and the notion of a dream that belongs to night as opposed to sleep. (The key passage in Blanchot that Deleuze does not cite is "If you lack sleep, in the end exhaustion *{l'épuisement}* infects you; this infection prohibits sleep, translates itself into insomnia" [*L'Espace* 281].) Next Kafka provides Deleuze with an account of a doubled dreamer, which occasions the key observation that "one dreams alongside insomnia *{on rêve à côté de l'insomnie}*" (E 100/CC 171). (One recalls here the paralogic of Deleuze's remark that the Proustian essence "appears *alongside {à côté de}*" the individual elements through which it plays [PS 194/162], or in *Anti-Oedipus* the statement concerning the whole and its parts that "we only believe in totalities that are *to the side {Nous ne croyons à des totalités qu*'à côté}" [AO 50/42].) Finally, Deleuze reads Beckett's image of hands touching the Dreamer's head as an image of the dream of insomnia, "a dream of the mind [*un rêve de l'esprit*], which must be made, fabricated" (E 101/CC 172). As Deleuze articulates the components of the concept, a certain consistency emerges, a notion of a constructed, mental, nocturnal, waking dream. Over the components the oscillating point of the term "insomnia" "pass[es] back and forth" in "a state of *overflight*" (QP 26/20–21). And in the midst of this process of conceptual unfolding appear other interrelated concepts—*exhaustion,* the *possible,* the *image*—each indicating a line of movement inherent in the concept of insomnia that sends it beyond itself to other concepts.

The movement of the concept described in *What Is Philosophy?* is not dependent on the concept's mode of exposition. But there is also in Deleuze's writing a shape to the unfolding of concepts, a dramatic, dynamic form that is part of his style. Deleuze says that he tries to write in such a way that a page "flies off in all directions *{fuie par tous les bouts},* and yet such that it is closed in upon itself like an egg" (PP 25/14). The egg, of course, plays an important role in Deleuze's treatment of individuation in *Difference and Repetition;* and in *Anti-Oedipus* and *A Thousand Plateaus* the Body without Organs is said to be an egg. The egg "is traversed by axes and thresholds, by latitudes, by longitudes, by geodesic lines, it is traversed by *gradients* that mark the becomings and the passages" (AO 26/19); "the full egg before the extension of the organism and the organization of the organs" is "defined by axes and vectors, by gradients and thresholds, by dynamic tendencies with mutations of energy, by kinematic movements with the displacement of groups, by migrations" (MP 190/153). The egg is implicated, or enfolded, difference, and in its unfolding we trace the passage from the virtual to the actual, from an initial differentiation (a set of "differential relations or virtual matter to be actualized" [DR 323/251]) through incipient individuation (an "intensive field") and dramatization ("spatio-temporal dynamisms") to the specific and organic differentiation whereby species characteristics and organic parts are given actual form.

Obviously, if the page is this kind of an egg, it necessarily "flies off in all directions," moving along its various axes, thresholds, vectors, and gradients. But the page-egg is also *"bien fermée sur soi,"* closed in upon itself, an explicated entity that eventuates in a determinate form. The problem is to fashion a leaking egg, one that continues to flee even as it closes in on itself. One way of understanding this problem is in terms of the refrain, whose three aspects are the point, the circumambient space, and the line of flight. The refrain may provide a single point of order in a field of chaos; it may organize a stable domain around that point; or it may open a way out of that organized circle, "as though the circle itself tended to open onto a future, as a function of the working forces it shelters" (MP 383/311). These are "not three successive moments in an evolution," but "three aspects of a single and same thing, the Refrain" (MP 383/312), yet they do trace a drama that one can follow on the Deleuzian page. An incipient point of order—the definition of a term, the establishment of a binary opposition, a suggestive quotation, an image, an example—determines the gradient, threshold, or axis of individuation that the page will follow. As the implications of this initial point are developed, a structured territory begins to form, and the egg closes in on itself (although vacuoles of diverse conceptual components, virtual points of alternative individuations, remain suspended in the ovular protoplasm). Then something unexpected happens—a spark, a break, a crack, a leap—a line of flight opens onto the next page.

"In philosophy, it's like in a novel," says Deleuze; "you have to ask 'What's going to happen?' 'What happened?' Except the characters are concepts, and the settings, the landscapes, are space-times. One is always writing to give life to something, to liberate life where it's imprisoned, in order to trace lines of flight" (PP 192/140–41). Each page creates the drama of imprisonment and escape, of a territorializing systematization of an initial distinction, and a liberating zigzag toward a new terrain. Creation, Deleuze observes, entails "tracing one's path between impossibilities. . . . It's Kafka who explains it: the impossibility of a Jewish writer speaking in German, the impossibility of speaking in Czech, the impossibility of not speaking" (PP 182/133), yet from these impossibilities Kafka was able to fashion new possibilities for the use of the German language: "A creator is someone who creates his own impossibilities, and who creates the possible at the same time. . . . You have to work away at the wall, because without a set of impossibilities, you won't have that line of flight, the exit that constitutes creation, that power of the false that is truth" (PP182–83/133). The page is a theater of created impossibilities and possibilities, a stage of self-imposed, perilous constraint and unanticipated freedom[4]—Houdini in straitjacket and chains miraculously escaping from his self-imposed bonds.

In *L'Épuisé*, for example, one can follow a sequence of escapes, initially modest but increasingly daring as the essay progresses. Deleuze opens with the following page-egg:

> The exhausted [*l'épuisé*] is much more than the tired [*le fatigué*]. "It's not just tiredness, I'm not just tired, despite the climb" [*Nouvelles et textes pour rien*, 128; *Stories and Texts for Nothing* 76]. The tired person no longer disposes of any possibility (subjective): hence he cannot realize the least possibility (objective). But possibility remains, because one never realizes all of the possible, one even causes it to be born to the extent that one realizes it. The tired person has only exhausted the realization, whereas the exhausted person exhausts all of the possible.

> The tired can no longer realize, but the exhausted can no longer possibilize. "That the impossible should be asked of me, good, what else could be asked of me?" [*L'innommable* 104; *Three Novels* 338]. There is no more possible: a raging Spinozism. Does he exhaust the possible because he is himself exhausted, or is he exhausted because he has exhausted the possible? He exhausts himself in exhausting the possible, and inversely. He exhausts that which *is not realized* in the possible. He puts an end to the possible, beyond all tiredness, "in order to end yet again." (E 57–58/CC 152)

First we encounter a point of order—the opposition of *l'épuisé* and *le fatigué*—followed by a citation indicating the source of the opposition and perhaps justifying the distinction (although the innocuousness of the cited passage suggests a parody of the learned reference, a playful reading-along-with-Beckett rather than a demonstration of the judiciousness of the commentary). Then Deleuze performs a Ciceronian *partitio*, dividing *le fatigué* into its subjective and objective dimensions while generating the key terms *possibility* and *realization*. Two symmetrically balanced sentences contrast *le fatigué*'s exhaustion of realization and *l'épuisé*'s exhaustion of possibility, a second quotation punctuates the paragraph, and then a spark—"a raging Spinozism"—flashes from the page, an unexpected leap toward an outside (in this case a virtual vacuole unactualized in the essay). A closing treatment of the objective and subjective dimensions of *l'épuisé* echoes the opening discussion of *le fatigué*, a chiastic play on various forms of the word "exhaustion" lending a Baroque air to the passage (somewhat unusual in Deleuze, no doubt inspired here by the Beckettian play of permutations that Deleuze later identifies as one means of exhausting the possible). The paragraph then ends with an ending, *l'épuisé* putting "an end to the possible," albeit only (in Beckett's words) "in order to end yet again."

By the paragraph's last sentence, the egg has closed in on itself, a structure has been individuated—a complex of symmetrically opposed clauses, sentences, and groups of sentences, interspersed with quotations and a scintillating fragment. "What just happened?" "What will happen next?" By no means has definitive closure set in, but neither is the way out self-evident. Only with the leap to the next paragraph is the line of flight revealed: "God is the originator or the totality {*l'ensemble*} of all possibility" (E 58/CC 152). With this unexpected move (who would have anticipated God?), new possibilities unfold, and the dimensions of the essay's organizational structure expand, the page-egg now including several paragraphs within it. A paragraph elaborating on the realization of the possible is followed by paragraphs describing the exhaustion of the possible, the function of the combinatory in generating exhaustive permutations, and the role of language in such combinatories. As this section comes to an end, a more daring escape becomes necessary. How does one go beyond language when discussing a writer? Where can Deleuze go next? First he differentiates between language and a Beckettian metalanguage, "atomic, disjunctive, cut up, minced" (E 66/CC 156), *langue I,* then he invents a new possibility, a line of flight into a fresh domain for exhausting the possible, *langue II,* the voice that speaks the words. When in turn that section closes, a final, spectacular escape occurs with the disclosure of *langue III,* a language of anonymous space and pure images, the nature of which Deleuze details to the conclusion of the first half of the essay.

Water, Fire, and Air

If there is a repeating form to the movement of the Deleuzian concept, that movement is not at all uniform; it proceeds at variable speeds and in differing modes. One means of approaching those speeds and modes is through categories Deleuze fashions to characterize Spinoza's style. Deleuze notes that Spinoza is often said "to have no style, using as he does a very scholastic Latin in the *Ethics*. But you have to beware of those said to 'have no style'; as Proust noted, often they are the greatest stylists" (PP 224/165). In "Spinoza and the Three 'Ethics'" (in *Essays Critical and Clinical*), Deleuze elaborates on this observation, arguing that three coexisting elements make up the style of the *Ethics*. One's first impression of the *Ethics* is of "an incomparable power and serenity, passing and repassing through definitions, axioms, postulates, propositions, demonstrations, corollaries and scholia, bearing everything along in its grandiose course. It's like a river which now spreads out, and now divides into a thousand branches; now accelerates and now slows, but always affirming its radical unity" (CC 172/138). Yet in addition to this river of definitions, there is also a fiery sequence of scholia, polemical and combative, "like a broken, discontinuous, subterranean, volcanic chain, which at irregular intervals interrupts the chain of demonstrative elements, the great fluvial and continuous chain. Each scholia is like a lighthouse that exchanges signals with others, at a distance and across the flux of demonstrations. It's like a language of fire which is distinct from the language of the waters" (CC 181/146). Finally, there is an "aerial" *Ethics* which, though only manifest in part 5, is still virtually present throughout the entire work.

In part 5 Spinoza seems to proceed via a sequence of logical deductions, but the movement of his argument is so rapid, the leaps from point to point so great, that the chain of deductions breaks down and a new style emerges, a thought "in which signs and concepts vanish, and things begin to write by themselves and for themselves, as they leap across the intervals of space" (CC 186/150). No longer operating in the realm of concepts, Spinoza now speaks "pure, intuitive, direct percepts" (PP 224/165). Thus there are three books in the *Ethics,* a "river-book" of definitions, a volcanic "book of fire," and "an aerial book, a book of light, which proceeds by lightning flashes" (CC 187/151).

With certain modifications and transmutations, the same schema may be applied to Deleuze. There is in Deleuze an *esprit de système,* the philosopher's love of the well-formed structure. Much of his work reads like an extended definition, a sequence of descriptions of interconnected terms whose nature, function, and relation are extensively detailed through a shifting play of discriminations, oppositions, similes, examples, and intertextual references. "It is the Planomenon, or the Rhizosphere, the Criterium (and still other names, according to the increasing number of dimensions). At n dimensions, one calls it the Hypersphere, the Mechanosphere" (MP 308/252). "One calls the *longitude* of a body the collection of particles belonging to that body in a given relation" (MP 313/256). "There is a mode of individuation very different from that of a person, of a subject, of a thing or a substance. We reserve the name *haecceity* for it" (MP 318/261). "And then there is an entirely different plane. . . . Thus, we call it the plane of Nature" (MP 326/266). A is B, X is Y, seldom has "is" *(est)* been used so often to create an "and" *(et)*![5] But unlike Spinoza, Deleuze does not generate definitions as components of arguments, demonstrations, and proofs, since for him philosophy involves the invention of concepts, not discussions, counterarguments, and responses to objections.[6] His interest is less in defeating the opposition than in showing how concepts function, how they cohere, how they move.

And if there is in Deleuze an *esprit de système,* it is often directed toward objects that would seem to defy systematization. *The Logic of Sense* is a logic of *nonsense, Francis Bacon* a logic of sensation (and not even the sensation of the *corps vécu,* but that of the *corps sans organes*). *Anti-Oedipus* details the elaborate structural relationship between paranoid desiring machines, the catatonic body without organs, and the schizophrenic nomadic subject. In Proust Deleuze finds a philosophy of essences and a taxonomy of signs, in Sacher-Masoch a clinical symptomatology and a theory of contracts and law. And even when Deleuze turns to other philosophers, it is to discover a countersystem in their work, to take a transverse path through their thought, against the bias, commencing in the middle rather than with first principles—looking first at incorporeals rather than *ataraxia* (the Stoics), relations instead of sensations (Hume), faculties rather than a priori synthetic judgments (Kant), folds rather than monads (Leibniz), expression and bodies instead of substance, modes, and attributes (Spinoza). Finally, if Spinoza's stream of proofs and demonstrations flows with a calm, majestic serenity, Deleuze's river of definitions is more turbulent, full of eddies and whirlpools ("What interests me are . . . the retentions, the resonances, the headlong rushes, and all the larvae you find in a book" [PP 25/14]), the tone more intense. In *L'Épuisé* Deleuze says at one point of Beckett's exhaustion of words, "This second movement, very complex, is not without relation to the first" (E 67/CC 157), and in that simple aside, "very complex," we hear that intensity—the analyst's absorption with his object, his fascination at its functioning, his surprise at its intricacy, his cautionary respect for its seriousness ("don't take this lightly, dear reader; pay attention") mixed with the slightest touch of wry amusement.

If Spinoza's book of fire is isolated in the scholia of the *Ethics,* the Deleuzian counterpart is interspersed throughout his texts. We have already encountered this fire in *L'Épuisé* with the sentence "There is no more possible: a raging Spinozism." The fire is not that of a polemical or combative passage, as in Spinoza, but that of a flash of insight, a change in speed, a break, a gap. The distance between flashes varies from work to work, but no book is without them. Even the "dry" *Difference and Repetition* has its arresting moments when the abstract analysis shifts speed: "The entire world is an egg" (DR 279/216). "Difference is not negation, it is the negative, on the contrary, that is difference inverted, seen from below. Always the candle in the eye of the cow" (DR 303/235). "The embryo is a sort of phantasm of its parents. . . . Dreams are our eggs, our larvae or our properly psychic individuals" (DR 322/250). Sometimes it is a matter of a distant allusion ("a raging Spinozism"), at others, an unexpected image ("the candle in the eye of the cow"). At times, the flash develops slowly, culminating in an epigrammatic conclusion: "Sometimes the veins are folds of matter that surround living beings held in the mass, so that the marble tile is like a rippling lake full of fish. Sometimes the veins are innate ideas in the soul, like folded figures or powerful statues caught in the block of marble. Matter is marbled, the soul is marbled, in two different manners" (PL 6/4). At others, the spark leaps across microintervals, as in this cascade of appositives and exhortations describing imperceptibility: "What is needed is much asceticism, much sobriety, much creative involution: an English elegance, an English fabric, blend in with the walls, eliminate the too-perceived, the too-much-to-be-perceived" (MP 342/279).

The "aerial" Spinoza emerges in part 5 of the *Ethics* when the geometric method gives way to "a method of invention that proceeds by intervals and leaps, hiatuses and contractions, like a dog searching for something rather than a reasonable man expostulating" (CC 185/149). The aerial Deleuze is most clearly evident at the culmination of his analyses, when a sequence of distinctions eventuates in the most abstract of observations. One thinks for example of Deleuze's treatment of the three forces in Bacon's paintings—the force that isolates a single figure within a structure, the force that couples pairs of figures in a relation of fact, and the force of separation that plays between the triptych's canvases—and of the climactic, ethereal evocations of that third force which makes possible "the separation of bodies in universal light, in universal color, which becomes the common fact of the Figures, their rhythmic being, second 'matter of fact' or Reunion that separates" (FB 56). Or one recalls Deleuze's description of Beckett's *langue III*, the pure image which is "not defined by the sublimity of its content, but by its form, that is, by its 'internal tension,' or by the force that it mobilizes in order to create the void or bore holes, loosen the grip of words, dry up the oozing of voices, disengage from memory and reason a small alogical image, amnesic, almost aphasic, now standing in the void, now shuddering in the open" (E 72/CC 159).

I would argue that much of the final chapter of *Foucault*, "Folds, or the Inside of Thought (Subjectivation)," is in this aerial mode, but above all the brilliant, cryptic paragraph on "absolute memory" and the self as a temporal fold. Here Deleuze opens with a reference to Leiris's "absolute memory" and then quickly ties it to the *hypomnemata* of the ancient Greeks. After briefly identifying memory as "the affect of self by self" (F 115/107), he leaps to Kant's characterization of time as "auto affection," at which point the tenuous links in the chain of association begin to break apart. Deleuze says that in part 5 Spinoza no longer speaks in concepts, or "new ways of thinking," but "in pure, intuitive and direct percepts," or "new ways of seeing and hearing/understanding {*d'entendre*}" (PP 224/165). Something similar takes place here, as Deleuze articulates the relationship between time and the self through the image of the fold: "But time as subject, or rather subjectification, is called memory. Not that short memory that comes afterward, and is opposed to forgetfulness, but the 'absolute memory' that doubles the present, that redoubles the outside, and which is made only with forgetfulness, since it is itself and ceaselessly forgotten in order to be remade: its fold in effect is confused with the unfold, because the one remains present in the other as that which is folded. Only forgetfulness (the unfold) rediscovers that which is folded in memory (in the fold itself)" (F 115/107). It is as if thought at this point were taking place within and through the image, as if time, self, and memory were being directly and intuitively apprehended as folds—a speech not in concepts but "in pure, intuitive and direct percepts."

Stuttering

Frequently Deleuze identifies style with stuttering, not so much stuttering in one's speech as making "language as such stutter" (CC 135/107). A great writer "is a foreigner in his own language: he does not mix another language with his own; he fashions *in* his language a foreign language that does not preexist it. To make language in itself cry, stutter, stammer, murmur" (CC 138/110). To fashion a foreign language in one's own tongue is to induce "a becoming-other of language, a minorization of that major language, a delirium that carries it away, a sorcerer's line that escapes the dominant system" (CC 15/5). And such a becoming is essentially syntactic: "Syntactic creation, style, such is the becoming of language: no creation of words, no neologisms have value outside the effects of syntax in which they are developed" (CC 15–16/5). Hence style in literature has a dual function: "It effects a decomposition or a destruction of the maternal tongue, but also the invention of a new language in the language, through syntactic creation" (CC 16/5). Deleuze cites Gherasim Luca and Beckett as exemplars of such syntactic creation. In his poem "Passionnément," Luca disrupts the linguistic rules of paradigmatic selection and syntagmatic combination by creating inclusive disjunctions and reflexive combinations from the phrase "Je t'aime passionnément": "Passionné nez passionnem je / je t'ai je t'aime je / je je jet je t'ai jetez / je t'aime passionnem t'aime" (CC 139/110). Here, "each word divides, but into itself *(pas-rats, passions-rations)* and combines, but with itself *(pas-passe-passion)*" (CC 139/110). Beckett, by contrast, works by accretion, adding words to the middle of phrases and sentences, while repeating them with slight alterations in exhaustive permutations.

One looks in vain for this kind of linguistic experimentation in Deleuze, but that is because style in philosophy, as opposed to literature, is determined by the movement of the concept, and if there is stuttering in Deleuze, it is a conceptual stuttering, a stuttering of thought itself. In *What is Philosophy?*, one of the characteristics of the modern "image of thought" is identified as "an 'Incapacity' *{Impouvoir}* of thought" which imparts a specific movement to concepts: "As Kleist or Artaud suggests, it is thought as such that begins to snarl, squeal, stutter, speak in tongues, scream, which leads it to create, or to try to. And if thought searches, it is less in the manner of someone who makes use of a method than that of a dog that one would say is making uncoordinated leaps" (QP 55/55). One might argue that stuttering is fundamental to Deleuze's thought, in that paradox in his view is basic to the creation of concepts. The only constraint on the formation of concepts, says Deleuze, "is that these should have a necessity, as well as a strangeness, and they have both to the extent they respond to real problems. The concept is that which keeps thought from being a mere opinion, a view, a discussion, idle chatter. Every concept is necessarily a paradox" (PP 186–87/136). The oxymoron is the simplest form of paradox, a disjunctive synthesis through a conjunction of opposite terms, neither of which alone is adequate to express the idea in question. And as Deleuze shows in *The Logic of Sense,* no conjunction of opposites is stable and self-sufficient; each conjunction leads to another in an infinite regress. Often, Deleuzian definitions are explicitly oxymoronic (for example, the "waking dream" of insomnia), but we may take the oxymoron as a general figure for a way of thinking, a halting, obsessive, repetitive effort to name that which has no name (yet): "It's this, but it's also that; it's not this, yet it's not that either; it's like this, but it's also like this, and this, and this. . . ." Hence the frequent use of appositives in Deleuze, the proliferation of different names for the same thing (for example, "a becoming-other of language, a minorization of that major language, a delirium that carries it away, a sorcerer's line that escapes the dominant system" [CC 15/5]). Each term is juxtaposed to the preceding, each an apparent equivalent, but actually an addendum, an adjunct, a rider: "AND . . . AND . . . AND, stammering" (D 73/59).

There is also in Deleuze a conceptual stuttering between works, what we might call a "Proust effect." As Deleuze says in *Proust and Signs,* "Style is not the man, style is essence itself. . . . In truth, difference and repetition are the two inseparable and correlative powers of essence" (PS 62–63/48–49). In a great writer like Proust, "we say: it's the same thing, on a different level—but we also say: it's something else, but to the same degree" (PS 63/49). Concepts Deleuze develops in one book reappear in another, enter into new combinations, then dissolve and form further alliances and interconnections in a third. In each work, the concepts undergo a slight metamorphosis, as if each repetition of a concept were a mere approximation, an effort once again to give it a name, but also a discovery of something new in the concept that only emerges with its restatement in a different context. The body without organs is one thing in *Anti-Oedipus,* but considerably more in *A Thousand Plateaus,* and something slightly different in *Francis Bacon*. Insomnia in *L'Épuisé* is a waking dream, but in "To Have Done with Judgment," it is a "dreamless slumber in which however one does not sleep" (CC 163/130). What we meet are themes in constant variation, or variations without themes, a ruminative, meditative differential repetition, halting, stammering, stuttering from work to work.

But the clearest instances of stuttering in Deleuze appear in those aerial passages when he strains to describe the ineffable—the Outside, pure light, sound in itself, and so on. Literary style, says Deleuze, involves not only the destruction of the mother tongue and the creation of a new syntax, but also a third aspect, that of pushing language "to a limit, to an outside or an underside consisting of Visions and Auditions which are no longer those of any language" (CC 16/5). "There is a painting and a music proper to writing, as the effects of colors and sonorities that rise above words. It's across words, between words, that one sees and one hears" (CC 9/lv). "Words paint and sing, but at the limit of the path they trace in dividing and combining. The words make silence. . . . Style is the economy of language. Face to face, or face to back, make language stutter, and at the same time carry language to its limit, to its outside, to its silence" (CC 142/113). Deleuze does not attempt to paint and sing through words, as do literary writers, but he does push language to its limits as he tries to say the unsayable and think the unthinkable. In *Difference and Repetition* Deleuze characterizes his transcendental empiricism as a disjunctive use of the faculties, repeatedly utilizing the same paradoxical figure: the *sentiendum* is the insensible that the senses alone can experience; the *memorandum* is the immemorial that memory alone can remember; the *cogitandum* is the inconceivable that understanding alone can conceptualize, and so on. This figure recurs in all of Deleuze's discussions of the arts: the object of painting is to render visible invisible forces (FB 39); that of music, to render sonorous nonsonorous forces (MP 423/343); of cinema, to push the visible "to a limit which is at once invisible and yet can only be seen" and disclose a speech that "is at once, as it were, the unspeakable and yet what can only be spoken" (IT 340/260).

This is a conceptual stuttering basic to Deleuze's thought, and one that frequently forms the subject of the most aerial passages, those poetic flights in which Deleuze attempts to make palpable the insensible, the invisible, the inaudible, the unsayable through various devices—the combining of abstract nouns, concrete adjectives, and active, physical verbs, the use of arresting similes, metaphors, oxymorons, and so on—but above all through evocative, incantatory rhythms. At times the rhythms are rough and muscular, as in this sequence of phrases from the final paragraph of *Foucault*: "Ce dehors informel, c'est une bataille, c'est comme une zone de turbulence et d'ouragan, où s'agitent des points singuliers, et des rapports de forces entre ces points" [This informal outside, it's a battle, it's like a zone of turbulence and of a hurricane, where singular points, and relations of forces between these points, move about] (F 129/121). At other times, the rhythms are quiet and self-effacing, like the subtle, complex pulsations and reverberations that play through *L'Épuisé*'s description of visions and sounds imperceptible in ordinary language: "Des visions ou des sons, comment les distinguer?, si purs et si simples, si forts, qu'on les appelle *mal vu mal dit,* quand les mots se percent et se retournent d'eux-mêmes pour montrer leur propre dehors. Musique propre de la poésie lue voix haute et sans musique" [Visions or sounds, how can one distinguish between them? So pure and so simple, so strong, that one calls them *ill seen ill said,* when words pierce themselves and turn by themselves so as to show their own outside. Music proper to poetry read aloud and without music] (E 105/CC 173). But always in these invocations of the ineffable, one hears something of the shaman, the magician casting spells through a hypnotic musical cadence.

Most often when Deleuze discusses style, he is speaking about literary style, and it is only with difficulty that one teases out the implications of his remarks for an analysis of style in philosophy. Such an effort is necessary if one wishes to characterize Deleuze's style, since in an important sense he is a philosopher and not a writer. As he and Guattari make clear in *What Is Philosophy?*, there is a basic difference between philosophy and literature, in that philosophers work with concepts whereas artists work with percepts and affects. Yet Deleuze also remarks elsewhere that "the affect, the percept, and the concept are three inseparable forces; they go from art to philosophy and from philosophy to art" (PP 187/137). Style in philosophy, he says, "is stretched toward three different poles: the concept, or new ways of thinking; the percept, or new ways of seeing and hearing/understanding; and the affect, or new ways of feeling. They're the philosophical trinity, philosophy as opera: you need all three to *create movement*" (PP 224/165). Of all the arts, literature is closest to philosophy, for literature and philosophy share language as their common medium—and their common enemy. Deleuze admires writers who create a foreign language within their native tongue, but who do so only in an effort to push language beyond itself, to auditions and visions, percepts and affects, that form the outside of language. The longer Beckett wrote, says Deleuze, "the less he could put up with words" (E 103/CC 172). There is a similar impatience with language in Deleuze, a desire to do as Beckett and "'bore holes' in the surface of language" (E 103/CC 172), to seek an outside of language, a silence proper to speech, that makes possible a thought like Spinoza's in part 5 of the *Ethics,* a thought not of concepts but of percepts and affects, new ways of seeing, construing, and feeling, which form the outside of concepts, their inherent surface and limit. It is at the limits of language, at the edge of the ineffable, that philosophy and literature interpenetrate, that Deleuze and Beckett join forces as philosopher-writer and writer-philosopher.[7]

Who Is Deleuze?

"Style is the man," says Buffon, but Deleuze says style is essence, event, becoming-imperceptible, effect. Is Deleuze's style dry, cold, objective, austere? At times, yes—occasionally to such an extent that it is indistinguishable from an anonymous expository prose. And always it is impersonal. But there are at least three Deleuzes: the fluvial Deleuze of definitions and systems, absorbed, fascinated, amused by the structures he is creating; the fiery Deleuze of epigrammatic flashes, scintillating, arresting; and the aerial Deleuze of cryptic speculation, thought in percepts and affects, sensually abstract, poetic, incantatory. Style in philosophy is defined by the movement of the concept—its endoconsistency, auto-*survol,* and involvement with other concepts—and by the syntax of arguments, the unfolding of lines of thought. Each of the three Deleuzes moves at a different speed and in a different mode, but there is a repeated movement in the Deleuzian page-egg, from individuating point of actualization, through explicating structure, to mutating line of flight, a perpetual drama of created impossibilities and unexpected possibilities, of self-imposed constraint and miraculous escape. And always there is stuttering, a halting, lurching movement from appositive to appositive (and, and, and), a differential repetition of themes in constant variation, a conceptual stuttering at the limits of language and thought.

In *What Is Philosophy?*, Deleuze and Guattari say that the true subjects of thought are not the philosophers who sign their works but the conceptual characters *(personnages conceptuels)* through which the thought unfolds: "Conceptual characters are the 'heteronyms' of the philosopher, and the philosopher's name is the simple pseudonym of his characters" (QP 62/64). Who are Deleuze's conceptual characters? One would be Houdini, the magician/illusionist obsessed with madness and death ("As soon as you begin thinking, you necessarily confront a line where life and death, reason and madness, are at stake, and that line draws you on" [PP 141/103]), constantly binding himself in straitjackets and chains, imprisoning himself in coffins, boxes, and jars, and escaping from behind a screen, unseen. A secret identity, hidden, imperceptible. Another would be Alice, the naive, prim girl of metamorphic body and perpetual good sense, exploring with bemused equanimity the surfaces of Wonderland nonsense—but a mutating Alice, splitting into Sylvia and Bruno (Bruno, the lefthanded, stuttering child). A Stoic, empiricist character, but above all, a humorous identity. ("In all great writers you find a humorous or comic level that coexists with the other levels, not just seriousness, but even something shocking {*l'atroce*}" [PP 107/145].) And then there's Professor Challenger, Deleuze/Guattari's spokesman in "The Geology of Morals," the mad scientist who conceives of the earth as a living being and travels to lost worlds of untimely coexistence, the uncouth professor on the fringes of the academy, but also a two-headed, simian animal-man subject to monstrous becomings. "The destiny of the philosopher is to become his conceptual character or characters" (QP 62/64). So who is Deleuze?

Style him Alice H. Challenger.

❖ 2

Is Deleuze a Postmodern Philosopher?

The Problem of Postmodernism

In *The Logic of Sense,* Gilles Deleuze's 1969 "essai de roman logique et psychanalytique" (LS 7/xiv) devoted to Stoic incorporeals and the logic of Alice in Wonderland, Deleuze defines a "minimal structure" as two divergent series related to each other by an aleatory point. Each series may be visualized as a line formed of points whose interrelations are determined by their differences from one another. The two lines in turn are set in resonance by a differential relation that causes them to diverge and intersect with yet other lines belonging to other series, the network of lines forming the plane of a general Question or domain of problems. The generative force of this chaotic structure is the aleatory point, a paradoxical element that partakes of both series but without occupying any specific space. Like the object in the Looking-Glass shop that is always on the shelf above the one Alice is looking at, the aleatory point "lacks its own place": "it lacks its own identity, it lacks its own resemblance, it lacks its own equilibrium, it lacks its own origin" (LS 55/41). A mobile element or empty slot, the aleatory point is a self-differentiating difference that generates divergent series and structures them across a dispersional field.

The concept of postmodernism, I would argue, is such an aleatory point, and its dispersional field constitutes our postmodern condition. From its initial development as a characterization of recent trends in architecture, the concept has been extended to describe movements in contemporary literature, art, cinema, photography, theater, and dance. Philosophy, it is now sometimes said, has entered a postmodern phase, inaugurated by

Nietzsche, Heidegger, Wittgenstein, and Dewey, and explored by deconstructionists, poststructuralists, and neopragmatists. Ecological, holistic science has been identified as postmodern by some commentators; and theorists like Lyotard, Jameson, and Baudrillard have formulated general accounts of postmodernity that encompass most dimensions of contemporary social life.[1] In each of its applications, the term has undergone subtle mutations, and as Linda Hutcheon astutely notes, its formal and logical manifestations in any one domain are often explicitly paradoxical. The postmodern play with genres and representation in literature and art, for example, simultaneously asserts the categories it subverts, since the violation of generic and mimetic codes requires at least an ironic recognition of the existence of such codes in the first place. In postmodern theory, similar puzzles emerge in what Hutcheon describes as "now familiar and inherently self-contradictory theories such as those Foucauldian totalizing negations of totalization or essentializations of the inessentializable (power, for instance), or those Lyotardian master narratives whose paradoxical plot is our loss of faith in master narratives" (Hutcheon 2). The aleatory point of postmodernism, it seems, generates differential series within specific areas and diffusive disturbances across multiple domains.

Some might regard the instability of the concept of postmodernism as a symptom of the inherent muddle of critical theory or the opportunism of academics cashing in on the latest fad. But from a Deleuzian perspective the lack of consensus about the term is a sign of intellectual health. For Deleuze, genuine thought only begins with a disturbance that impinges on thought, with a perplexing and paradoxical question that forces thought into motion. Such a paradoxical question is not amorphous, nor is the field of problems it delineates vague and without contours. But that disturbance is a difference rather than an identity, and the field it reveals is likewise a field of unfolding differences rather than fixed entities. When such a paradoxical question is finally settled, when all the problems of a domain are solved, then thought is dead and difference has played itself out. At present, postmodernism is a generative difference that is disclosing a specific field of problems; once its multiple and contradictory senses are resolved, its use will be over. Then it will be merely another reductive period concept that helps us master history by emptying it of its contradictions.

Whether Deleuze would agree with this description of postmodernism or not is difficult to tell, since he never wrote about postmodernity—or, for that matter, any of the other "post" concepts of recent discussions (poststructuralism, postindustrialism, postcolonialism, postmarxism, and so on).[2] This is hardly surprising, given Deleuze's general reluctance to delineate fixed and stable historical periods. Yet as others have noted, periodization is in some sense antithetical to postmodern thought, in that periodization presumes a disinterested vantage from which historical epochs may be demarcated. Deleuze's silence on postmodernity, then, may make him more postmodern than such writers as Lyotard, Baudrillard, and Jameson, with their various accounts of our postmodern historical situation, and may lend support to the paradoxical conclusion that true postmodernists can never declare themselves postmodern.[3] And as I have already suggested, Deleuze's notion of the aleatory point and the differential field may finally provide a better description of the phenomenon of postmodernism than any of the elaborate historical models that have yet been put forward.

But my object in this essay is less to propose a Deleuzian definition of postmodernism than to explore the possible resonances and divergences between Deleuze's thought and various treatments of postmodernism by other critics and theorists. Deleuze was a prolific writer and an influential figure in recent French philosophy, but in the United States his thought has not received the critical-historical analysis it deserves, and Deleuze did little to suggest how his work might be related to that of his contemporaries. By considering him first as a postmodern philosopher and then as a postmodern commentator on literature, painting, and cinema, I hope to provide a context for assessing the nature of his work and for judging its relation to the thought of his time. Such an evaluation will demonstrate, I believe, that if ours is the era of postmodernism, then Deleuze is indeed a philosopher of his time, and hence a postmodern philosopher—albeit postmodern with a difference, in that his work enriches, enlarges and ultimately modifies our conception of postmodernity.

Postmodern Thought

What might it mean to be a postmodern philosopher? According to Jean-François Lyotard, postmodern thought is characterized by an "incredulity regarding metanarratives," specifically, those metanarratives "that have marked modernity: the progressive emancipation of reason and liberty, the progressive or catastrophic liberation of labor (source of alienated value in capitalism), the enrichment of humanity as a whole through the progress of capitalist technoscience, and, even, if one includes Christianity itself within modernity (as opposed to Classical antiquity), the salvation of creatures through the conversion of souls to the Christological narrative of the martyr's love" (*Condition postmoderne* 7). In Lyotard's estimation, the philosophy of Hegel brings all these narratives together in a totalizing form, "and in this sense it concentrates within itself the whole of speculative modernism" (*Postmoderne expliqué* 37–38).

If such narrative incredulity is the measure of postmodernity, then Deleuze is decidedly postmodern. Throughout his work, he holds that truth is "not something that preexists, that is to be discovered, but must be created in each domain" (PP 172/126). Deleuze resorts to no *grand récit* to legitimate his thought, and although a critique of the metanarratives of modernity is not central to his project, he does frequently challenge them in his work. Take, for example, his seminal *Nietzsche and Philosophy* (1962), which enunciates the fundamental themes of all of Deleuze's thought and inaugurates the Nietzschean moment in contemporary French philosophy.[4] Here Deleuze not only establishes Nietzsche as a philosopher of difference but also questions the Hegelian summation of speculative modernity, positing in Nietzsche's thought an antidialectical affirmation of affirmation that directly responds to Hegel's negation of negation. Nietzsche, in Deleuze's reading, rejects the Hegelian *Aufhebung* of difference within an overarching totality and seeks a double affirmation of difference, first as a local affirmation of becoming, multiplicity, and chance within a single moment, and then as a general affirmation of becoming, multiplicity, and chance as universal ontological principles. The concept of the Overman, or the individual who affirms difference, says Deleuze, "is directed against the dialectical concept of man, and transvaluation against the dialectical appropriation or suppression of alienation. Anti-Hegelianism traverses the work of Nietzsche like a constant thread of aggressivity" (NP 9/8). Or consider Deleuze and Guattari's collaboratively written *Anti-Oedipus* (1972), which, of course, is a direct assault on the master narrative of Oedipalization in both its Freudian and Lacanian guises, but which also, as Lyotard points out, "subverts most profoundly what it doesn't criticize: Marxism" ("Energumen Capitalism" 11). Base/superstructure, use-value/exchange-value, labor, class struggle, the primacy of production, the inevitable limits of the capitalist mode of production—all the themes of traditional Marxism's great narrative are challenged in this book and submitted to a paralogic of flows, machines, and disjunctive synthesis.[5]

In a broad sense, then, we may easily say that Deleuze is postmodern in that he is a post-Enlightenment, post-Hegelian philosopher. But perhaps a more specific indication of his postmodernity lies in the way he thinks the "unthought." At least since Heidegger, most twentieth-century philosophers have been concerned with examining the unthought presuppositions that underlie their thought and function as its ground of possibility. David Couzens Hoy, in an essay on Foucault as a postmodern philosopher, has argued that what distinguishes modern from postmodern philosophers is the fact that postmoderns abandon the modern project of thinking the "great unthought" in its entirety and recognize the heterogeneity of the unthought and the lack of privilege that any one approach to it might have (Hoy 12–41). In Hoy's analysis, Foucault is a thinker who straddles the gap between modern and postmodern philosophy, his archeological studies manifesting a modern, neo-Kantian stance toward the unthought, and his later genealogical works a postmodern, Nietzschean stance. In Foucault's *Archaeology of Knowledge,* the notion of the *episteme* is granted a global comprehensiveness within a given epoch and archeology is defended as the sole legitimate means of uncovering the conditions of possibility of a given discursive formation. In *Discipline and Punish* and later works, by contrast, the power relations that inform the production of knowledge are multiple and untotalizable, and the genealogical analysis of power is but one of an undetermined number of possible approaches to the problem.

A similar movement may be traced in Deleuze's philosophy, an early phase of his "thought of the unthought" receiving its most complete articulation in *Difference and Repetition,* and a later phase finding its fullest development in *A Thousand Plateaus.* It would be inaccurate to assert that Deleuze is truly modern at any point in his approach to the unthought, but in *Difference and Repetition* he does offer an account of the groundless ground of thought whose implicit claims to comprehensiveness are unmatched in his later writings. For the early Deleuze, difference is the great unthought of Western philosophy, something that common sense can only grasp as a secondary deviation from a primary identity. This commonsense understanding of difference as secondary deviation, however, is the product of a transcendental illusion, which can only be overcome through what Deleuze calls a "transcendental empiricism," in which the various mental faculties are not engaged in a common functioning, a *sensus communis,* but in a disjunctive functioning, each faculty experiencing that which it alone can encounter and which the faculties in their common employment discount as error, illusion, or madness. The faculty of sensibility is jolted by intensities, the faculty of imagination by fantasies, the faculty of memory by the virtual past, the faculty of reason by problems.[6] And in each case, what is revealed is a domain of virtual differences, a metaphysical field which is immanent within the real and which is composed of zones of possible individuation that manifest themselves in specific and concrete forms within the actual world. Each zone of possibility is an enfolded, self-differentiating difference that unfolds itself as it is actualized, but that appears only in the form of a disguised difference, one that is interpreted by common sense as a manifestation of identity, save in those occasional moments of disequilibrium when the faculties function disjunctively. Proustian involuntary memory, for example, is not in Deleuze's reading the gateway to the recovery of a personal history, but the revelation of a Bergsonian virtual past that has never been present, a paradoxical, essential past that coexists with each present moment and all other virtual past moments as a single temporal field, and that the faculty of memory alone can encounter in moments of disorientation, such as those when Marcel eats a madeleine or steps on uneven paving stones.

At no point in *Difference and Repetition* does Deleuze attempt the modernist gesture of validating thought through some form of self-grounding—which the theory itself automatically rules out—but he does perhaps show a modernist tendency in his effort to grasp the unthought as a whole, even if that whole is a dispersional multiplicity. (One could argue just as well, however, that this total picture of an untotalizable thought is a typically postmodern theory, similar to Lyotard's master narrative of the loss of faith in narratives.) In later work, however, and especially in the two volumes of *Capitalism and Schizophrenia, Anti-Oedipus* and *A Thousand Plateaus,* one can see a movement away from such a totalizing theory to something much more akin to Foucault's genealogical analyses of power.

In *Anti-Oedipus* and *A Thousand Plateaus* it is no longer difference but desire that is the unthought. Like Foucauldian power, desire for Deleuze and Guattari is both intentional and nonsubjective, immanent within heterogeneous assemblages of bodies, institutions, discourses and objects (which Foucault calls *"dispositifs"* and DeleuzeGuattari *"agencements machiniques"*), more horizontal than vertical in its manifestations, inseparable from knowledge and disciplinary regimes, and unstable in its manifestations, both reinforcing coercive relations and providing points of resistance to such coercion.[7] Desire, like power, is ubiquitous, but there is no presumption that desire comprises the whole of the unthought or that other ways of thinking the unthought are impossible. In *Anti-Oedipus,* Deleuze and Guattari do seem to offer a grand synthesis of world history in terms of desiring production, but as Eugene Holland has argued, this totalizing impulse should be seen as part of a postmodern strategy of "allegorical" enactment of "the very objects and processes it describes in society at large" (Holland 291). Deleuze and Guattari argue that capitalism manifests two tendencies, a schizophrenic tendency toward the disorganization and decoding of social relations, and a paranoiac tendency toward the reorganization and recoding of such relations, and in Holland's reading, the systematic aspect of *Anti-Oedipus* dramatizes the "paranoia characteristic of the capitalist mode of production" (Holland 291). In *A Thousand Plateaus,* however, virtually all signs of totalization are absent. The book is made up of fifteen "plateaus," each of which traces a specific "intensity" across several traditional disciplinary domains. In each plateau a concept is developed—faciality, rhizomes, regimes of signs, becoming-animal, nomadism, and so on—and though the various plateaus are interrelated, there is no systematic way in which these various manifestations of desire may be unified. In one plateau the unthought is explored in terms of biological territories and musical refrains; in another, it is traced across the smooth and striated spaces revealed in quilt making, maritime warfare, Mandelbrot's fractals, Epicurean physics, and Gothic art. And in each of its guises, the unthought functions as a germinal disturbance that generates one of a theoretically unlimited number of compossible plateaus.

If Deleuze is a postmodern philosopher in his narrative incredulity and in his treatment of the unthought, he is equally a philosopher of the postmodern in that his works provide a philosophical exposition of many of the concepts often associated with postmodernity. Indeed, if one looks at Fredric Jameson's influential essay "Postmodernism, or The Cultural Logic of Late Capitalism," which offers a fairly comprehensive, synthetic description of postmodern art and culture, one finds a catalogue of motifs that reads like a checklist of Deleuzian themes and practices. In Jameson's view, postmodern art is characterized by a play of surfaces and a loss of interpretive depth; an obsession with simulation and mass-produced images; a replacement of emotive affect with libidinal intensities; a predilection for pastiche over parody; a treatment of difference as a mode of relation; a "derealized" sense of history; and a schizophrenic splintering of subjectivity. While all of these elements could be isolated in Deleuze's work, I would like to concentrate on three—simulation, intensities, and schizophrenia—and indicate the ways in which Deleuze's treatment of these themes differs from that of most theorists of the postmodern.

Since Benjamin's "Work of Art in the Age of Mechanical Reproduction," it has become something of a commonplace in cultural criticism to remark on the derealizing effects of the mass media, advertising, and the proliferation of images in Western societies. Perhaps no one has made more of this point than Jean Baudrillard, who claims that we inhabit a postmodern world of universal mediation, in which the real has disappeared and been replaced by simulacra, copies of copies with no originary referent: "Simulation is no longer that of a territory, a referential being or a substance. It is the generation by models of a real without origin or reality: a hyperreal. The territory no longer precedes the map, nor survives it. Henceforth, it is the map that precedes the territory—PRECESSION OF SIMULACRA—it is the map that engenders the territory" (Baudrillard 253).

Deleuze, too, writes about simulacra, but not as peculiarly postmodern objects. He notes that in Plato a distinction is made between the *eikon* and the *phantasma* (see the *Sophist* 598b), the good copy that imitates its model and the bad copy or simulacrum that only appears to resemble an original, and Deleuze argues that Plato's denigration of the *phantasma* represents a rejection of difference.[8] For Deleuze, the world of coherent representations and docile copies is the product of the transcendental illusion of common sense, and simulacra belong to a realm of becoming and difference from which representations and copies issue as secondary effects. In a cosmos of universal flux and becoming, there can be no fixed identities, no stable models from which copies may be generated, for everything is part of a constant process of becoming-other. From the perspective of becoming and the ubiquitous unfolding of difference, there never have been anything but simulacra, and our contemporary culture of simulation is simply a context in which the existence of simulacra becomes increasingly undeniable. Hence for Deleuze, the function of art in our age is to exacerbate the play of cultural simulacra and extract from them the generative force of difference: "The more our everyday life appears to be standardized, stereotyped, subjected to an accelerated reproduction of consumer objects, the more art must attach itself to everyday life, and wrest from it that little difference which plays elsewhere and simultaneously between other levels of repetition, . . . so that finally Difference expresses itself" (DR 375/293). As examples of such artistic practice, Deleuze cites "the manner in which all repetitions coexist in modern music (thus already the development of the leitmotiv in Berg's *Wozzeck*)—the manner in which pop art in painting has managed to push the copy, the copy of the copy, and so on to the extreme point at which the copy reverses itself, and becomes a simulacrum . . .—the manner in which {*nouveaux romanistes*} seize from the brute and mechanical repetitions of habit small modifications, which in turn animate repetitions of memory, and then an ultimate repetition" that extends to the limits of the work (DR 375–76/293-94).

Besides a widespread fascination with simulation, Jameson notes in postmodern art a decline in the expression of deep, personal emotion and the appearance of new feelings "which it may be better and more accurate to call 'intensities,'" feelings that are "free-floating and impersonal, and tend to be dominated by a peculiar kind of euphoria" (64). Deleuze and

Guattari often speak of intensities in *Anti-Oedipus* and *A Thousand Plateaus*, and in ways that seem to accord with Jameson's sense of the term, but it is only in *Difference and Repetition* that Deleuze fully defines the word. An intensity is a "pure difference in itself" (DR 187/144) that the senses alone can experience, and only when the senses are employed in disjunction from common sense. The intensity, in other words, is the transcendental object of the faculty of sensibility (just as the virtual past is the transcendental object of the faculty of memory). Any *dérèglement des sens* could serve as an example of the intensity, but the most elemental instance of it comes in moments of vertigo when one experiences what Deleuze labels *la profondeur*, a dimensionless depth from which dimensional space issues as a secondary product. This depth "is indeed space as a whole, but space as intensive quantity," that is, before it takes on the coherent properties of extension and quality, a "pure *spatium*" as opposed to a dimensional *"extensio"* (DR 296/230). What is most important to note here is that intensities, like simulacra, are not peculiarly postmodern entities, but ubiquitous elements that simply surface in a particularly striking fashion in contemporary art and culture.

In *Anti-Oedipus* Deleuze and Guattari speak often of intensities, and clearly as instances of a "sensible difference in itself," but their primary goal in that work is to develop a vocabulary for describing the body of desire that escapes the rational regulation of subjectivity. They see the domain of desiring-production and libidinal intensities as akin to the affective dimension of schizophrenia, and their argument is that the decoding of fluxes and flows that characterizes schizophrenia is also manifested in the fundamental processes of capitalism. Everywhere capitalism develops, it undermines traditional social codes—kinship systems, religious beliefs, class hierarchies, taboos, ritual trade relations, and so on—and releases uncoded fluxes of heterogeneous matter, ideas, affects, and fantasies. But unlike schizophrenia, it constantly recodes fluxes and flows within new forms of social organization (such as the Oedipal family) in an effort to maintain a controlled and universal exchange of commodities. It would seem that we have here a properly historical account of what Jameson has labeled a postmodern phenomenon—the schizophrenic "breakdown of temporality" in which "the present of the world or material signifier comes before the subject with heightened intensity, bearing a mysterious charge of affect" (Jameson 73). Yet the schizophrenic decoding of flows in Deleuze and Guattari, although most evident in advanced Western capitalism, represents the limit of every form of exchange, a latent possibility that haunts all social systems and threatens their dissolution (see AO 180/153). Capitalism is simply the first social system to institutionalize such decoding on an unlimited scale, and the emergence of schizophrenic affectivity, temporality and fragmentation in postmodern art merely partakes of the accelerating tendency toward decoding that informs multinational capitalism.

It would be a mistake to regard Deleuze's assertion of the universality of simulacra, intensities, and schizophrenic decoding as signs of essentialism in his thought, for such concepts are merely tools for mapping possible worlds, not irreducible constituents of ultimate reality. But it is evident that for Deleuze there is no decisive break with which postmodernity is ushered in and no peculiarly postmodern phenomena that characterize our culture. Deleuze articulates postmodern themes and exemplifies postmodern practices, in short, but he does not offer a historicized theoretical account of postmodernity. From Jameson's perspective, no doubt, Deleuze's thought is symptomatic of postmodernity but insufficiently self-critical to recognize its grounding in its own historical situation. Deleuze would counter, I believe, that he is simply incredulous of all historical narratives, including the one that might account for the shape of thought in our present postmodern condition.

Postmodern Arts

Andreas Huyssen has wisely cautioned us against assuming too quickly that poststructuralism is necessarily the philosophical counterpart of aesthetic postmodernism. French poststructuralists especially, he notes, are relatively silent about postmodernity, devoting most of their attention to the works of high modernism. He argues, in fact, that French poststructuralism "provides us primarily with an archeology of modernity, a theory of modernism at the stage of its exhaustion" (Huyssen 209). He points out that critics like Roland Barthes not only concentrate most often on modernist writers and the problem of modernity, but also reinforce modernist aestheticism in certain theorizations of *écriture* and reinstate the modernist distinction between high culture and low culture in such schemas as the Barthesian opposition of *jouissance* and *plaisir*. Deleuze is a poststructural philosopher, and he resembles other French poststructuralists in his fondness for modernist art and his interest in the question of modernity, but I do not believe that Deleuze articulates "a theory of modernism at the stage of its exhaustion," for his sense of the modern, I would argue, is decidedly postmodern, a point that may be demonstrated through a brief consideration of Deleuze's books on Proust, Kafka, Francis Bacon, and the cinema.

Proust is one of Deleuze's favorite writers, frequently discussed throughout his works and treated at length in *Proust and Signs,* published in 1964 and augmented in subsequent editions in 1970 and 1971. Proust, of course, is one of the established luminaries of high modernism, but for Deleuze he is not the modernist aesthete of subjectivity, the self-reflexive recluse who recaptures the past and creates in his novel an autonomous verbal icon. Deleuze treats the *Recherche* as the account of Marcel's apprenticeship in the understanding of signs, which are enfolded, implicate differences that Marcel interprets as he unfolds and explicates them. Marcel discovers the differential nature of worldly signs through lies; of amorous signs through jealousy; of sensual signs through involuntary memory; and of artistic signs through the Vinteuil sonata. And what he finally learns through artistic signs is that difference is the generative force from which issue the multiple compossible worlds that make up the real. Marcel, far from functioning as the consciousness that holds the *Recherche* together, is dispersed across the multiple signs of the text. The work itself does not express deep meanings or feelings, but operates as a machine. For, says Deleuze, "the modern work of art is a machine, and functions as such. . . . The modern work of art has no problem of meaning, but only a problem of usage" (PS 175–76/145–46). The *Recherche* is filled with machines that produce fragments and partial objects, and machines that set them in resonance, while itself being a machine that produces various effects (in the sense that one speaks of the Doppler effect): truth effects, reader effects, and unity effects of "a One and a Whole which [are] not principal, but on the contrary 'the effect' of the multiple and its disconnected parts" (PS 195/163). "In truth," says Deleuze, "the narrator is an enormous Body without Organs," a spider within the web of the *Recherche,* the web and the spider forming "a single and same machine" (PS 218/181).

Kafka is another of Deleuze's favorite writers, whose works he and Guattari examine at length in their 1975 book, *Kafka: Toward a Minor Literature.* For Deleuze and Guattari Kafka is not the modernist prophet of *Angst* and existential gloom, nor the advocate of a tragic, negative theology, but instead a joyous, humorous writer whose works constitute a political experimentation on the real. Kafka's writings, they argue, are rhizomelike in their structure and machinelike in their function, and hence constituted of multiple fragments and pieces that form unified wholes only as secondary effects. Deleuze and Guattari's Kafka, in this sense, resembles Deleuze's Proust. But in Kafka Deleuze and Guattari also find a theorist and practitioner of what they call "minor literature," an avant-garde form of political writing that undermines the high modernist distinction of elite and mass culture and its separation of life and art. In Kafka's language, Deleuze and Guattari discover a minor usage of German, a Prague Jew's deliberate impoverishment of a foreign culture's "paper language" that induces unexpected mutations in the dominant, major tongue. And in such works as *The Trial* and *The Castle,* they see a political experimentation on the social forces of Kafka's day, a minor practice that functions as a means of "prolonging, of accelerating an entire movement that already traverses the social field: it operates in a virtual realm, already real without being actual (the diabolic powers of the future which, for the moment, are only knocking at the door)" (K 88–89/48). If one accepts Huyssen's characterization of postmodern art as informed by a critique of the imperialism of enlightened modernity and the domination of minorities and marginal cultures by cultural majorities (see Huyssen 219–220), then the Kafka that Deleuze and Guattari describe—Kafka, the exponent of minor literature—must be considered postmodern.

In his *Francis Bacon: The Logic of Sensation* (1981), Deleuze may not discuss one of the classic examples of high modernism, but he certainly treats a figure who is much more commonly associated with modernist than postmodernist trends in painting. Yet what Deleuze regards as the basic problem addressed in Bacon's paintings is essentially a postmodern concern—that of representation in a world of ubiquitous images—even if Deleuze labels it a "modern" dilemma. Modern painting, says Deleuze, "is invaded, besieged by photos and clichés which are already on the canvas even before the painter begins his work" (FB 14).[9] The great task faced by painters is that of escaping received codes of representation and figuration. In Deleuze's analysis, Bacon rejects the strategies of abstract formalism or abstract expressionism, and instead tries to wrest the figure from the clichés of figuration, to paint a portrait of a human being, for example, but to allow a catastrophic zone of chaos to invade the representation as it takes form, to follow the line of mutation induced by a chance brushstroke or haphazard color and allow it to deform the figure, to introduce "a zone of Sahara into the head," to split "the head into two parts with an ocean" (FB 65) in between, to turn a torso into a piece of meat or a leg into a puddle of purple ink. The representations that emerge may resemble certain objects in the world, but they are simply instances of a resemblance that "surges forth as the brutal product of non-resembling means" (FB 75). What Bacon ultimately paints, in Deleuze's view, is the network of invisible forces that play through visible forms. Hence in Bacon's various portraits of screaming individuals, Deleuze does not find an expressionistic rendering of psychological anguish, but a figural mutation that seeks to "put the visibility of the cry, the open mouth as shadowy abyss, in relation with the invisible forces which are still only those of the future" (FB 41). In this regard, the Francis Bacon that Deleuze describes is a practitioner of Lyotard's postmodern negative sublime, which "invokes the unpresentable within the presentation itself; which refuses the consolation of good forms and the consensus of a taste that would allow the common experience of a nostalgia for the impossible; which explores new presentations, not in order to enjoy them, but in order to convey better the existence of the unpresentable" (*Postmoderne expliqué* 32).

In his books on film, *Cinema 1: The Movement-Image* (1983) and *Cinema 2: The Time-Image* (1985), Deleuze raises the question of modernity once again, this time by distinguishing two broad movements in the history of film—the classic cinema of conventionally coded narratives and coherent spatiotemporal coordinates, and the modern cinema of undecidable narratives and irreconcilable disjunctions in space and time. Yet here, too, as in his analyses of Proust, Kafka and Bacon, what Deleuze labels "modern" could easily be classified as postmodern. This is perhaps most evident in Deleuze's account of the relation between sound and image in classic and modern films. According to Deleuze, space and time in the classic cinema are regulated through a "sensorimotor schema," an organization of the world in terms of human goals, purposes, obstacles, actions, and reactions, and it is this sensorimotor schema that coherent narratives presuppose as their condition of possibility. Sound and image reinforce one another in the classic cinema, and together they map a coherent world. In the modern cinema (beginning with Italian neorealism), the sensorimotor schema breaks down, and the elements of film begin to be related to each other differentially rather than synthetically. The cut, for instance, no longer connects two shots that belong to a single space and time, but functions instead as a gap or blank that asks the viewer to discover a relation between two heterogeneous images based on their differences from one another. Sound and image also develop in a differential manner, the audio and the visual in modern film functioning as autonomous strata that test the limits of what can be seen and what can be heard. In the films of Duras, Straub/Huillet, Godard, and others, Deleuze finds separate levels of sounds and images, bound in "an incommensurable or 'irrational' relation which ties them to one another, without forming a whole, without proposing the slightest whole" (IT 334/256), that relation being based on the differences between the two levels and the ways in which each of the levels approaches its limits. Clearly, each level tends toward the Lyotardian postmodern negative sublime. But more importantly, what Deleuze sees as the characteristic relation between sound and image in modern film is a perfect example of what Jameson identifies as "the postmodernist experience of form," in which the viewer or reader is expected "to rise somehow to a level at which the vivid perception of radical difference is in and of itself a new mode of grasping what used to be called relationship: something for which the word collage is still only a very feeble name" (Jameson 76).

Untimely Postmodernism

In many respects Deleuze is a postmodern philosopher: he abandons, and occasionally challenges, the *grands récits* of the Enlightenment; he thinks the unthought, but with no nostalgia for a missing whole and no claims to possess a privileged methodology; and he gives philosophical articulation to a number of postmodern themes—simulacra, intensities, and schizophrenic decoding, among others. He does not, however, offer any theoretical accounts of postmodernity, and like many of his French contemporaries, he shows much greater interest in the problems of modernity and the monuments of high modernism than in postmodernism and postmodern art. Yet his treatment of modernist literature, painting, and film differs from that of many French poststructuralists in that the aesthetic features Deleuze values and discovers in such artists as Proust, Kafka, and Bacon are distinctively postmodern rather than modern.

Should we conclude, then, that Deleuze merely subscribes to a new theory of modernism, one that treats the twentieth century as a single period with characteristics that we are now beginning to label postmodern? I think not, for it assumes in Deleuze a willingness to periodize that simply is not there. He often speaks of modernity and modern art, but little that he identifies as characteristic of such art is exclusively so. As any section of *A Thousand Plateaus* makes readily apparent, the features that Deleuze finds in Proust, Kafka, Bacon, and modern film he also discovers in different guises in art works from various eras and diverse cultures. One cannot say that Deleuze is uninterested in history or historical distinctions, but it is evident that he has no desire to formulate a single global history or even a limited history whose demarcations are hard and fast. Unlike Fredric Jameson, who sees a need for "cognitive maps" as guides for future political action, and who offers his account of postmodernism as a contribution to the cartography of our age, Deleuze attempts a cartography of desire that charts the fissures and rifts of metamorphoses and becoming wherever and whenever they appear. The maps Deleuze draws are less emplotments of our era than diagrams of force, which function as do *A Thousand Plateaus'* "maps of regimes of signs: we can turn them around, retain this or that coordinate, this or that dimension, and depending on the case we will have a social formation, a pathological delusion, a historical event, etc." (MP 149–50/119). Such cognitive maps have historical coordinates, but they are tentative, hypothetical, and strategically drawn, for they are always constructed to induce a mutation, to discover a locus of difference that will generate unexpected transformations. The task of modern philosophy, says Deleuze, is "to overcome the alternatives temporal-nontemporal, historical-eternal, particular-universal. Following Nietzsche, we discover the untimely as something that is more profound than time and eternity: philosophy [in this regard] is neither the philosophy of history, nor the philosophy of the eternal, but untimely, always and only untimely, that is, 'against this time, in favor, I hope, of a time to come' " (DR 3/xxi). It is perhaps in this sense that Deleuze is most thoroughly postmodern.

❖ 3

Deleuze, Foucault, and the Playful Fold of the Self

In his 1986 tribute to his friend and fellow philosopher Michel Foucault, Gilles Deleuze offers an especially dense and challenging account of the Foucauldian self as the product of a process of subjectivation and as a "fold" that constitutes an "inside" of thought. Concentrating on volumes 2 and 3 of Foucault's *History of Sexuality,* Deleuze not only situates these late studies of the ethics of self-formation in relation to the Foucauldian archaeologies of knowledge of the 1960s and the genealogies of power of the mid-1970s, but also provides, as I hope to show, a means of bringing together Foucault's disparate remarks on subject formation, politics, and the history of thought within the general theoretical context of a Nietzschean affective physics of force. The self that emerges from Deleuze's analysis—a subject of desire, political resistance, and ecstatic thought—ultimately is hardly a self at all in any conventional sense, but instead the locus of an internalization of chance, becoming, and force. And if in certain respects it is truly a Foucauldian self, it is above all a Deleuzian creation that occupies an important position in Deleuze's own thought.

The points raised in Deleuze's commentary on the Foucauldian subject are particularly useful in illuminating the relationship between mimesis, play, and the self, both in ancient Greek thought and in contemporary theory. In Foucault's analysis of the Greek desiring subject one can see equally the workings of an archaic mentality, in which mimesis is above all "coming-into-being," agonistic play, and the manifestation of power, and a median mentality, in which mimesis entails representation and the mediation of reason.[1] As Deleuze's commentary makes clear, Foucault finds valuable the Greek ideal of aesthetic self-formation and the conception of the desiring subject as a locus of force—both of which are consonant with an archaic mimesis of play and power. What Foucault rejects in the Greek subject is the median mentality of rational self-regulation, but also the archaic constitution of the self through asymmetrical, hierarchical power relations. The conception of the self as a fold of forces, explicit in Deleuze's thought and implicit in Foucault's, ultimately may be seen, then, as a contemporary transformation of archaic mimesis, one that attempts to salvage the positive aspects of mimetic play while rejecting the negative effects of an aristocratic power mentality.

The Greek Self

When volumes 2 and 3 of *The History of Sexuality* appeared in 1984, many were caught off guard, even those who had studied closely Foucault's remarks in interviews and articles during the years following the publication of volume 1 in 1976. Not only had Foucault abandoned his usual investigatory domain of sixteenth- through nineteenth-century northwestern Europe for the broad expanses of classical Greek and Roman antiquity; and not only had he apparently departed from his genealogical methodology and chosen to focus much more on texts than on practices; but he had also elected to concentrate his attention on the "desiring *subject*," thereby deflecting the initial orientation of his analysis in *The History of Sexuality* from the formation of the modern concept of sexuality to the constitution of the ethical self.

Throughout his early archaeological work Foucault had remained an inveterate enemy of the subject, opposing his own histories of discontinuity and rupture to the continuities of traditional historiography which are grounded in the sovereign cogito. As he states in *The Archaeology of Knowledge,* "Continuous history is the indispensable correlative of the founding function of the subject.... Making historical analysis the discourse of the continuous and making human consciousness the original subject of all historical development and all action are the two sides of the same system of thought" (12). And in his genealogical studies he had sustained his attack on the subject, following Nietzsche's lead in creating histories that are, as he says in "Nietzsche, Genealogy, History," parodic, dissociative and sacrificial—parodic, in regarding the historical actor as a carnival mask; dissociative, in treating individual identity as heterogeneous multiplicity; and sacrificial, in making the subject of knowledge the object of a necessary liquidation.[2]

Yet Foucault was in no way reverting to a foundational subject in his ethical studies, for his purpose was to examine the ways in which subjects are produced, the "forms and modalities of the relation to self by which the individual constitutes and recognizes himself *qua* subject" (*Use of Pleasure* [henceforth abbreviated as UP] 6). If in his archaeologies Foucault delineates the discursive formations that produce knowledge, and in his genealogies the networks of power that are immanent within knowledge, in his ethical studies he shows how the individual is summoned as a locus of knowledge and power to an elaborate process of self-coding, self-discipline, and self-formation that varies across broad historical periods. The specific domain of the summons on which Foucault concentrates is that of the ethics of sexuality—how it is that sexual conduct becomes a problem that solicits an individual's moral concern and thereby requires an active molding and shaping of the self. By focusing on the question of the constitution of the desiring subject Foucault hopes to detail the ways in which an archaeology of problematizations and a genealogy of those practices that make problematizations possible may be interrelated within an "etho-poetics" of self-creation.

Foucault adopts a loosely Aristotelian schema in his investigation of the desiring subject, analyzing the self's relation to itself in terms of its *ethical substance* (material cause), its *mode of subjection* (efficient cause), its *forms of elaboration* (formal cause) and its *telos* (final cause). The ethical substance is that part of oneself, whether it be one's desires, feelings, sensations, or intentions, that requires one's moral concern, and hence that functions as a matter or substance upon which one must bring to bear one's formative energies. The mode of subjection is "the way in which the individual establishes his relation to the rule and recognizes himself as obliged to put it into practice" (UP 27), whether in response to social conventions, the claims of reason, divine law, the aesthetics of a beautiful life, and so on. The forms of elaboration are the self-shaping practices that guide ethical work—those, for example, of an ascetic regime of sudden renunciations, a hermeneutics of continuous self-examination, an agon of relentless psychic combat, or a perpetual indulgence in therapies of self-expression and self-discovery. The telos, finally, is the mode of being to which the ethical subject aspires, whether it be that of tranquility and detachment, mastery and autonomy, oneness with God, or some other moral ideal. Foucault's project, then, is to show how in each age, a specific dimension of an individual's life is taken to constitute the domain of the ethical, a specific relation of the individual to this domain is established, and specific means and ends are recognized as appropriate for directing the individual's actions within that domain.

Foucault's primary task in volume 2 of *The History of Sexuality* (to which I will restrict my attention here) is to characterize the desiring subject of the ancient Greeks in terms of these four aspects of the self. He argues that the ethical substance for the Greeks must be understood in terms of *aphrodisia,* or "the acts, gestures, and contacts that produce a certain form of pleasure" (UP 40). The principal constituents of *aphrodisia* are the pleasures of eating and sex, for these are the pleasures that involve the sense of touch and hence are liable to self-indulgence *(akolasia).* Rather than concentrating on proscribed acts, shameful desires, or forbidden pleasures, the Greeks viewed acts, desires, and pleasures as naturally joined in a dynamic, circular relationship and hence as indissociable components of a single process. Their ethical attention was drawn instead to the "force that linked together acts, pleasures, and desires," to "this dynamic relationship that constituted what might be called the texture of the ethical experience of the *aphrodisia*" (UP 43). The Greek ethics of sexuality, then, focused on the regulation and management of this circuit of forces, on questions of the frequency or intensity of the circuit's functioning, and of the active or passive role that one assumed within it.

Hence the Greek mode of subjectivation, the second aspect of the self, involved a style or proper use of *aphrodisia*. It was not "a question of what was permitted or forbidden, among the desires that one felt or the acts that one committed, but of prudence, reflection, and calculation in the way one distributed and controlled his acts" (UP 54). Since need arose naturally in the circuit of *aphrodisia,* one might manage the circuit by allowing need to increase and thereby intensify pleasure at the same time that one avoided creating unnatural desires that go beyond need. One might also intervene in the circuit by regulating its tempo, by finding the proper time of day, time of year, or time of life for the use of specific pleasures. Finally, one might control the circuit in a qualitative fashion by selecting pleasures, engaging in acts, and satisfying desires that were suited to one's way of life, "which was itself determined by the status one had inherited and the purposes one had chosen" (UP 60).

The forms of elaboration of Greek sexual ethics centered on the concept of *enkrateia,* an active type of self-mastery "located on the axis of struggle, resistance and combat," which may be referred "in general to the dynamics of a domination of oneself by oneself and to the effort that this demands" (UP 65). The forces of *aphrodisia* were seen as natural and necessary, but always given to revolt and excess; therefore, ethical conduct inevitably entailed "a battle for power" (UP 66), an internal struggle between the higher and lower parts of the soul for domination and mastery. The ethical subject was to seek a stable state of rule within the soul, which mirrored the proper hierarchy of the well-governed household and state. And the subject was to attain such mastery through rigorous training, which would "enable the individual to face privations without suffering, as they occurred, and to reduce every pleasure to nothing more than the elementary satisfaction of needs" (UP 73).

The telos of Greek sexual ethics was *sophrosyne,* the freedom of self-mastery that allowed one to rule oneself and thereby rule others; hence, "in its full, positive form," this freedom "was a power that one brought to bear on oneself in the power that one exercised over others" (UP 80). A virile, active quality, *sophrosyne* also entailed a relation to truth, since "to rule one's pleasures and to bring them under the authority of the *logos* formed one and the same enterprise" (UP 86). The freedom of self-mastery required the structural dominance of reason over the appetites, the instrumental use of reason as a dialectical tool of discovery, and the ontological recognition of the logos as the soul's true being. Finally, *sophrosyne* made possible an aesthetics of existence, in which the well-governed life "took on the brilliance of a beauty that was revealed to those able to behold it or keep its memory present in mind" (UP 89).

As one can see, Foucault's account of the Greek desiring subject makes little use of the median concepts of representational mimesis so often associated with discussions of the self—unity, identity, the self-same, imitation, reflection. In his treatment of the ethical telos of *sophrosyne,* Foucault does acknowledge the well-known Platonic motifs of rational self-formation, especially that of the soul's imitative doubling of the logos within. But in general, Foucault situates the Greek ethical subject in an archaic, aristocratic mentality. That self emerges in an agonistic play of forces. It is constituted as a manifestation, or mimetic "coming-into-being," of power. And in every respect it is grounded in the values of a hierarchical, aristocratic culture: its ethical substance is defined in terms of active and passive *aphrodisia;* its mode of subjection presupposes class-specific styles of self-regulation; its forms of elaboration are framed in terms of domination and submission; and its telos of self-mastery *(sophrosyne)* is founded on the opposition of freedom to slavery.

Forces and the Self

Yet despite this clear articulation of the aristocratic features of the Greek desiring subject, and despite Foucault's protestations that the ancient world was no golden age,[3] many readers have seen in Foucault's description of Greek sexual ethics a nostalgic "return to the Greeks," and understandably so. Clearly, Foucault finds sympathetic an ethics that is "not directed toward a codification of acts, nor toward a hermeneutics of the subject, but toward a stylization of attitudes and an aesthetics of existence" (UP 92). His description of the ethical substance of the Greeks as a dynamic relationship among forces that link together desires, acts and pleasures is consonant with the fundamentally Nietzschean orientation of his own thought. His treatment of the mode of subjection as a stylistics of self-regulation of one's *aphrodisia* suggests the possibility of conceiving morality along aesthetic rather than juridical lines, and hence of imposing a greater distance between sexual behavior and disciplinary institutions than exists in most Western societies at present, something Foucault no doubt would have found attractive. His characterization of the forms of elaboration of Greek ethics in terms of an agonistic struggle for power and self-mastery, even as it brings to light those classist and sexist aspects of Greek ethical life that Foucault found most objectionable, at the same time reinforces his claims in *Discipline and Punish* and volume 1 of *The History of Sexuality* that power is ubiquitous and unavoidable. And in his discussion of freedom and self-creation as the telos of Greek ethics one senses that Foucault is positing values that are as much his own as those of the ancient Greeks.

It would seem, then, that Deleuze is justified in reading Foucault's late studies in the ethics of the self as more than mere histories and in treating them instead as essential components of a single philosophical project of a decidedly Nietzschean cast. In his book *Foucault,* Deleuze constructs an elaborate map of Foucauldian thought, describing the early archaeological works in terms of strata of the statable and the visible, the later genealogies in terms of strategies of unformed forces, and the final ethical studies in terms of folds that constitute an inside of thought. In order to explore in detail Deleuze's analysis of the Foucauldian self, it is necessary first to plot that self on the coordinates of this general map.

Deleuze argues that Foucault's conception of knowledge, developed in his archaeologies and utilized in his later works as well, is informed by a basic distinction between the statable *(l'énonçable)* and the visible *(le visible),* or that which can be stated and that which can be seen. The strata of historical formations that the archaeologist of knowledge excavates are composed of statements and visibilities, which are closely interrelated and intertwined in a complex fashion, but which have separate modes of constitution and histories of emergence. In any age, only a limited number of things can be said and seen, and what Foucault reveals in his archaeologies are the conditions that make possible the articulation of statements within a particular discursive field and the disclosure of visibilities within a particular regime of light.

Statements are serious speech acts which have as their condition the regularities of a discursive formation, a pattern of practices that determines the possible referents, subject positions, conceptual networks, and nondiscursive relations of statements that may occur in a given historical domain of knowledge. Visibilities, in turn, are "forms of luminosity, created by light itself and allowing things or objects to exist only as flashes, mirrorings, scintillations" (F 60/52), and they have as their condition the regularities of nondiscursive practices "which distribute the clear and the obscure, the opaque and the transparent, the seen and the not-seen" (F 64/57) within a particular historical period. According to Deleuze's analysis, then, what Foucault does in *Madness and Civilization*, for example, is to examine the strange body of statements that make up the science of madness of the seventeenth and eighteenth centuries and the peculiar collection of self-evident visible entities that the age saw in the domain of unreason, and then disclose those regularities of discursive and nondiscursive practices that made possible the formation of the complex of statements and visibilities that constituted the period's knowledge of madness. He then shows how a reconfiguration of practices in the nineteenth century makes possible a new body of statements and a new collection of visibilities, which combine to form a psychiatric knowledge of insanity that is incommensurable with the preceding century's science of madness.

Deleuze insists that Foucault's statements and visibilities, despite their intimate interconnections, cannot be related to one another as signifiers to signifieds or signs to referents, for they have no common origin or isomorphic, unifying structure. What puts them in relation to one another is power, which constitutes a domain immanent within knowledge but irreducible to its categories of analysis. Deleuze defines power as relations between forces, each force having a varying capacity to affect and to be affected by other forces. Unlike statements and visibilities, which have concrete forms and specified functions, forces constitute an unformed matter with nonformalized functions. The relationship between the strata of knowledge and the unstratified field of power may be clarified, perhaps, if one compares statements and visibilities to the macroscopic objects of our everyday world and forces to the molecules of which they are formed, with the exception that forces are less molecular particles than vectors or zones of becoming, unstable, mobile and nonlocalizable elements imbued with a constant microagitation.

To specify further the nature of force, Deleuze makes use of a mathematical model which is worth exploring briefly. He describes forces as singular points, that is, as foci or nodes of curves or parabolas, the curves or parabolas being analogous to the regularities of statements and visibilities. Singular points, Deleuze argues, belong to a domain of problems that should be distinguished from the domain of specific equations and concrete solutions. For every general species of curve or parabola one may determine the existence of a singular point, Deleuze points out, but one cannot specify the coordinates of such a point until a particular curve or parabola is generated through the assignment of a given set of values. Thus, the singular point, before specific values are assigned, may be seen as a real but virtual entity that delimits a problem, or a zone of possibilities, with any number of concrete curves or parabolas actualizing that problem as various values are assigned to the basic equation that generates that species of curve or parabola. Although the location of the singular point is determined as a secondary result of the generation of a specific curve or parabola, the singular point has priority over individual curves or parabolas in that it is the focal element of the general problem of which various curves and parabolas are only so many instantiations.

Forces, then, are like singular points, real but virtual, nonlocalizable entities that determine the regularities of statements and visibilities while remaining themselves elements of a qualitatively distinct realm of problems and zones of possibility. Forces instigate the formation of statements and visibilities, even as these statements and visibilities consolidate, integrate, and actualize relations of forces within the complex regularities of large-scale regimes of signs and regimes of light. What puts statements and visibilities in relation to one another is the field of forces which they have in common. These forces, however, are not intrinsic components of statements and visibilities; hence the relation between the statable and the visible, since it passes through the intermediary of force, may be described as a nonrelation, and since that nonrelation is formed in a domain of nonlocalizable elements, it may be described as a nonrelation in a nonplace.

An instructive example of the relationship between strata of statements and visibilities and vectors of forces may be found in Foucault's *Discipline and Punish* (1975). One of Foucault's objects in this book is to describe the emergence of the modern penal system in the nineteenth century. He demonstrates that the prison became the standard form of punishment in Europe only as the result of a complex series of events quite separate from those that generated the discourse on delinquency which regulated the juridical mechanisms of penal detention. The prison found its conceptual ideal in Jeremy Bentham's "Panopticon; or, the Inspection House" (1787), a blueprint for a prison with a central observation tower and encircling cells that would allow guards to observe the prisoners without themselves being seen and hence to exercise a perpetual and ubiquitous surveillance over their charges. The panoptic prison served as a machine for creating visibilities, and its function gradually was duplicated in barracks, factories, hospitals, and schools. The discourse of delinquency generated a body of statements that became interconnected with the visibilities created by the prison machine, but what instigated the formation of statements and visibilities and what put them in relation to one another was a particular field of forces, a general dimension of nonformed matter and nonformalized functions. That nonformed matter found actualization within various forms of visibility, including the architectural structures of prisons, barracks, factories, and schools, as well as the human forms of prisoners, soldiers, workers, and students; and it also found actualization within various forms of enunciability, including the discursive categories of the delinquent, the deviant, the malignant, and the normal. The nonformalized function that characterized the nineteenth-century field of forces was that of a universal panopticism, a function of "seeing without being seen," which manifested itself in diverse regulative and normalizing practices within a heterogeneous collection of institutions.

Forces generate the forms of the strata of knowledge, but they remain separate from those strata. They constitute what Deleuze calls an Outside—not that which is outside of and removed from strata, but the outside of strata itself, at the limit of the knowable (since strata comprise knowledge) and the determinable. The Outside is immanent within strata, intimately interfused at a molecular level, yet nonlocalizable, and hence, as Deleuze cryptically remarks, "*an outside more distant* than any exterior world and even any form of exteriority, and consequently infinitely closer" (F 92/86). In his genealogical studies Foucault demonstrates the intimate ways in which power infiltrates the strata of knowledge by isolating the various subtle means whereby forces discipline bodies in a micropolitics of normalization and regimentation. But the internalization of power, that most intimate application of forces to oneself, Foucault only treats in his ethical studies. In Deleuze's schema, this internalization of power constitutes an inside of the Outside, and its figure is that of the fold.

The fold Deleuze has in mind is that of an invagination of a surface, such as the alveoli of the lungs, or the bays and harbors of a coastline. The fold is a topological figure of a single surface that forms two volumes, an inside and an outside, yet two volumes that communicate with one another as the inside of the outside and the outside of the inside. What Deleuze finds in the Greek ethical self that Foucault analyzes, then, is no foundational interiority, no discrete inner subject, but a fold that forms an inside of the outside, an invagination of forces. If the Greeks may be credited with having invented the self, it is because they managed to detach forces from collective networks of power and explicitly coded strata of knowledge and to turn forces back upon themselves. The activity of self-formation attained a relative autonomy among the Greeks that allowed a reflexive use of forces, and it is this doubling of forces that created the fold of the Greek ethical self. In these broad terms, therefore, the gradual shift in emphasis that Foucault detects—from the optional, unstructured forms of subjectivation of the classical world to the mandatory, juridical applications of social codes of behavior of the Christian and modern world—represents a slow unfolding of the Greek ethical self, a return of detached forces of self-formation to the general network of social forces. Yet this shift is only relative, and even among Christians and moderns the fold of the self remains an isolable dimension of the relation of forces.

The four aspects of self-formation that Foucault identifies, the ethical substance, mode of subjectivation, forms of elaboration, and telos of the desiring subject, Deleuze treats as four folds of the self. Of these four folds, however, it is the fold of the telos that Deleuze regards as most important. The ethical substance he reads simply as a material fold. The mode of subjectivation he labels "the fold of the relation of forces, properly speaking, for it is always according to a particular rule that the relation of forces is bent back to become a relation to oneself" (F 111/104). The forms of elaboration Deleuze identifies as "the fold of knowledge, or the fold of truth, in that it constitutes a relation of the true to our being, and of our being to the true" (F 111/104). And the telos he regards as "the fold of the outside itself, the ultimate fold" (F 112/104). In essence, what Deleuze has done is to redistribute the elements of Foucault's analysis, first by extracting those agonistic elements that appear in all four aspects of the self and assigning them to a single fold of forces, and then by removing the self's relation to truth from the telos of Greek ethics and classifying it with other codifications of behavior within a fold of knowledge. Thus, the telos, which Foucault discusses in terms of self-mastery, virility, truth, and aesthetics, becomes in Deleuze's reformulation a fold of freedom and aesthetic self-creation. Since the first fold simply establishes the matter of ethical labor, and the second and third folds are folds of power and knowledge, the only fold that adds anything new to Deleuze's map of Foucault is the fourth fold of the outside itself.

The Creative Self

Deleuze is somewhat free in his handling of the details of Foucault's analysis, yet his purpose obviously is not to recapitulate the minute points of the final volumes of *The History of Sexuality* but to make sense of those works as parts of a general philosophical project. As we have seen, Deleuze systematizes Foucault's thought by establishing the relationship between the archaeological strata of knowledge, the genealogical domain of power and the ethical folds of the self. In his discussion of the self, however, Deleuze also posits a relationship between Foucault's ethical studies and his numerous political interventions in roundtables, interviews, and discussions and his scattered remarks about a projected history of systems of thought. Deleuze's conjectures on this relationship between the self, politics, and thought are necessarily rather speculative, given the paucity of evidence he has to go on, yet it is perhaps here that Deleuze's analysis is at its most profound.

As Foucault indicates at several points, his genealogies are histories of the present, studies that commence with an intolerable situation in the contemporary world and seek a moment of discontinuity in the history of that situation, one that will defamiliarize existing practices and make it possible to imagine alternatives to them. So, in *Discipline and Punish* he starts with the intolerable institution of the modern prison, traces its history to its problematic formation at the beginning of the nineteenth century, demonstrates its arbitrary logic and its perpetual complicity with movements for prison reform, and hopefully opens up possibilities for undoing this institution—possibilities, of course, which Foucault himself encouraged by forming the *Groupe d'Information sur les Prisons* in 1971. Yet in Foucault's genealogies, the oppressive networks of power seem to grow ever more constraining as the analysis proceeds, and one soon comes to wonder how resistance of any kind is possible if power is as pervasive and insidious as he claims. What Deleuze sees in Foucault's ethical studies is an effort to envision the self as a locus of resistance, a point at which thought itself can become a political force. Hence, Deleuze concludes that the question Foucault's final books pose is, "If power is constitutive of truth, how can one conceive of a 'power of truth' which would not be the truth of power, a truth that would flow from transverse lines of resistance and not from integral lines of power?" (F 101/94–95).

Resistance is fundamental to force, Deleuze argues, since force is by nature unstable, mobile, and metamorphic. The regularities of statements and visibilities may consolidate and organize forces, but a contrary movement of forces toward dispersion and disorganization is immanent within all strata of knowledge, and resistance is merely a matter of accelerating this movement. (In his theoretical remarks on power, in fact, Foucault always recognizes the instability of relations of force and the existence of lines of resistance inherent within power, even if he does not stress this dimension of power in his genealogies.) If the self, then, is an internalization of forces, it necessarily may function as a locus of resistance. But what have forces and the self to do with thought?

In his introduction to volume 2 of *The History of Sexuality*, Foucault speaks briefly of all his works as so many parts of a general "history of truth" which analyzes "the games of truth and error through which being is historically constituted as experience; that is, as something that can and must be thought" (UP 6–7). His archaeologies and genealogies, he says, articulate "the *problematizations* through which being offers itself to be, necessarily, thought—and the *practices* on the basis of which these problematizations are formed" (UP 11). Yet these studies do more than simply describe problematizations and practices, for Foucault sees philosophical activity as "the critical work that thought brings to bear on itself," as "the endeavor to know how and to what extent it might be possible to think differently, instead of legitimating what is already known" (UP 9). Foucault's effort is to think differently and to satisfy a certain kind of curiosity, "not the curiosity that seeks to assimilate what it is proper for one to know, but that which enables one to get free of oneself" (UP 8). Thought, then, is an act of freedom, a way of seeing otherwise and of escaping oneself. As Foucault remarks in a late interview, "Thought is not what inhabits a certain conduct and gives it its meaning; rather, it is what allows one to step back from this way of acting or reacting, to present it to oneself as an object of thought and question it as to its meaning, its conditions, and its goals. Thought is freedom in relation to what one does, the motion by which one detaches oneself from it, establishes it as an object, and reflects on it as a problem" (*Foucault Reader* 388). Thus, in summary we may say that problematizations and practices constitute being as experience; problematizations instigate thought; and thought in turn frees one from problematizations, thereby making it possible for one to think otherwise and to initiate an aesthetics of self-formation.

Deleuze sees in these scattered remarks of Foucault's a way of bringing together Foucault's practice of thought—his histories of knowledge, power, and the self—and his theory of thought and its relation to the self. What Foucault refers to as problematizations are the conditions of possibility of statements and visibilities, the regularities of discursive formations and regimes of light that allow some things to be said and seen and others not. That which determines the forms of the statable and the visible and which puts them in relation to one another is the field of forces operative within a given historical period. The general configuration of such a field of forces may be described in terms of a distribution of singular points, an arrangement of various problems or zones of possibility which find actualization and consolidation in the specific strata of knowledge. The great epistemological shifts that Foucault studies—those, for example, from classical unreason to nineteenth-century psychiatry, or from royal torture in the ancien régime to nineteenth-century penal discipline—entail new distributions of singular points, each of which may be seen as a large-scale throw of the dice. Only at the level of forces, of the continuous throw of dice of the Outside, does thought gain autonomy from statements and visibilities, for only then can thought grasp them in terms of their conditions of possibility and modes of relation.

Yet if Foucault's thought is a thought *of* the Outside, it is also a thought *from* the Outside. In an early essay on Blanchot, Foucault details the many ways in which Blanchot's work constitutes a *"pensée du dehors,"* a "thought from without" or "thought from outside," which does not have its origin in a subject but emerges from the anonymous murmur of language itself, or from language's confrontation with the mute world that always escapes it. Deleuze argues that for Foucault as well thought comes from the Outside, from a disruptive play of forces that sets thought in motion. And to the extent that thought is able to arrive at something new, "to think differently," as Foucault says, "instead of legitimating what is already known" (UP 9), thought itself is a play of forces. Just as the epistemological shifts Foucault describes in his histories entail an aleatory redistribution of singular points, so his own thought aspires to induce a similar reconfiguration of singular points, one equally unpredictable in its arrangement and its ultimate effects. Hence Deleuze's conclusion that "to think is to emit singularities, to throw the dice" (F 124–25/117).

The subject of thought is a fold in the domain of forces, a topological inside of the Outside, but the fold must be understood temporally as well as spatially, argues Deleuze, for the redoubling of force creates an "absolute memory" that makes it possible "to put time on the outside, and to think the outside as time" (F 115/108). The term "absolute memory" Deleuze takes from Foucault's 1963 book *Death and the Labyrinth: The World of Raymond Roussel,* in which Foucault contrasts the fiction of Roussel and Michel Leiris by noting that while Roussel strives through various radical textual strategies to reach the "unbreathable void" of a pure Outside, Leiris adopts a slower and more patient methodology for reaching the Outside, in his autobiographical *Les règles du jeu,* for example, gradually gathering together, as Foucault says, "from so many things without social standing, from so many fantastic civil records . . . his own identity, as if in the *folds* of words there slept, with dreams never completely dead, an absolute memory" (*Death* 28–29). In his histories of the self Foucault follows Leiris's practice, seeking among the disparate records and documents of the Western archive the lingering trace of the Greek and Christian subject within the modern self. But in these histories Foucault also discovers an absolute memory, claims Deleuze, a "memory of the outside, beyond the short memory which is inscribed in strata and archives, beyond the relics still caught in the diagrams [of power]" (F 114/107).

Deleuze's analysis of absolute memory focuses on the relationship between thought, memory, and forgetting, a topic of clearly Heideggerian provenance, but one that owes much less to *What Is Called Thinking* than to Maurice Blanchot's *L'Entretien infini*. Blanchot approaches the theme of memory and forgetting through an intriguing discussion of Tristan and Iseult, in which he notes that the effect of the fatal love potion, according to one of the principal accounts of the tale, is said to last only three years. And in fact, in that version of the story at the end of three years the lovers awake from their spell, part, and proceed to the pursuit of their separate lives. Yet their passion does not die, but continues its own existence, as if their separation itself formed a new relation between the two lovers—a nonrelation—as if in forgetting their love "they approached the true center of their passion," a passion of impossibility and darkness, in which "it is the infinity of night itself that continues to desire itself, a neuter desire that has nothing to do with you or me" (*L'Entretien* 287). What this tale reveals is that desire is a forgetting that is retained, an enfolded, ineffable infinity that can never be known directly: "Forgetting: the movement of forgetting: infinity which opens up, in closing shut, with forgetting—provided that it is gathered together, not through the lightness that liberates the memory of memory, but, in the reminiscence *{souvenir}* itself, as the relation with that which is hidden and which no presence would be able to retain" (*L'Entretien* 288). That which can be retained only as a forgetting is what Blanchot calls the Outside, that stubbornly resistant dimension of experience that defies signification, and yet inhabits language as its shadowy, anonymous unthought.

Blanchot finds a similar structure of forgetting and remembering on a social scale in Foucault's account of the relationship between seventeenth- and eighteenth-century *déraison* and *raison* in *Madness and Civilization*.

During the Great Internment of the early seventeenth century, Foucault reports, madmen, perverts, prostitutes, libertines, beggars, and blasphemers were gathered together and placed in asylums that had formerly housed lepers. Through this internment, loci of "unreason" were established, sites for sequestering those who had lost the proper use of reason and who "thought wrongly." The asylum, says Blanchot, created a magic circle which enclosed "a truth, but a strange one, a dangerous one: the extreme truth which threatens all power of being true" (*L'Entretien* 293). It also enclosed death, not the living death of the lepers who formerly inhabited the asylums, but a death that was "more interior . . . the empty head of the fool substituted for the macabre skull, the senseless laugh instead of the funereal rictus, Hamlet facing Yorick, the dead jester, two times a jester" (*L'Entretien* 293). Those who were sequestered were forgotten by the world of reason but retained within it. And though the world of reason could establish no relation with unreason, since the mad refused to speak the language of reason, the asylum functioned as a foundational nonrelation between reason and unreason that made possible the delineation of reason through the expulsion and forgetting of its Other, the Outside.

For Blanchot, then, the thought of the Outside entails a paradoxical relation between memory and forgetting, in that this thought requires a retention of that which is necessarily forgotten. The asylum preserves the Outside at the same time that it relegates the Outside to forgetfulness; hence, one might say, the asylum is a memory of the Outside that is simultaneously a site of forgetting. Likewise, the passion of Tristan and Iseult is forgotten after three years, but its forgetting is retained as an anonymous and ongoing desire, a memory of the Outside that enfolds within it its own forgetting. This structure of retention and expulsion, of memory and forgetting, is unavoidable in thinking the Outside, for the Outside is that which is excluded through signification but which nevertheless continues to insist and persist even if it cannot exist in any articulable present.

Deleuze makes use of Blanchot's investigation of memory and forgetting in his treatment of the Foucauldian subject, arguing that the self, like the asylum, is an enclosure of the Outside, a way of constituting "an *interiority* of waiting and exception" (*L'Entretien* 292; cited by Deleuze, F 104/97). But Deleuze extends Blanchot's analysis to consider the structure of time itself in the thought of the Outside, a structure framed in terms of an enfolding and unfolding of the pure becoming of the Outside that constitutes a memory (a folding) of forgetting (an unfolding). That structure, though it is met with through history and historical analysis, is finally outside history, or rather, the Outside of history, for it is the structure of the untimely, or the Eternal Return.

Memory, claims Deleuze, "is the true name of the relation to self, or the affect of self by self" (F 115/107). The Outside is a dimension of pure becoming ruled by chance, a "moving matter animated by peristaltic movements, by folds and foldings that constitute an inside" (F 103–04/96–97). The inside, as fold of the Outside, doubles the Outside and is coextensive with it, in that the chaotic, unformed Outside and inside together compose an undifferentiated matter. The present of the Outside is doubled on the inside, but it is perpetually forgotten and at each moment reconstituted anew. The Outside, however, is retained in the past, in an absolute memory.

The forgotten present is the present of what Deleuze calls "the event," a time of pure becoming that qualitatively differs from measured, chronological time. In *What Is Philosophy?* Deleuze elaborates on this concept of the event by comparing it to Bergsonian *durée*. Bergson argues that if time is continuous, an atomized conception of time is inadequate, for if time consists simply of a succession of discrete moments or instants, there must always be time between any two instants. In the case of the time of the event, by contrast, "It is no longer time which is between two instants; it is the event which is a between-time [*entre-temps,* "meanwhile, meantime"]: the between-time is not of the eternal, but it is no longer (of) time either, it is (of) becoming. The between-time, the event, is always a dead time, where nothing happens, an infinite waiting {*attente*} which is already infinitely passed, waiting and reserve. This dead time does not succeed that which arrives; it coexists with the instant or the time of the accident, but as the immensity of empty time {*temps vide*} where one sees time both as still to come and as already arrived" (QP 149/158). The time of the event is a between-time, a dead time of pure becoming, a gap in chronological time that, as gap, eludes any present and functions as a forgetting. The virtual time of the event, however, is retained within an absolute memory. This absolute memory resembles what Deleuze refers to elsewhere as a Bergsonian virtual past, a past which has never existed as present, but which doubles every present moment and extends to include all virtual past moments within a single, coexisting dimension. Such a past constitutes the condition of possibility of all memory, a real but virtual dimension of pure memory within which specific, actual memories may arise.

The Outside, then, is forever forgotten as present but continually retained as past, its retention constituting a folding of the Outside, and its forgetting an unfolding. One may say, then, that the forgetting or unfolding of the present is that which is folded within memory. Hence, Deleuze argues, "That which is opposed to memory is not forgetting, but the forgetting of forgetting, which dissolves us in the outside, and which constitutes death" (F 115/107–08). It is through this interplay of memory and forgetting that we discover time as subject, for time "is the folding of the outside, and, as such, makes every present pass into forgetting, but conserves every past in memory, forgetting as the impossibility of return, and memory as the necessity of recommencement" (F 115/108). This interplay of necessary recommencement and impossible return, of course, is the interplay of the Eternal Return, the time of the perpetual repetition of difference.[4]

The Outside is the unthought of thought, and when the thinking subject discovers this unthought the subject problematizes itself and becomes an ethical subject with a new relation to time. The topological fold of the inside of the Outside, says Deleuze, "liberates a time that condenses the past in the inside, brings about the advent of the future from the outside, and confronts the two at the limit of the living present" (F 126–27/119). Through an ethics of thinking the Outside as the unthought of thought the subject is summoned first to analyze the past in terms of forces, to discover the distributions of singular points that form the conditions of strata of knowledge and hence to recognize those conditions as the Outside; and then to think "the past against the present, to resist the present" (F 127/119) by challenging the forms of knowledge, the relations of power and the codifications of the self that are sedimented in the present and that make up our identity, with the hope that something new may come about, an unpredictable and unforeseeable redistribution of singular points, a thought from the Outside. Thus, Deleuze concludes, "thought thinks its own history (past), but in order to liberate itself from that which it thinks (present), and to be able finally to 'think otherwise' (future)" (F 127/119).

The Self of Resistance

Deleuze always thinks with other philosophers rather than about them. Hence his commentaries on Hume, Nietzsche, Bergson, Spinoza, and Leibniz are as much expositions of his own thought as explications of theirs. Deleuze's *Foucault* is no exception to this practice. Yet I would argue that Deleuze's thought is as close to Foucault's as to anyone else's, and that his reading of Foucault remains one of our best guides to the Foucauldian corpus as a philosophical project. It is difficult to separate Deleuze from Foucault, to locate precisely the point at which Deleuze swerves to pursue his own distinct ends, although clearly in his development of the concepts of absolute memory and the Outside as the unthought of thought he is elaborating an argument that has only the most tenuous of connections with actual texts of Foucault's. Yet even here, I believe, Deleuze is pursuing a line of investigation that is in accord with the basic ends of Foucault's thought. It has been argued that in his description of the Foucauldian self Deleuze "errs in linking Foucault too closely with Nietzschean aspirations" (Bernauer 230), and that he takes no account in his portrait of the "critical maturity" (Bové, "The Foucault Phenomenon" xxxiv) of Foucault's cautious political activism. But ultimately these objections are matters more of emphasis and tone than of substance, for there is nothing in Deleuze's ethics of the Outside to preclude the establishment of solidarity with group struggles or the engagement of a prudent politics that goes beyond the easy rhetoric of liberation.

Foucault's thought is Nietzschean, and Deleuze is right in arguing for the centrality of force in the development of Foucault's archaeological, genealogical, and ethical studies. The conception of the self as a fold of forces, as an inside of the Outside, not only relates subjectivation to the domains of knowledge and power, but also makes possible a description of thought as a mode of resistance. Yet this Nietzschean thought of the self, as we have seen, may also be situated within the broad context of a modern transformation of archaic mimesis. In his description of the Greek desiring subject, Foucault shows sympathy toward the ancient aesthetics of self-formation and the notion of the self as a manifestation or production of force, even as he distances himself from the archaic structuration of the subject within the asymmetrical power relations of gender and class. The unstructured, aleatory fold of forces, which Deleuze identifies as the Foucauldian self, is finally a version of the ecstatic manifestation of power inherent in archaic mimesis, but one that is anarchic rather than aristocratic, conceived of as a mode of resistance to asymmetrical power relations rather than an integral part of such relations. Something of the archaic agon of forces remains in this conception of the self as fold, and it is in this regard that Deleuze differentiates himself and Foucault from Heidegger. ("In Foucault there has always been a Heraclitism that is deeper than in Heidegger, for finally phenomenology is too pacifying, it has blessed too many things" [F 120/113].) Yet this agon of forces is seen as a means of subverting fixed power relations rather than supporting them. Whether an ecstatic play of forces may be opposed to asymmetrical power relations, or whether the manifestation of force is inseparable from a stratifying power mentality, remains to be seen. This is the great wager that Deleuze and Foucault venture, the throw of the dice that is the playful fold of the self.

Tributaries

4

Minor Writing and Minor Literature

What is the role of theory in what some regard as a posttheoretical era? Or more specifically, what is the relevance of the Grand Theory of Poststructuralism for the set of analytic practices emergent in the last two decades that we might loosely label "cultural studies"?[1] The question is intriguing when considered in relation to the thought of Deleuze, whose philosophy is often regarded as poststructural, and whose concept of minor literature has been of some use to students of postcolonial, ethnic, minority, and marginal literatures. As I hope to show, though Deleuze's epistemology is antifoundational, his views of language, matter, and time put him at odds with much of poststructuralism, and though the concept of minor literature has been sympathetically received in cultural studies, the theoretical implications of the concept have not been generally recognized. It may be that Deleuze is simply an anomalous figure in French philosophy, but it is also possible that the movement from poststructural theorization to its application in cultural studies is less certain than might at first appear.

Poststructural Deleuze

There can be no doubt that Deleuze likes grand theories and that he builds abstract systems with a kind of profligate abandon—*Difference and Repetition, The Logic of Sense, Anti-Oedipus, A Thousand Plateaus,* and *What Is Philosophy?* would perhaps be the most striking examples of this aspect of his work. Is he a poststructuralist? In many ways, yes.[2] His epistemology is certainly antifoundational, as one can see from this 1985 interview: "This idea that truth is not something that pre-exists, that is to be discovered, but must be created in each domain, is obvious, for example in the sciences.

Even in physics, there's no truth that doesn't presuppose a symbolic system, be it only one of coordinates. There is no truth that does not 'falsify' established ideas. To say that 'truth is a creation' implies that the production of truth passes through a series of operations that amount to working on a material—in the strictest sense, a series of falsifications" (PP 172/126). A book of philosophy, he says in *Difference and Repetition,* "should be in part a very particular species of detective novel, in part a sort of science fiction" (DR 3/xx), a detective novel in that it "should intervene to resolve a local situation" (DR 3/xx), and a work of science fiction in that it should experiment on the real through an invention of concepts "at that point of our knowledge, at that extreme point which separates our knowledge from our ignorance and *makes each pass into the other*" (DR 4/xxi). Guattari speaks equally for Deleuze when he describes their work in *Anti-Oedipus* as that of a functionalist, for whom the question of meaning is irrelevant: "We are strictly functionalists: what interests us is how something works, functions, what machine it is. As for the signifier, that's still something from the domain of 'What does it mean?' . . . But for us, the unconscious does not mean anything, nor does language" (PP 35/21–22).[3]

Deleuze also characterizes his thought as a form of constructionism, which he opposes to the reflective activity of traditional philosophy: "What for me replaces reflection is constructionism. . . . To create concepts is to construct a region of the plane, to add a new region to existing ones, to explore a new region, to fill in what's missing. The concept is a composite, a consolidation of lines, of curves. If concepts must constantly be renewed, it's precisely because the plane of immanence has to be constructed region by region, it is a local construction, going from one contiguous point to the next" (PP 201/147). If one exercises the term with some caution, one might call his thought "aesthetic," and thereby ally him with the artist-metaphysicians whom Megill studies in *Prophets of Extremity*—Nietzsche, Heidegger, Foucault, Derrida. Besides stressing truth as creation, Deleuze argues for example that what is important in philosophy is not whether a statement is right or wrong, accurate or inaccurate, but whether it is relevant, interesting, and new: "But what someone says is never wrong, it's not that some things are wrong, but that they're stupid or of no importance. That they've been said a thousand times before. The notions of importance, of necessity, of interest, are a thousand times more significant than the notion of truth. Not at all because they replace truth, but because they measure the truth of what I'm saying" (PP 177/130).[4]

But there is much in Deleuze that separates him from the rest of his generation of poststructural philosophers. In commenting on Foucault's well-known statement, "One day, perhaps, the century will be seen as Deleuzian," Deleuze remarks that Foucault

> may perhaps have meant the following: that I was the most naive among the philosophers of our generation. In all of us, one finds themes like multiplicity, difference, repetition. But I put forward almost raw concepts, while others work with more mediations. I have never been concerned about going beyond metaphysics or the death of philosophy, and the renunciation of Totality, Unity, the Subject has never been a big deal for me. I've never broken from a kind of empiricism, which proceeds to a direct exposition of concepts. I haven't approached things through structure, nor through linguistics or psychoanalysis, through science or even through history, because I think philosophy has its own raw materials that allow it to enter into external, more fundamental, relations with other disciplines. (PP 122/88–89)

Deleuze perhaps exaggerates his distance from other disciplines, for he has certainly worked at length with the themes of structuralism, linguistics, psychoanalysis, and science, and he is somewhat disingenuous in saying that Totality, Unity, and the Subject have not preoccupied him, given his development of such concepts as the "open whole" *{tout ouvert}* (see IM 29–30/16–17), the whole as added part (see PS 195–98/163–65 and AO 50/42) and the various prepersonal, preindividual becomings that a subject may undergo (MP 284–380/233–309). Yet Deleuze does seem somewhat unconcerned about the metaphysics of presence as he builds his elaborate systems and makes apparently unqualified ontological assertions about the nature of matter, force, power, and so on. And it is not at all evident that he has even made "the linguistic turn," as Rorty has put it.

Throughout his work, Deleuze is obsessed with the limits of language. In *Proust and Signs* he examines the interpenetration of bodies and words in terms of signs, yet his is not a semiology of ubiquitous structured codes, but of hieroglyphic, concealed differences enfolded in words and things. In *The Logic of Sense,* his most extended treatment of language, he regards meaning *(sens)* as the incorporeal surface between bodies and words, the "expressed" of words whose "expression" is the event. It might seem that we have here a kind of textualism, in that Deleuze posits at times an indissociable link between meaning as the incorporeal surface of words and the event as the incorporeal surface of things, but it is evident at least in his later work that for him the statement "il n'y pas de hors texte" does not hold.

In *A Thousand Plateaus,* Deleuze and Guattari argue that language is a mode of action whereby speech acts modify the world by inducing "incorporeal transformations" of bodies. The set of regular patterns of speech action in effect in a given society forms a "collective assemblage of enunciation," or "regime of signs," whose function it is to intervene in bodies, which themselves are organized according to patterns of nondiscursive practice, or "machinic assemblages" (also referred to as "social technological machines"). There is interaction between the two strata of linguistic regimes of signs and nondiscursive machinic assemblages, but they remain separate and irreducible to one another. And immanent within the two strata is a virtual, unformed matter of pure speeds and intensities, a plane of consistency on which no differentiation can be made between words and things, signs and bodies. (Readers of Kristeva will recognize certain similarities between the plane of consistency and the semiotic *chora,* with the difference that Deleuze/Guattari subscribe to no developmental model of the psyche and regard the Kristevan semiotic as always immanent within the real.) Even, then, if one were to argue that the nondiscursive stratum of machinic assemblages is structured like a language or code (and it is not at all certain that a pattern of practices should be considered a language or code), the plane of consistency is clearly outside language and any form of semiotic organization.

Deleuze, then, is in some regards peripheral to the mainstream of poststructural thought, although one must also wonder whether such a mainstream is itself not a fiction. In a 1961 essay titled "The History of Philosophy and Historicity," Paul Ricoeur makes a useful distinction between two models of philosophy inherent in any history of philosophy: philosophy as system and philosophy as singularity. On one hand, historians of philosophy approach their subject as a system, according to which "the sum total of philosophies would only form one single philosophy in which historical philosophies would be particular moments" (Ricoeur 64). On the other, they regard each philosopher's thought as unique or singular, determined by the problem or question the individual philosopher alone was able to formulate. "From this point of view, singular philosophies are radically isolated from one another; each one constitutes a total world into which it is necessary to penetrate slowly by means of a kind of familiarity which is never totally achieved" (Ricoeur 65). Histories of philosophy continually shuttle between the two extremes of system and singularity, ceasing to be histories at all if they fully embrace either extreme, in that a single system of all philosophy is ultimately a static structure and a sequence of totally unrelated singularities forms an unstructured and meaningless aggregate. Ricoeur does not deny that philosophers live in a social and material world, it should be noted, but he argues that any "reflective" theory of history is inadequate to the origin of a philosophical problematic: "The theory of the 'reflection' is valid only as long as it is merely a question of explaining the social import of a philosophy, its social selection, its success or efficacity. It is not valid when it is a question of explaining the radical origin of a philosophy" (Ricoeur 68). The social import of philosophy is the legitimate subject of a sociology of knowledge, but "the history of philosophy is a philosophical activity" (Ricoeur 69).

Deleuze, of course, is in many regards far from Ricoeur, but he does share Ricoeur's interest in problems and singularity in thought. For Deleuze, philosophy is the invention of concepts, and the object of a history of philosophy is to identify various concepts and to articulate the problems to which they are responses. "Philosophy is not communicative, any more than it is contemplative or reflective: it is creative or even revolutionary, by nature, in that it is ceaselessly creating new concepts. The only condition is that these should have a necessity, as well as a strangeness, and they have both to the extent they respond to real problems" (PP 186–87/136). Although Deleuze recognizes thought's embeddedness in concrete situations, and hence sympathizes with Foucault's genealogical practices, he also stresses the singularity or newness of genuine thought.[5] An efficacious problem is a disruptive event, an enfolded, implicate difference, immanent within the real, whose time is that of Aion as opposed to Chronos, a delirious time "out of joint" *(hors de ses gonds)*, a pure becoming that is neither historical nor eternal but *"intempestif,"* or "untimely" (as in Nietzsche's *Unzeitgemässe Betrachtungen*).[6] "There is no act of creation that is not transhistorical and does not come up from behind or pass by way of a liberated line. Nietzsche opposes history not to the eternal but to the subhistorical or superhistorical: the Untimely, another name for haecceity, becoming, the innocence of becoming (that is, forgetting as opposed to memory, geography as opposed to history, the map as opposed to the tracing, the rhizome as opposed to arborescence)" (MP 363/296).

Clearly, for Deleuze any history of philosophy must be a paradoxical enterprise, for it must be a history of the untimely, or that which escapes history—and indeed, this is the kind of "history" Deleuze himself fashions in his many studies of other philosophers. Rather than offering a narrative of the development of ideas, arguments, positions, and so on, he describes the functioning of specific problems and sets them in resonance with one another through the unfolding of the problems proper to his own thought. In this manner Deleuze creates his own precursors—among whom one would number especially the Stoics, Spinoza, Hume, Nietzsche, and Bergson—and brings them into a kind of untimely, interactive coexistence within the problems he articulates. To the extent that Deleuze himself is successful in formulating genuine problems, his thought should disrupt conventional narratives of the history of philosophy, and his accounts of others' thought should bring into existence an idiosyncratic, untimely network of precursors that constitutes an "antihistory" of his own thought. Given Deleuze's views and practices of philosophy and history, then, it is not surprising that we should find his position within poststructuralism to be problematic.

Minor Literature

The concept of minor literature, which Deleuze and Guattari first enunciate in *Kafka: Toward a Minor Literature,* is perhaps the notion of theirs that has best lent itself to accommodation within cultural studies.[7] Deleuze and Guattari list three characteristics of minor literature: "Its language is affected with a high coefficient of deterritorialization" (K 29/16); "everything in [a minor literature] is political" (K 30/16); and in it "everything takes on a collective value" (K 31/16). Via the first characteristic the concept of minor literature engages the "language question," which has been at the center of many discussions of postcolonial literature. As Deleuze and Guattari point out, Kafka is caught between several languages and at home in none. The German he speaks with his family is a bureaucratic, "paper language"; the Czech through which he communicates with servants is the language of his father's disowned rural Jewish heritage; the Yiddish of Löwy's theater is an uncanny, slightly frightening language; and the Hebrew of the synagogue is a distant language he only learns later in life. Yet this linguistic dispossession allows Kafka to discover a minor usage of German, an intensive, unsettling disequilibrium within the language that opens it to creative deformations. Kafka's situation is analogous to that of Indian writers who must choose between their regional, Indian tongues and a pan-Indian, bureaucratic English, or African writers who must decide whether to communicate widely through the colonizer's tongue or reach a more limited audience through a specific tribal language. And Kafka's deterritorialization of German represents a particular strategy for dealing with this widespread postcolonial linguistic dilemma. The closely related second and third characteristics of minor literature have proven germane to discussions of gay, lesbian, and women's literatures in that these aspects of minor literature stress the inseparability of the personal and the political as well as the unavoidably collective dimension of any individual effort by members of a marginalized group.

One of the original features of the concept of "minor literature" is its rapprochement of three distinct categories of literature: *secondary literature,* whether it be that of a minor nation or linguistic group in relation to a major tradition, or that of a humble, minor movement or tendency (for example, American local colorists) within a larger tradition; *marginal literature,* or the literature of minorities; and *experimental literature,* which "minorizes" a major language (in the sense that a minor key in music may be said to chromaticize and destabilize the harmonic order of a major key). The effects of this rapprochement have been salutary in the study of high modernism, whose chief practitioners have all too often been regarded as politically disengaged cosmopolitan aesthetes. By treating Kafka as a minor writer, Deleuze and Guattari call attention to his status as a member of an ethnic minority and citizen of a minor region/protonation within a foreign-based empire, while insisting that his formal and thematic innovations in literature have direct social and political implications. As this analysis is extended to other modernists—Joyce and Beckett, for example—the seeming unity of European modernism comes into question, as does its supposed remove from the domain of social and political struggle.

Yet if the syncretism of the concept of minor literature has given it power in dislodging presuppositions about modernism, it also has occasioned critique. In his study of Sarah Orne Jewett as a minor American writer, Louis A. Renza provides a detailed and sympathetic account of Deleuze and Guattari's concept of minor literature, but he concludes that their battle against the canon of major literature betrays an unconscious desire to form a countercanon of anti-Oedipal literature—a subset of great oppositional writers, such as Kafka and Beckett, within the set of great modernists. It seems highly debatable that praise of an author must entail a desire for a canon, and as Bensmaïa points out, Renza's critique does not sufficiently take into account the politico-historical forces that have summoned minor literature into existence, and hence the extent to which the category of minor literature is descriptive rather than arbitrarily prescriptive. But whatever the shortcomings of Renza's argument, his ultimate goal is to preserve the distinction between primary and secondary literature. Hence he must oppose the inclusion of any "great" writer within the category of minor literature, something Deleuze and Guattari invite by bringing together secondary literature and experimental literature in a single concept.

A similar uneasiness with minor literature's conceptual syncreticism underlies Caren Kaplan's critique of Deleuze and Guattari—in this case, however, from the perspective of minority literatures. Kaplan argues that for many people "becoming minor" is not a choice but something forced upon them, and that in positing a universal potential for linguistic deterritorialization Deleuze and Guattari obscure the real differences between privileged and disempowered writers: "What is lost in Deleuze and Guattari's formulation is the acknowledgement that oppositional consciousness (with its benefits and costs) stems from the daily, lived experience of oppression" (Kaplan 191). Deleuze and Guattari do not ignore this distinction, but they do make possible an inclusion of privileged and oppressed within a single category by suggesting a common ground between experimental and minority literatures and by asserting the feasibility of a "becoming minor" of white first-world males. Kaplan's insistence on the importance of oppression, then, has the effect of reinstating the distinction between minority and majority discourses that the concept of minor literature blurs.

Although references to the concept of minor literature are frequent in discussions of postcolonial, minority, and marginal literatures, it is not at all certain that the concept has been thoroughly assimilated within these fields.[8] Renza and Kaplan offer critiques of the concept, but without fully acknowledging the presuppositions that underlie it and make necessary the syncretism they oppose. The concept of minor literature is only one element of Deleuze and Guattari's study of Kafka, an element whose coherence depends on a number of interrelated concepts that are seldom mentioned in others' treatment of the idea. In *A Thousand Plateaus* Deleuze and Guattari develop those concepts at length and thereby clarify the larger theoretical assumptions that feed into the notion of minor literature. In Deleuze's last book, *Essays Critical and Clinical*, those assumptions are neatly summarized in the brief essay "Literature and Life," which describes the function of literature in terms of stuttering, becoming, fabulation, and visions/auditions.

Great writers stutter in their own language, says Deleuze, or rather, they make the language itself stutter. Such writers create within language "a sort of foreign language, which is not a different language, nor a rediscovered patois, but a becoming-other of the language, a minorization of that major language, a delirium that carries it away, a sorcerer's line that escapes the dominant system" (CC 15/5). At various times Deleuze offers as examples of this "becoming-other of the language" the grammatical anomalies of e. e. cummings ("He danced his did" [CC 89–90/68]), the fractured variations of Gherasim Luca ("Passionné nez passionnem je / je t'ai je t'aime je / je je jet je t'ai jetez / je t'aime passionnem t'aime" [CC 139/110]), and the obsessive repetitions of Beckett ("Le meilleur moindre. Non. Néant le meilleur. Le meilleur pire. Non. Pas le meilleur pire. Néant pas le meilleur pire. Moins meilleur pire. Non. Le moins. Le moins meilleur pire" [E 106/CC 174]).

But these are not simply instances of an aestheticist experimentation with form. In Deleuze's view, language is charged with power relations. The object of language is not communication, but the inculcation of *mots d'ordre*—"slogans," "watchwords," but also literally "words of order," the dominant, orthodox ways of classifying, organizing, and explaining the world. Far from being a mere collection of ideological signifiers, language is a mode of action, the various *mots d'ordre* of a culture being enforced through regular patterns of practice, "collective assemblages of enunciation," or "regimes of signs." These patterns or regimes of signs are themselves in constant interaction with nondiscursive forces that shape the material world, practices that form "social technological machines," or "machinic assemblages." Immanent within language are "lines of continuous variation," virtual oscillations of difference, real without being actual, that regimes of signs actualize in specific, disciplinary forms.

At the phonological level, a line of continuous variation may be conceived of as the range of possible pronunciations of a phoneme, a sonic spectrum of articulations with a central band of dominant, prestigious enunciations, outer bands of regional, occupational, racial, class, or gender-specific pronunciations, and liminal zones of deformed articulation in which the phoneme shades indiscernibly into the sonic spectrum of a neighboring phoneme. A syntactic line of continuous variation would include a spectrum of combinatory patterns whose liminal members merge with alternative syntactic options or fade into as yet unactualized patterns. At the semantic level, a line of continuous variation may be thought of as the range of possible instantiations of a given speech act, the collection of practice contexts through which a particular phrase takes on its various shades of meaning. Regimes of signs limit and control these lines of continuous variation, channel them into acceptable pragmatic patterns, and discipline deviant oscillations and perturbations. Yet the lines of continuous variation remain immanent within the regimes of signs, available for actualization at any time.

When writers efficaciously experiment with language, then, they do not simply manipulate signifiers. They experiment on the real; they activate lines of continuous variation immanent within language. And in so doing, they engage the same forces of creative deformation that various minorities utilize in fashioning their own speech within a dominant language—Czech Jews in German, the Irish in British English, African-Americans in white American English. Linguistic experimentation is directly political, and it is this fact that makes possible the inclusion of secondary, experimental, and marginal literatures within the single category of minor literature. That which is deemed secondary, whether within a single national literature or within an international world system of literatures, is that which deviates from dominant regimes of signs or falls within the parameters of unprestigious patterns of variation. Marginal discourses likewise either break with ruling linguistic practices or conform to ghettoized minor usages. Minor literature is a minor *usage* of language, one that may be practiced across a wide range of discourses, including those commonly classified as secondary, avant-garde, or marginal.

What is essential to note is that the theory of minor literature entails ontological claims about the nature of language and its relation to the world. The lines of continuous variation immanent within language are virtual—real without being actual, not mere potentials or possibilities but existing vectors of force actualized through various patterns of discursive practice. The virtual constitutes a domain of unformed matter and nonformalized functions in which no differentiation can be made between the discursive and the nondiscursive; only as the virtual is actualized in various regimes of signs and machinic assemblages does it becomes associated with the formed matter and formalized functions of discursive or nondiscursive pragmatic patterns. A minor usage of language thus involves an engagement not only with sociopolitical forces but also with a nonlinguistic outside characterized solely by differential speeds and affective intensities. As one can see, the theoretical presuppositions underlying the concept of minor literature are antitextualist and unabashedly metaphysical (albeit in a problematic way), something deconstructive cultural critics seldom acknowledge as they make occasional use of the term.

Linguistic stuttering induces a becoming-other of language, but according to Deleuze this is only one of a series of becomings that are central to the function of literature—becoming-woman, becoming-child, becoming-black, becoming-animal, becoming-molecular, becoming-imperceptible: "Writing is inseparable from becoming: in writing one becomes-woman, one becomes-animal, or vegetable, one becomes-molecular to the point of becoming-imperceptible" (CC 11/1). Value-laden binary oppositions regulate social codes: male/female, white/nonwhite, European/non-European, adult/child, human/animal, and so on. A becoming is a passage between things, a decoding that proceeds via a mutative interaction with the stigmatized term of a binary power relation. A becoming-woman is a passage between male and female that undoes gender codes, but a passage away from the dominant values of maleness, and hence a becoming-*woman*. (That passage must take place *between* man and woman since both terms are coded within a male-dominated power structure—hence Deleuze's statement that even women must undergo a becoming-woman.) Likewise, a becoming-black undoes racial codes, a becoming-child decodes adult norms of behavior, and a becoming-animal scrambles cultural codes of properly human action.

To the extent that social codes are embedded in language, a becoming-other of language necessarily involves a becoming-woman, a becoming-black, or a becoming-animal, but such becomings are not exclusively linguistic, since they partake of the virtual. The goal of writing, says Deleuze, is becoming-imperceptible (D 56/45), and all other forms of becoming are simply means of attaining such imperceptibility. Becoming-imperceptible is a process of elimination whereby one divests oneself of all coded identity and engages the abstract lines of a nonorganic life, the immanent, virtual lines of continuous variation that play through discursive regimes of signs and nondiscursive machinic assemblages alike. The camouflage fish, according to Deleuze and Guattari, far from illustrating mimeticism in nature, is an exemplary practitioner of becoming-imperceptible: "it is crisscrossed by abstract lines that resemble nothing, that do not even follow its organic divisions; but thus disorganized, disarticulated, it forms a world with the lines of a rock, with the sand, and with plants, becoming imperceptible" (MP 343/280). Writers follow the practice of the camouflage fish, eliminating all identifying marks until they engage the abstract lines of virtual force that play through language and the world.

The concept of becoming is inseparable from that of minor literature, in that minor literature's deterritorialization of language necessarily entails a dissolution of cultural codes. (In Deleuze and Guattari's study of Kafka, in fact, considerable time is devoted to instances of becoming-child and becoming-animal in his work.) The notion of becoming-imperceptible also clarifies minor literature's relationship to secondary literature and its status as a collective enterprise. Major literatures view great authors as strong personalities, superior individuals with unique identities, whereas secondary authors are seen as insufficiently individuated, generic hacks. Minor literature embraces the anonymity of the secondary, but pushes it to an extreme, turning the generic into the imperceptible, the clichéd into the collective, for by engaging the abstract lines of continuous variation immanent within a regime of signs the minor writer manipulates the same forces that marginal groups activate in their creative deformation of a major language. Yet if minor literature is an inherently collective activity, it is one that in its very operation dissolves the collectivity, since minor literature's various becomings have as their function the decoding of all fixed identities. Further, such becomings are untimely, transhistorical events that manifest the time of Aion, creative acts that "are like mutant abstract lines that have disengaged themselves from the task of representing a world, precisely because they assemble a new type of reality that history can only repossess or resituate in punctual systems" (MP 363/296). It is not surprising, then, that the concept of becomings has not featured prominently in cultural studies,[9] since it puts in question all identity formation and problematizes any critical approach that is grounded in history.

There is, however, another sense in which minor literature is collective. Besides being a form of stuttering and a process of becoming, writing (that is, minor writing, or the minor usage of language) is a kind of fabulation: "Health as literature, as writing, consists of the invention of a people that is lacking. The fabulative function of literature is to invent a people" (CC 14/4). If minor literature is immediately political and collective, its primary problem is that the collectivity as subject of a genuine becoming does not exist. In this sense, the writer must invent a people, create the subject of a collective decoding of its own externally imposed identity. Such a people "is not called to dominate the world. It is a minor people, eternally minor, seized in a becoming-revolutionary" (CC 14/4). Whenever minor writers enter a process of becoming, they engage collective lines of continuous variation within a regime of signs, and in so doing invent the voice of a minor people: "It's the *becoming* of the writer. Kafka for central Europe, Melville for America—both present literature as the collective enunciation of a minor people, or of all minor peoples, who only find their expression in and through the writer" (CC 15/4).

It would seem, then, that fabulation represents a compensatory restitution of identity following the dissolution of codes induced by the various becomings that tend toward a general becoming-imperceptible. But we must be cautious. Literature as becoming is delirium, says Deleuze, and if "there is no delirium that does not pass through peoples, races and tribes, and does not haunt universal history" (CC 15/4), likewise there is no fabulation that is not also delirious: "The ultimate goal of literature is to disengage in delirium this creation of a health, or this invention of a people, that is, a possibility of life" (CC 15/4). The people to be invented will be perpetually minor, forever in the process of becoming other, possessed of the delirious identity of an event. The event has a specificity, a mode of individuation that is singular but "very different from that of a person, of a subject, of a thing, or of a substance" (MP 318/261). Events are like hurricanes, battles, or seasons, phenomena that are made up entirely "of relations of movement and rest between molecules or particles, the power of affecting and being affected" (MP 318/261). We may label a hurricane "Hugo," but it is less a thing than a movement, or better, a concatenation of multiple, heterogeneous movements. To name an event requires three components: an indefinite pronoun to suggest its nonentitative principle of individuation; a proper name to indicate its singularity; and an infinitive to denote its untimely, transhistorical temporality. If minor writers invent a people, then, it is only in the sense that their fabulation creates a people as movement and event, a singular vector of a continuous becoming-other.

Writing is stuttering, becoming, and fabulation, according to Deleuze, but it is also a mode of "vision and audition," a way of pushing language to its limits and revealing its own outside. The problem of writing, says Deleuze, is inseparable "from a problem of *seeing* and *hearing*: when another language is created in language, it is the language as a whole that tends toward an 'asyntactic,' 'agrammatical' limit, or that communicates with its proper outside" (CC 9/lv). A minor deterritorialization of language entails the destruction of one's native tongue and the creation of a new language within that tongue (CC 16/5), and it proceeds via a dynamic syntactic line of variation, or "grammar of disequilibrium" (CC 141/112), which is inseparable from a linguistic limit of pure intensities toward which it tends. At that limit, a painting and a music proper to language emerge, visions and auditions that form the outside of language. These sights and sounds are not external to language but themselves constitute the outside surface of language. Painters such as Rembrandt, Cézanne, and Van Velde, according to Deleuze, find a way to pierce the surface of their paintings so that "the void or the visible in itself" appears; composers like Beethoven or Schubert pierce the surface of their music to reveal "silence or the audible in itself" (E 103/CC 172–73). So also do writers like Kafka and Beckett "bore holes in language" and disclose "colors and sonorities that rise above words . . . across words, between words" (CC 9/lv). The visions and auditions that form language's limit "are not phantasms, but veritable Ideas which the writer sees and hears in the interstices of language, in the gaps of language" (CC 16/5). They are sights and sounds proper to language, an in itself of language that renders language silent: "The words paint and sing, but at the limit of the path they trace in dividing and combining. The words make silence" (CC 142/113).

In *What Is Philosophy?* Deleuze and Guattari state that the object of the arts is to render sensations in matter, "to extract a block of sensations, a pure being of sensations" (QP 158/167). Sensations are percepts and affects, which are not to be confused with perceptions and affections. Percepts and affects "are *beings* that have value in themselves and exceed any lived reality. . . . The work of art is a being of sensation and nothing else: it exists in itself" (QP 154–55/164). Such percepts and affects are like Erwin Straus's phenomenological "sensations," fusional, primary apprehensions in which subject and object are indissociable, but with the exception that percepts and affects are beings, nonhuman, preindividual entities that pass through human beings and constitute them: "*Affects are precisely these nonhuman becomings of man,* just as percepts (including the town) are *nonhuman landscapes of nature.* . . . One is not in the world, one becomes with the world, one becomes by contemplating it. Everything is vision, becoming. One becomes universe" (QP 160/169). What artists do is to extract percepts from perceptions, affects from affections, and give them material embodiment, either by realizing sensation within the material they manipulate or by making the material pass into sensation (QP 182–83/193).

Clearly, the visions and auditions of the limits of language are percepts that find embodiment in the material of language, just as the becomings of minor writing are affects that pass through linguistic matter. These visions and auditions are percepts proper to language in the sense that they are percepts that language alone can actualize, but they have their own being, which is one with the play of forces immanent within the real, the vectors of unformed matter and unformalized functions that trace the movement of a nonorganic life. Visions and auditions form the limits of language, but they are actualized only with the engagement of the immanent nonlinguistic forces of the plane of consistency. It is for this reason that Deleuze says of visions and auditions, those "veritable Ideas which the writer sees and hears in the interstices of language," that "it is the passage of life into language that constitutes the Ideas" (CC 16/5).

Minor Writing

Minor literature is a way of writing, more a usage of language than a product, a process rather than a form. It is perhaps more accurate, then, to speak of minor literature as minor writing rather than minor literature (although Deleuze uses the words "writing" and "literature" interchangeably to refer to the verbal art he admires). Such a designation helps as well to clarify Deleuze's focus as a commentator on writing and literature, for his orientation is seldom that of a critic reading a text—explicating, interpreting, or deciphering a completed work of art—but instead that of someone trying to think with the writer about the process and logic of the text's becoming. One might argue that Deleuze is simply engaging in a version of the Romantic expressive aesthetics that Abrams outlines in *The Mirror and the Lamp,* an aesthetics that focuses on the artist rather than the audience, universe, or work. If so, however, it is an unusual expressive aesthetics, in that what is expressed is not "the poet's perceptions, thoughts, and feelings" (Abrams 22) but the nonhuman percepts and affects that pass through the world and artist. There is indeed a certain Romantic line of descent evident in Deleuze's focus on the creators of art, one that passes through Nietzsche, whose remarks about art are generally statements about artists and the way they view their creative activity. But Deleuze's focus is exclusively on the problem of art from the artist's perspective, the goals artists pursue and effects they achieve, not on the artists themselves.

A brief look at one of Deleuze's essays from *Essays Critical and Clinical,* "The Shame and the Glory: T. E. Lawrence," should suffice to delineate his method of commentary. Early in this study of Lawrence's *Seven Pillars of Wisdom,* Deleuze cites a letter from E. M. Forster to Lawrence, in which Forster describes Lawrence's book as "granular": "Dividing literature into fluid and granular, you come into the latter class. It's not merely your subject matter that makes me say this. You do present (though you don't see) life as a succession of items which are organically connected but yet have some sort of intervals between them, i.e., you give a series of pictures. I see people on camels, motionless, I look again and they are in a new position which I can connect with its predecessor, but is similarly immobile. There never can have been a Movement with so little motion in it!" (A. W. Lawrence 58). It is typical of Deleuze to cite writers about writing; seldom does he quote critics. Forster comments on the compositional problem of structuring a work of prose, and though his orientation is not antithetical to that of a mere reader, his perspective is clearly that of a fellow author. And though Forster points to objective, concrete aspects of the text—the succession of static images through which Lawrence tells his story—his main concern is to convey an impression he has of the work—that of a granular, motionless movement. It is precisely the impressionistic nature of Forster's remarks that Deleuze values, for what Forster is isolating is an effect, a "feel," an "atmosphere" that pervades Lawrence's book. This is not a subjective, emotive impressionism, as one finds in the connoisseurship of many nineteenth-century commentators on *les beaux arts,* but a necessarily imprecise description of what Deleuze calls an event—something whose mode of individuation is not that of a thing, but a hurricane or a battle—a becoming. This is where Deleuze usually starts his literary analyses, with the evocation of an atmosphere, an intuitive impression of the event of a work, and his task from that point on is to articulate the logic of its unfolding and the artistic problem that informs its creation.

The granularity Forster identifies permeates *Seven Pillars of Wisdom*, not only in its succession of static scenes, but also in its style, "which sounds like a foreign language, less Arabic than a phantom German" (CC 149/119). And in these static scenes, through this granular "phantom German," appear "aesthetic percepts as veritable visions" (CC 146/116), absolute landscapes of pure light and movement. Lawrence also "projects into things, into reality, in the future and up to the sky, an image of himself and others intense enough so that *it lives its own life*" (CC 147/117–18). Far from being a mythomaniac, Lawrence is a fabulator inventing a revolutionary people, projecting enlarged images of a collective becoming on a landscape of visionary percepts. But Lawrence's specific problem goes beyond that of embodying percepts and fabulative images, for *Seven Pillars of Wisdom* is really two books, "one concerning images projected into the real that live their own life, the other concerning the mind that contemplates them, delivered to its own abstractions" (CC 149/119). For Lawrence, abstract ideas are "entities that inspire powerful spatial dynamisms, and which mix intimately in the desert with projected images, things, bodies or beings" (CC 149/119). These abstract entities "which pass into the desert, *double the {projected} images,* mixing with images and giving them a visionary dimension" (CC 150/120).

A crucial abstract entity in Lawrence's book is shame, which manifests itself in three different ways. There is first the shame of betrayal, the shame of betraying the Arabs by making promises Lawrence knows the British will not honor, and the shame (mixed with pride) of betraying the British by training partisans capable of turning on their colonial masters. There is also the shame of command and subordination, Lawrence as commander "stealing souls to send them to suffering," yet as follower "being submitted to inferiors" (CC 152/122). But most important is Lawrence's shame for the body. The Arabs scorn the body because it is separate from the mind, but Lawrence is ashamed of the body because it is inseparable from the mind. The body is an animal living its own life, whereas the mind is an observer suffering the body's appetites and sensations: "The mind begins by coldly and curiously regarding what the body does; at first it is a witness; then it is moved *{il s'émeut}*, an impassioned witness, that is, it undergoes in its own right affects that are not simply the effects of the body, but veritable *critical entities* hanging over the body and judging it" (CC 155/124). It is in this shame of the body, then, that the true nature of abstract entities is revealed: they are "emotions, affects" (CC 155/124). Their intensity permeates Lawrence's style and the visionary images he project into the world. "They are not only the eyes of the mind, but its Powers *(Puissances)*, and its Words. It is the shock of [such abstract] entities that one hears in the style of Lawrence. But because they have no other object than the body, they stir up at the limit of language the apparition of great visual and sonic Images that hollow out animate and inanimate bodies, in order both to humiliate and magnify them at the same time" (CC 156/124).

The problem for Lawrence, then, is that of embodying percepts and affects, the percepts of visions (absolute landscapes of pure light and movement) and images (projections of a future revolutionary people), and the affects of abstract entities (affective ideas such as shame). Deleuze's task is to think with Lawrence, to extract from his practice a logic of percepts and affects that explains the specific way in which Lawrence brings together body and mind, image and abstraction, vision and style. Forster's impression of granularity points toward the work's complex atmospheric identity—the desert dust of sand and light, the halting movement of successive static images, the rough cadences of a phantom German. And as Deleuze articulates the relationship between visions, images and entities, the specific nature of that granularity unfolds, the peculiar intensity and quality of the luminous landscapes and fixed tableaus resulting from the superimposition of hallucinatory visions, fabulative images, and palpable affective abstractions, the grinding rhythms of the style arising from the shock of abstract entities rubbing against one another: "It is as if [abstract] entities people an inner desert which is applied to an external desert, where fabulous images are projected across bodies, men, beasts, and rocks. Entities and Images, Abstractions and Visions combine to make Lawrence another William Blake" (CC 156/124).

Deleuze's writing about literature often seems impressionistic, replete with evocative imagery and vague in its indications of what aspects of the text precisely create the effects he describes. In part this is a function of the object of his analysis. Stutterings, visions, and auditions are at the limits of language; becomings by their nature defy exact description; percepts and affects are beings that literally interfuse animals, plants, landscapes and people. But Deleuze's impressionism stems as well from his basic approach to literary commentary. He may offer poetic evocations of textual effects or cite occasional examples, but never does he attempt to demonstrate that his is the best reading of a passage or the proper way of interpreting a text. Rather, he simply invents a way of thinking about a work, one that has the dual purpose of articulating the logic of a work's construction from the perspective of the artist and of formulating philosophical concepts of sufficient inner consistency to sustain that logic. The purpose of his analyses is to think alongside the work of art, not to explain it or to stand in for it, but to create a philosophical analog that invites the reader to imagine the work in a new way that necessarily entails a new understanding of the world. Hence the tendency of Deleuze's commentaries to read like manifestos, tools to help writers conceive of new possibilities for their art, yet at the same time to function simply as moments in the unfolding of the single problem that constitutes his philosophical project.

The Minor

Minor literature is not a specific kind of literature—the literature of minorities, the literature of secondary authors or small nations, the literature of the avant-garde—but a way of writing, a use of language. What Deleuze and Guattari call "minor literature" in *Kafka* is simply what Deleuze elsewhere refers to as "writing" or "literature," that is, the linguistic practice that he admires and promotes. That cultural studies should find minor literature an appealing concept is not surprising, but the full implications of the concept have not always been recognized. By relating Deleuze's remarks on writing as stuttering, becoming, fabulation and vision/audition to the notion of minor literature as a political, collective deterritorialization of language, I have tried to show that implicit in the concept of minor literature are a number of theoretical assumptions about the nature of language, matter, force, time, and history that are idiosyncratic to Deleuze's philosophy. I have also tried to demonstrate that Deleuze's conception of literature is bound up with a specific kind of commentary, an artist-oriented, impressionistic, poetic thinking-alongside-texts that functions as both literary manifesto and philosophical essay. That critics should appropriate the concept of minor literature for their own purposes is not objectionable. There is nothing inherently wrong with eclecticism or bricolage, but it is important to be aware of the presuppositions that underlie the concepts one appropriates, if only to be cognizant of the alterations one has imposed on them in adapting them for different uses. If one takes seriously the concept of minor literature, I believe, either one must embrace the concept and thereby adopt a theoretical stance that requires a rethinking of fundamental aspects of literary criticism, or one must significantly reconfigure the concept to make it serve other ends.

There can be no doubt that over the last forty years Grand Theory has generally given way to various forms of cultural studies, yet it seems less evident that we have entered a posttheoretical age. Certain theories have been assimilated within cultural studies, but others have not, and though a theoretical consensus has emerged among some practitioners of cultural studies, I doubt that the assumptions underlying that consensus will long go unchallenged. Anomalous figures like Deleuze, I suspect, will continue to appear, and when they do, philosophical events will transpire, untimely perturbations will disturb the even flow of our histories, and theory will begin anew.

❖ 5

Becoming Metal, Becoming Death . . .

> *Metal is neither a thing nor an organism,
> but a body without organs.*
> —Deleuze and Guattari, *A Thousand Plateaus*

In *A Thousand Plateaus,* Deleuze and Guattari assert that "all becomings commence with and pass through becoming-woman. It is the key to all other becomings" (MP 340/277). One means of testing this assertion is through an examination of death metal music, a form of heavy metal rock music that has emerged in the United States and Europe during the last twenty years.[1] Performed almost exclusively by men for majority male audiences, death metal features high-adrenalin, high-volume songs with often violent, aggressive, and angry lyrics. Yet musically death metal offers instances of a genuine becoming, I believe, even though in many ways it is strongly coded as masculine. In *Running with the Devil,* easily the best book available on heavy metal music and an essential contribution to the study of popular music in general, Robert Walser observes that most treatments of heavy metal concentrate almost exclusively on the lyrics and say little about the music, despite the fact that performers and audiences alike regard the music as primary. Since a thorough consideration of both the lyrics and music of death metal is well beyond the scope of a single chapter, my focus will be mainly on the music. Not only will this reverse the trend of most metal music commentary, but it will also afford an opportunity to explore the elusive notion of musical becoming. Death metal is not necessarily the best, the most popular, or the most representative form of music, nor are all the efforts of its practitioners successful, but it does provide illuminating instances of a musical becoming, a becoming-metal that produces a sonic plane of consistency of affective intensities and qualitative and quantitative speeds.

Names

Abscess, Affliction (Sweden), Amorphis (Finland), Asphyx (Holland), Atheist, Atrocity (Germany), Blood Duster, Broken Hope, Brutality, Brutal Truth, Cancer (England), Cannibal Corpse, Carcass (England), Convulse, Cynic, Dead Infection (Poland), Dead Orchestra, Death, Deceased, Deicide, Destruktion (Germany), Disembowelment (Australia), Disharmonic Orchestra (Austria), Disincarnate, Dismember (Sweden), Desultory (Sweden), Dissection, Dying Fetus, Embalmer, Entombed (Sweden), Epidemic, Evoke (England), Exit-13, Exmortem (Denmark), Gorfest, Gorguts, Grave (Sweden), Haemorrhage (Spain), Human Remains, Hypocrisy (Sweden), Immolation, Incantation, Infernal Torment (Denmark), Invocator (Denmark), Konkhra, Krabathor (Czech Republic), Kreator (Germany), Macabre, Malevolent Creation, Mangled Torsos, Monstrosity, Morbid Angel, Morgoth (Germany), Obituary, Obliveon (Canada), Oppressor, Pestilence (Holland), Possessed, Pungent Stench (Austria), Purge, Regredior (Lithuania), Revenant, Sinister (Holland), Sodom (Germany), Suffocation, Uncreation (Spain), Vader (Poland), Vomitory (Sweden).

These are some of the names of death metal, most of them representing currently active groups from the United States and Europe who began issuing professionally produced and distributed CDs during the last twenty years. *RIP Magazine*'s Jon Sutherland says of death metal names, "The neverending list of extreme metal band names related to death has been growing for years. Each new band who picks such an evil, degrading, socially unacceptable moniker is certainly not looking for acceptance from the moral majority. Instead they are surely trying to shock the hell out of anyone who would be so inclined to indulge in what Jeremy Wagner of Broken Hope once called in RIP 'the heaviest, fullest, fastest, most brutal, intense, horrifying, aggressive, extreme form of music known to mankind'" (Sutherland 4). Sutherland is right: the names by and large are meant to offend, and that offense often has a political edge, directed at the moral majority in general and, in the United States, the Christian Coalition in particular.[2] Above all, the names evoke the music, which, as Wagner succinctly remarks, is meant to be heavy, full, fast, brutal, intense, horrifying, aggressive, and extreme.

History

Most commentators trace the emergence of heavy metal music to the 1969–1970 release of Led Zeppelin's *Led Zeppelin II,* Deep Purple's *Deep Purple in Rock,* and Black Sabbath's *Paranoid.* Of these three, Black Sabbath, with its "slab-of-sound riffing and doom-laden lyrics" (Shapiro 8), was the clear forebear of death metal. After an initial rise in popularity, heavy metal slumped in the late 1970s, but with the advent of such groups as Van Halen, Def Leppard, Iron Maiden, Saxon, and Motörhead in 1978–80, metal in the 1980s "was transformed from the moribund music of a fading subculture into the dominant genre of American music" (Walser 11), with record sales and concert receipts exceeding those of any other form of popular music during that period.[3] England's Venom produced what is arguably the first death metal album, *Welcome to Hell,* in 1981. Other important forces in the first wave of death metal included Los Angeles's Slayer, among whose early albums were *Show No Mercy* (1983), *Hell Awaits* (1985) and *Reign in Blood* (1986), Switzerland's Hellhammer, formed in 1984 (and soon reconstituted as Celtic Frost), Sweden's Bathory, Germany's Kreator and Sodom, and Florida's Death, whose first album, *Scream Bloody Gore,* was issued in 1987. Disappointing releases by Venom and Celtic Frost in the late 1980s seemed to mark the demise of the genre, but a second wave of death metal began to form in 1989, with Florida (Obituary, Deicide, Morbid Angel, Atheist, Suffocation) and Sweden (Affliction, Dismember, Hypocrisy, Grave) emerging as hotbeds of the form. With well over five hundred groups recording and performing in the Americas, Europe, and Australia, death metal today would include among its dominant presences Morbid Angel, Deicide, Cannibal Corpse, Dying Fetus, Cryptopsy, Immolation, and Nile.[4]

Margins

During a July 1995 concert in Atlanta which I attended, Morbid Angel's David Vincent said to the crowd between songs, "Once upon a time on a distant planet there was a show called 'Headbanger's Ball,' and you might have seen our video on that show. But heavy music isn't fashionable anymore.... We've made a promise to you: we will never compromise, we will never change, we will never sell out!"

Vincent's reference to *Headbanger's Ball*—MTV's late-night metal program, which began in December 1986, became MTV's most popular show by 1989 (Walser 13) and, following slumping ratings, ended in January 1995—reveals the uneasy relationship all metal groups have with commercial success and mass appeal. Throughout its history, heavy metal has thrived despite a virtual absence of radio play and press coverage, its audiences thronging concert venues and purchasing millions of CDs largely as a result of word-of-mouth endorsements of the music. The anomalous success of *Headbanger's Ball* induced MTV to include more metal videos in its playlist and thereby furnish the music with a newfound mass-media presence, but while metal was enjoying growing exposure in the late 1980s, its hard edge was becoming increasingly dull, as many of the most successful groups of the period (such as Bon Jovi) combined metal textures with pop harmonies and romantic lyrics. As metal became more mainstream, pop metal bands migrated to prime-time slots and the midnight *Headbanger's Ball* came to specialize in rougher forms of metal, eventually narrowing its audience until the show was cancelled. At no time, however, did death metal feature prominently in the *Headbanger's Ball*, Morbid Angel being the only death metal group played regularly on the show.

Death metal is viewed by its practitioners and audience as extreme music, as marginal, proudly deviant, and socially unacceptable. Death musicians scorn the mainstream media and the recording industry, yet they want to make a living as musicians and bring their music to their audience; audiences in turn want to hear the music and buy recordings. Death metal, like all metal, depends on live concerts for its dissemination. In the mid 1980s, however, when few record labels would sign death metal groups,[5] an underground circulation of death demos and informal newsletters arose which eventually led to the formation of a death metal press that remains central to the genre's cultural life. A few glossy, professionally produced magazines, such as *Metal Maniacs, Metal Hammer, Pit,* and *Terrorizer,* cover death metal along with other extreme offerings (including punk, hardcore, thrash, industrial, black metal, gothic, and doom), but there are also a number of "fanzines," often rudimentary photocopied, mail-order publications, that are produced by death metal devotees themselves. (The glossy metal magazines all have a regular section providing readers with news about fanzines, including addresses for purchase.) A bare-bones example of the death metal fanzine is *Neptune,* launched in 1994 by then twelve-year-old Colin Conway, which consists of brief interviews (conducted by fax) and paragraph-long reviews of CDs and demos (with addresses for ordering demos from the bands). More elaborate is *The Grimoire,* edited by Bill Zebub (Turjancik) of Clifton, New Jersey, with contributions in one early issue from Rev. Al Ations, Metal Monster, Lou Siffer, and advice columns from

The Three Wise Men—Metal Dave, He Who is Wise, and Rev. Al Ations. Known for his campy archaisms and occasional silly interview questions ("Art thou familiar with the 'black metal' movement?" "If thy bologna had a first name, wouldst thou keep it a secret?"), Bill Zebub conducts lengthy interviews with artists, invites performers and record producers to comment on various topics (for example, "Is Death Metal Dead?"), prints bands' responses to negative reviews, and publishes letters from readers.

The death metal press, it should be evident, is a self-organizing communication system exhibiting varying degrees of integration in a market economy. In a loose alliance of artists, listeners, and record companies (primarily small labels, such as Century Media, Earache, Nuclear Blast, Metalblade, Relapse, and Roadrunner, which provide copies of CDs for fanzine reviews), this press promotes a circulation of commodities but also a nonprofit, autoregulating discourse of performers and listeners who interact in the formation of the genre. Fanzine reviewers constantly probe the limits of death metal, questioning whether a given recording is innovative or redundant, genuine death metal or black metal, an extreme statement or a sellout. Articles trace the history of the genre and its relation to other kinds of music, while readers offer critiques of performances and reviews, commenting not only on musical issues, but also on such questions as the sexist and homophobic attitudes exhibited in a given band's lyrics. In this manner, performers and listeners self-consciously, and often astutely, negotiate the development of the genre, ensuring its commercial viability while insisting that it remain extreme and marginal to the mainstream of pop music culture.

Volume

What is death metal? "The equation is fairly simple. It's guitar tuned down so low that only dogs can hear it. It's songs about the Devil, revenge from the grave, death by garden tools and other tales from the dark side delivered, for the most part, in a Linda Blair/*Exorcist*-like satanic growl" (Shapiro 8).

And like most rock music, it is extremely loud. Of course, this is nothing new. Frank Zappa offers the following insightful reminiscence of the early days of rock 'n' roll:

> But then I remember going to see *Blackboard Jungle*. When the titles flashed up there on the screen Bill Haley and his Comets started blurching "One Two Three O'Clock, Four O'Clock Rock . . ." It was the loudest rock sound kids had ever heard at that time. I remember

> being inspired with awe. In cruddy little teen-age rooms across America, kids had been huddling around old radios and cheap record players listening to the 'dirty music' of their life style. ('Go in your room if you wanna listen to that crap . . . and turn the volume all the way down.') But in the theater, watching *Blackboard Jungle,* they couldn't tell you to turn it down. I didn't care if Bill Haley was white or sincere . . . he was playing the Teen-Age National Anthem and it was so LOUD I was jumping up and down. (Zappa 85)

The loudness of metal music is of a specific sort, one that has been available to musicians only since the late 1960s when technological innovations made possible the amplification of very low frequencies at volume levels equal to those of mid- and high-level frequencies.[6] Virtually all metal music features an overpoweringly full bass guitar, heavily amplified bass kick drums, and the ubiquitous power chords of the electric guitar—thick, high-volume, high-distortion open fourths and fifths played primarily on the guitar's bottom two or three strings. Although recordings capture some of the music's sonic intensity, they convey little of the jolting corporeal presence of the live concert sound, which is heard with the ears but above all felt with the body, especially in the upper chest. In death metal, the force of the low frequencies is particularly intense, with the bass and guitars usually tuned a half step or whole step below standard tunings.

What death metal musicians seek in this volume is a music of intensities, a continuum of sensation (percepts/affects) that converts the lived body into a dedifferentiated sonic body without organs. Francis Bacon says that he tries in his paintings to allow the paint to work directly on the nerves and bypass the brain, to convey the violence and "brutality of fact" (Sylvester 182), and death metal aims at a parallel effect in music. Death metal develops a specific potential within the basic loudness of rock music, a line of variation that plays across an electronic-industrial-commercial machinic phylum and entails a continuing experimentation on the body. A simple increase in volume, of course, can be a mindless substitute for musical thought (witness the satire of *This is Spinal Tap*) as well as a danger to the ears (the well-publicized cases of Pete Townsend and Ted Nugent come to mind). Death musicians and concert technicians, however, through the careful manipulation of centrally controlled mixing boards, manage in most venues to sculpt a configuration of frequencies that pushes sonic intensity to its limits without causing permanent ear damage. The particular sound of death metal, its profile of highs and lows, emerges from a long process of corporeal-machinic testing and represents one dimension of a possible solution to the problem of creating an extreme music.

Sound

But volume alone is not enough to describe this music. Play Mozart loud and it's still Mozart. Death metal, like all rock, experiments with timbre. Various kinds of popular music—alternative, rap, grunge, r & b, soul, hard core, bubble gum—are known by their sound, the texture of their individual combinations of instruments and those instruments' electronic manipulations. The spectrum of popular music as a whole, one might argue, functions as a collective synthesizer, a machine that, while remaining for the most part harmonically and rhythmically conservative, explores timbral variations across a wide range of possibilities.[7] The sound of death metal is one complex of such timbral variations, a complex that shares many of the characteristics of heavy metal in general.

It is no accident that this music is labeled "metal." In addition to its venerable associations with metallurgy and chemistry, the term "heavy metal," as Walser points out, has been in use since the early nineteenth century to designate large artillery, and by extension, mental or bodily ability, power, and influence, as in the phrase, "He is a man of heavy metal." The term, "in each of its parts and as a compound, evoked power and potency" (Walser 1). Who first called the music "heavy metal" is not certain, but from the early 1970s the term has stuck, and various subcategories of the genre have tended to retain the reference to metal (speed metal, death metal, black metal, war metal). "Metal" connotes power and potency, but also industry and machines. It is trite but true that rock in its essence is electronic machine music, and the diverse exponents of metal music experiment on the timbre continuum of electronic sounds through the selection and manipulation of their machines. Death metal guitarists work with specific kinds of guitars (solid-body instruments by Ibanez, Jackson, and BC Rich, among others, that offer no natural accoustical amplification of sound, valued for their fast fretboards and sustain), pickups (DiMarzio Super Distortion, for example), amplifiers (Marshall, Mesa Boogie), effects units (for example, ART, Rat Distortion, Rocktron Intelefex), and so on, all in an effort to get a specific sound. That sound is the product of what might be called a becoming-metal of music.

Becoming-Metal

In *A Thousand Plateaus*, Deleuze and Guattari offer as an example of musical becoming in general, and the becoming-animal of music in particular, Olivier Messiaen's use of birdsong in his compositions.[8] Messiaen was an avid birdwatcher who could identify hundreds of birdsongs and accurately reproduce the refrains of dozens of species of birds. In a series of works written during the 1950s, *Reveil des oiseaux* (1953), *Oiseaux exotiques* (1956), *Catalogue d'oiseaux* (1958), and *Chronochromie* (1960), Messiaen chose birdsongs as his primary compositional materials, often "treating the bird song as malleable material," but also frequently "trying to outline the most exact musical portrait possible" (Samuel 94) of an individual species. Yet even in his most faithful musical reproductions of particular birdsongs, inevitable modifications and distortions were introduced. The rapid tempos of bird songs, their high pitch and microintervallic variations, their subtle play of timbre, require analogs that necessarily alter the material if they are to be used in instrumental music. Tempos must be slowed to a human pace, pitches must be brought within the register of normal human hearing, microintervals must be expanded to conform to the half-tone intervals of the even-tempered scale, and chord textures must be substituted for the subtleties of timbre inherent in a given bird's voice. What starts as a true and accurate representation of a birdsong emerges as an independent creation, a musical phrase created between composer and bird. "Becoming is never imitating," argue Deleuze and Guattari (MP 375/305). Becoming passes between things in a mutual deterritorialization. "Let's suppose a painter 'represents' a bird; in fact, this is a becoming-bird that can take place only to the extent that the bird itself is in the process of becoming something else, a pure line and pure color. Thus imitation destroys itself, since the imitator unknowingly enters into a becoming that conjugates with the becoming without knowing what he or she imitates" (MP 374/304–05).

The relationship between metal and metal music is not one of imitation. There is no inherent sound to metal, even if we may produce sounds by hammering on sheets of steel and speak of "metallic sounds." There is, perhaps, an affinity between metal and music in the development of certain instruments (brass, percussion, synthesizers), and Deleuze-Guattari suggest that metallurgy has an essential relation with music by virtue "of the tendency that traverses the two arts, a tendency to bring into its own, beyond separate forms, a continuous development of form, and beyond variable matters, a continuous variation of matter" (MP 510/411). But this has nothing to do with imitation. The sound of death metal is a response to metal, a modification of a sonic material that answers to a complex of sociohistorical forces which we can specify only with great difficulty, but whose general characteristics we can describe as powerful, industrial, machinelike, ahuman, android. The language of timbres, like the language of tastes and smells, is crude and limited, but practitioners of metal music frequently refer to the sound as crunching, grinding, and shredding, the guitars resembling buzzsaws, chainsaws, and (less frequently) jet engines. The project in this music is to create an aggressive sonic machine of destruction, an electronic, nonhuman sound shredder. Although the qualities that describe that sound may resonate with the network of connotations associated with "metal," we are still not talking about imitation. "We are in no way arguing for an aesthetics of qualities, as if the pure quality (color, sound, etc.) contained the secret of a becoming without measure. . . . A functionalist conception, on the contrary, considers in a quality only the function it fulfills in a specific assemblage, or in the passage from one assemblage to another" (MP 376/306). The variation set in motion within the sonic material of death metal follows its own line of mutation, whose designation "metal" simply gestures toward its instigative instants.

Ascetics

Deleuze and Guattari describe music as "the active, creative operation that consists in deterritorializing the refrain" (MP 369/300), the refrain (*ritournelle*) being any kind of rhythmic pattern that stakes out a territory. The song of a particular bird, for example, may function as a territorial marker, the composer's becoming-bird inducing an uncoding of that marker, and hence a deterritorialization of the refrain. Music, of course, has its own organizational system—its harmonic regularities, rules of counterpoint, formal conventions, generic expectations, and so on—which effects a secondary reterritorialization of sound: "When music takes hold of the refrain in order to deterritorialize it, and it deterritorializes the voice, when it takes hold of the refrain in order to make it fly off in a rhythmic sound block, when the refrain 'becomes' Schumann or Debussy, it is through a system of melodic and harmonic coordinates that music reterritorializes itself, within itself, as music" (MP 372/303). The great musician, however, "invents a sort of diagonal that passes between the harmonic vertical and the melodic horizon" (MP 363/296), thereby unsettling the regularities of musical practice and inaugurating a "generalized chromaticism . . . affecting not only pitches but all sound components—durations, intensities, timbres, attacks. . . . By putting all its components in continuous variation, music becomes itself a superlinear system, a rhizome instead of a tree, and enters the service of a virtual cosmic continuum, of which even its holes, silences, ruptures, and breaks form a part" (MP 120–21/95).

One might assume from these remarks that the ideal work of music would disrupt all musical conventions—all regularities of harmony, counterpoint, duration, intensity, timbre, attack—at the same time. Such is not the case, however. "At times one goes too far, adds too much, works with a jumble of lines and sounds; but then, instead of producing a cosmic machine capable of 'rendering sonorous,' one lapses back to a machine of reproduction that ends up reproducing nothing but a scribble effacing all lines, a scramble effacing all sounds" (MP 424/343–44). If all musical elements of a composition are simultaneously disrupted, only an amorphous white noise results, one without consistency or discernible components. What is needed is "a maximum of calculated sobriety in relation to the disparate elements and the parameters," a "sober gesture, an act of consistency, of capture, or of extraction that works on a material that is not meager but prodigiously simplified, creatively limited, selected" (MP 425–26/344–45). This point is especially important for any discussion of popular music, since the frequent complaint of elitist critics is that popular music is a mere repetition of the same, a commodity-driven circulation of identical products that never challenge audience expectations. The fact is that art music and popular music alike maintain certain continuities of form and regularities of organization that satisfy audience expectations and serve as the background against which innovations are situated. And in a world market economy, all music circulates (if it circulates at all) as a commodity in one way or another. Of course, the musical sophistication of audiences varies, as does the number of innovative elements one finds in a given composition, but dismissals of popular music often ignore components of experimentation (such as timbre) and mistake simplicity for a paucity of musical content. Frequently experimentation in popular genres proceeds via a deliberate impoverishment of materials, an intensification of a tendency through an ascetic reduction of its elements to their most basic level. In this regard, popular musicians resemble the minor writers Deleuze and Guattari describe in *Kafka: Toward a Minor Literature*—Kafka, who "opts for the German language of Prague, such as it is, in its very poverty" and "goes always further in deterritorialization . . . to the point of sobriety," and Beckett, who "proceeds through dryness and sobriety, a willed poverty, pushing deterritorialization to the point that nothing remains but intensities" (K 34–35/19).

Ascetic Extremes

As we have noted, rock music is loud, and death metal pushes this tendency to an extreme, seeking a specific configuration of frequencies that creates a full, heavy, physical sonic presence. Dynamic variations tend to be restricted to diverse levels of loud, with intensity differences occurring in juxtaposed blocks of sound. Dynamic contrasts are created through occasional bars of solo bass motifs, through sporadic antiphonal exchanges of solo power chords between the rhythm and lead guitars, and above all through alternations of chord sections of varying thickness and monophonic figures played in unison by bass and guitars. Crescendi and decrescendi are relatively rare, and for several reasons: whereas crescendi often express tender emotions and deep feelings, death metal seeks to eliminate any form of sentimentality and to evoke instead a distilled affective intensity; whereas crescendi subordinate elements of a phrase within a larger temporal-dynamic structure, death metal tends to emphasize each element of a phrase in a pursuit of pure speed; whereas crescendi often build to an orgasmic climax, death metal aspires to a music of constant orgasm, plateaus without rise or fall; whereas crescendi create continuities, death metal works in jolts, fits and starts, angular contrasts rather than smooth transitions. Death metal's dynamic vocabulary, in short, is deliberately impoverished, a limited set of permutations extracted from the range of possibilities within rock music and then carried to their extreme.

The timbre of high-distortion, long-sustain power chords common to all metal music also represents a particular line of development within rock, a specific realization of the synthetic sonic potential of the electric guitar. It might seem that the logical extension of this tendency would be to incorporate synthesizers within the music, but most metal musicians reject this option. Although guitar synthesizers exist, the units most commonly used in popular music are keyboard synthesizers, and keyboards have strong historical ties to art music and church music, whereas electric guitars, with few exceptions, are quintessentially rock instruments. Much of the synthesizer palette has been appropriated by pop, new age, disco, and even easy listening music, and hence has connotations that metal musicians find unacceptable. Groups do exist that combine metal and synthesizer textures, most notably the "industrial" group Ministry and, some might argue, Nine Inch Nails. And in their 1995 CD *Demanufacture*, the once conventionally death metal group Fear Factory deliberately sought a fusion of industrial and death timbres. But synthesizers lend themselves best to studio experimentation, whereas metal stresses live performance and the active, athletic manipulation of the instruments. Metal groups, and especially death metal bands, tend to be stripped-down, no-frills guitar-bass-drums units, intent on exploring a self-consciously limited number of textural and pragmatic possibilities within the traditional domain of rock.

Death musicians use a narrow harmonic language, working almost exclusively within the Phrygian and Locrian modes, which when combined make available in E the tones E-F-G-A-B♭-B-C-D. Besides sharing many of the musical connotations of traditional minor scales and the blues pentatonic scale (E-G-A-B-D), the Phrygian includes the half-tone interval between the tonic and second degree of the scale (E-F), an unstable interval with exotic, claustrophobic associations within the Western tradition. Death composers also stress the interval of the augmented fourth (E-A#), or tritone, known for centuries as the *diabolus in musica*, since in traditional counterpoint it was considered an undesirable interval that required great diligence to avoid. The tonal area most distant from the tonic, the augmented fourth provides maximum tension and dissonance within the language of classical harmony. Although a variety of triadic chords is available within the Phrygian and Locrian modes, death musicians generally drop the third from traditional triads, playing open fifths and fourths devoid of major/minor implications. Common major and minor progressions, including standard metal progressions such as VI-VII-i (C-D-Em in E), are largely absent, harmonic movement consisting primarily of an alternation between the tonic and the three tonal areas of the minor second, minor third, and augmented fourth. (As one might guess, monophonic and harmonic motifs that employ a tonic pedal point are extremely important in this music.) Compositions tend to be structured in motivic blocks of four, eight, or sixteen measures, each block stressing the tonic, with occasional shifts in the tonic center occurring between blocks.

Recognizable melodies are mostly confined to low registers, functioning essentially as bass motifs, whether played by the lead guitar alone or doubled by the bass. Heavy metal generally tends to stress melody less than do other forms of music, but in mainstream metal bands like Led Zeppelin or Van Halen the vocalist and lead guitarist do articulate clear melodies understandable within conventional harmonic structures. As Weinstein and others observe (Weinstein 25), heavy metal groups feature a strong vocalist and lead guitarist engaged in an affectionate rivalry with one another (for example, Led Zeppelin's Robert Plant and Jimmy Page, or Van Halen's David Lee Roth/Sammy Hagar and Eddie Van Halen), both contributing to the overall sound, but each serving as the source of individual melodic invention. Death metal groups have the requisite vocalist and lead guitarist, but sonically they tend toward anonymity. The death vocalist does not sing but talks or screams in a guttural growl, creating a deeply reverberant, low-pitched sound with scratchy, metallic overtones. If one listens to an early death metal recording, such as Venom's *Black Metal* (1982), an offering from the mid-1980s, such as Possessed's *Seven Churches* (1986), and virtually any recent death CD, one can trace a clear process of increasing vocal distortion in the genre, a general "machining" of the voice that renders it in many recordings so indistinct that the articulated words are indecipherable without reference to a lyric sheet. Many death metal songs feature guitar solos, but they are seldom more than thirty seconds long. With no conventional harmonic progression against which to develop their solos, death guitarists combine extremely rapid polytonal and atonal riffs with feedback shrieks and whining glissandi produced through intricate tapping techniques, harmonics, string bends, slides, pick slides, tremolo bar bends and other effects. Unlike the blues-based, expressive solos of mainstream metal, in which performers make their guitars "talk" or "sing," death metal solos function as frenetic emissions from the sonic blocks, brief spates of upper-register, organized noise that blur tonality and provide little in the way of a discernible melodic contour.[9]

It would be an exaggeration to say that death vocalists and guitarists are indistinguishable from one another, but they do tend to subordinate individual differences to the creation of a single ensemble sound (more so vocalists than guitarists), and though that sound varies from group to group, sufficient homogeneity within the genre exists to render those variations on occasion indiscernible. In death metal, the group is a machine whose parts work equally in the production of collective effects. Though guitarists fashion occasional solos and vocalists enunciate words, their primary function is as percussionists, the group machine being essentially a rhythm and speed machine.

Speed

In *A Thousand Plateaus,* Deleuze and Guattari define a body on the plane of consistency in terms of a longitude of speed and a latitude of affect, "that is, the whole of the material elements belonging to it under given relations of movement and rest, speed and slowness (longitude); the whole of the intensive affects of which it is capable at a given power or degree of potential (latitude)" (MP 318/260). Speed, however, is not a simple matter of quantity, that is, a measurable rate of movement. To emphasize the qualitative nature of speed, Deleuze and Guattari distinguish at another point between movement and speed: "movement may be very rapid, but that does not make it speed; speed may be very slow, or even immobile, yet still it is speed. Movement is extensive; speed is intensive" (MP 473/381).[10] Speed is a characteristic of the plane of consistency, the plane of events and becoming, whose time is not that of Chronos, "the time of measure that situates things and persons, develops a form, and determines a subject," but Aion, "the indefinite time of the event, the floating line that knows only speeds" (MP 320/262). To differentiate Chronos and Aion, Deleuze and Guattari cite Boulez's opposition of pulsed and nonpulsed time in music, suggesting that the pulsed time of metrically regular music corresponds to Chronos, the nonpulsed time of a floating, unmeasured music to Aion (MP 320, 326/262, 266).

Music that operates on a plane of consistency and effects a genuine becoming induces "a liberation of time, Aion, a nonpulsed time for a floating music, as Boulez says, an electronic music in which forms give way to pure modifications of speed" (MP 327/267). From this one might conclude that the music of speed is an exclusively nonpulsed music. If this conclusion is correct, then Boulez and Deleuze-Guattari part company here, for Boulez explicitly ties speed to pulsed time: "Only pulsed time is susceptible to speed, acceleration or deceleration: the regular or irregular referential system on which it is based is a function of a chronometric time of greater or lesser delimitation, breadth or variability. The relationship of chronometric time to the number of pulsations will be the index of speed" (Boulez 88). But whether Deleuze-Guattari and Boulez agree or not, it would seem that most Western art music and virtually all popular music are devoid of what Deleuze and Guattari regard as speed.

Rhythm

Boulez's opposition of pulsed and nonpulsed time owes much to Messiaen's distinction between rhythm and meter (as does Deleuze and Guattari's discussion of rhythm in *A Thousand Plateaus,* "Plateau 11. 1837: Of the Refrain"), and in Messiaen's treatment of rhythm the elitist implications of this conception of musical time are patent. Messiaen regards meter as the regular repetition of accents in a uniformly divided time, and rhythm as the irregular and uneven stress of incommensurable durations in an undivided time. Rhythmic music is "music that scorns repetition, squareness, and equal divisions, and that is inspired by the movements of nature, movements of free and unequal durations" (Samuel 67). Many consider works by Bach and Prokofiev to epitomize rhythmic music, but Messiaen claims that "they have no rhythm," for "in these works we hear an uninterrupted succession of equal durations that puts the listener in a state of beatific satisfaction; nothing interferes with his pulse, breathing, or heartbeat. So he is very calm, receives no shock, and all this seems perfectly 'rhythmic' to him" (Samuel 68). For the same reasons, Messiaen regards traditional jazz as fundamentally unrhythmic, and in this respect similar to the military march (Samuel 68). One would assume that Messiaen would also have to view all rock music as singularly devoid of rhythm.

Yet there are signs that Messiaen's opposition of rhythm and meter is less clear-cut than might at first appear. Mozart, he claims, "is the greatest rhythmician in classical music," which suggests that variable rhythm and regular meter can coexist, Mozart's conventional meters being offset by the shifting play of accent indicated in "the melodic line, harmonic devices, or a lot of variable signs too numerous to mention" (Samuel 69). And if one listens to Messiaen's own compositions, one often encounters strongly pulsed, regular temporal units, organized, however, in shorter sections than one commonly meets in traditional Western music and juxtaposed in unsettling patterns that disrupt an audience's calm.

Difference

For Messiaen, rhythm is temporal difference—the incommensurable, the unequal, the multiple—which shocks, jolts, and thereby undoes chronometric time. This, I would argue, is what Deleuze and Guattari mean by speed. Boulez's "nonpulsed time" is a name Deleuze and Guattari give Aion, but the range of musical devices available to composers in disrupting Chronos extends well beyond the specific practices Boulez associates with nonpulsed time. Composers can indeed break with chronometric time by organizing sound in unstressed, undifferentiated temporal units (what Boulez calls nonpulsed or amorphous time). But they can also follow Messiaen's lead and juxtapose pulses of varying duration, or do as Mozart and fashion layers of rhythmic variability within patterns of metrical regularity. They can adopt the minimalist strategy of a Philip Glass and push metrical repetition to an extreme, until a floating, unfixed time emerges from the trance-inducing drone. Or they can accelerate (or decelerate) metrical regularities until they collapse or run out of control.

These are only a few of the ways in which composers can escape chronometric time. But we must finally recognize that contextual factors affect musical time and that music has diverse uses in varying social situations. Western concert music divorces listening from corporeal action, audiences passively sitting while musicians perform. Historically, however, music has played an important role in many social functions, including ritual, war, and celebration. Most popular music is dance music, and as such designed for specific uses. The regular meters of various dance forms can reinforce rituals of harmony, control, and social integration (the minuet, for example), but they can also facilitate group experiences of frenzy and abandon. When decontextualized, dance rhythms may seem monotonous and stultifying, but as components of a collective, kinesthetic event they may help create an altered, incommensurable time. The high volume and driving pulse of much rock music are not meant to calm and soothe, but to impel to action, to shock and jolt. And though we may find in rock many of the techniques used in art music to experiment with duration, even the most primitive of pop meters and most regular of rock pulses can function within a collective assemblage to produce a floating, nonpulsed time.

Metal Speed

Death metal is dance music—music for headbanging and moshing—and hence generically constrained in its meters. Although groups play occasional slow songs, most death metal music is fast, a characteristic it shares with the "speed metal" (or "thrash") music of such groups as Metallica and Anthrax. Speed, of course, is relative, and various forms of music utilize rapid notes and fast tempos. Many pieces from the classical repertory feature prestissimo passages, and few can exceed concert virtuosi in sheer speed of execution. Frequently, however, the experience of such works is that of a managed, controlled speed, the soloist's dazzling figures grounded in a broader ensemble tempo, or the orchestra's accelerated motifs subsumed within more extended patterns of accent and harmonic rhythm. "Only pulsed time is susceptible to speed," as Boulez remarks, and the experience of speed (in the sense of measured rapidity) is a function of the subordination of rhythms and the dispensation of pulse. One of the effects of the high volume of death metal is that it allows relatively little subordination of one instrument to another, and thus of one rhythmic figure to another. The mind may recognize that the sixteenth-note tremolo motif in the bass is to be understood within the framework of the quarter-note snare beat and the four-bar rhythm of the vocal, but the body experiences each of those notes as an accent. Rapid, low-frequency percussive stresses are created by the bass and guitar, but above all by the highly amplified double kick drums, which the drummer plays with both feet. By using two kick drums, the drummer can produce extremely rapid figures that add rhythmic punch to the ensemble sound at speeds that are at times difficult to process. Even if a death group should play in a leisurely, rolling 3/4 meter, the kick drums will most likely fill with sixteenth- or thirty-second-note patterns that multiply the stresses per measure. The variations in the combinations of low-frequency accents produced by the instruments are innumerable, but as a rule the succession of accents is swift. In sum, death metal's emphatically pulsed, rapid tempos and multiple low-frequency accents produce the overall impression of a music played almost constantly at diverse levels of a breakneck speed.

But if death metal creates quantitative speed, it also produces the qualitative speed of differential rhythms and nonpulsed time. Occasionally, death groups play in a genuinely amorphous, nonpulsed time, suspending all regular accent and pulsation in thrashing, hyperaccelerated blasts of sound. They also exploit multiple rhythmic layers that at times combine irregular figures with more conventional motifs. More important, however, is the tactic of accelerating meters to the point of collapse. A standard element of death metal is the "blast beat," which features the drummer's cut-time alternation of downbeat kick drum and offbeat snare, the accent being heard on the offbeat but felt on the downbeat, creating the sensation of a frenzied, manic acceleration. Often, a blast beat section will culminate in an unaccented kick drum roll, which obliterates any sense of an organized pulse and creates the sensation of temporal dissolution. But death metal's central technique for creating rhythmic incommensurability is to change tempo frequently and to provide no common measure for the immediate comprehension of such changes. By this strategy, death groups are able to create within individual motivic blocks intensely felt, generically coherent popular dance rhythms, while intensifying the sense of quantitative speed and producing effects of differential, qualitative speed through the juxtaposition of these blocks. Deleuze and Guattari say that Kleist invented in his works a new rhythm of time: "an endless succession of catatonic fits or fainting spells, and flashes or rushes. Catatonia is: 'this affect is too strong for me,' and a flash is: 'the force of this affect carries me away,' so that the Self *(Moi)* becomes nothing more than a character whose actions and emotions are desubjectified, even to the point of dying" (MP 440/356). This is the rhythm of death metal, with its abrupt starts and stops, its disjunct plateaus of high-volume, fast-paced activity, its blocks of feverish acceleration, its zones of breakdown and collapse. Rush and catatonia, quantitative and qualitative speed.

Specific Speed

Consider Sinister's "Sadistic Intent," from their *Diabolical Summoning* (1993), a fairly representative example of the shifting tempos and rhythmic variations of death metal. (See table.) The song opens with a solo bass motif in E, an even eighth-note figure in a brisk 3/4 time (♩ = 156) in the Dorian mode (although all subsequent sections are in the Locrian mode). Following antiphonal exchanges between the bass and ensemble in which the lead doubles the bass, the rhythm guitar announces the second measure of the opening section's theme, a three-beat, sixteenth-note tremolo on the tonic. Although the 3/4 meter is clearly established (and emphasized by the vocal accents), its rolling, round quality is countered by the constant duple subdivisions of the beat into eighth- and sixteenth-note values. The interplay of duple and triple values is reversed in the second section, constructed around a two-bar tonic-tritone-dominant figure in 12/8 time (♩. = 108), with primary accents on the second and fourth beats of each bar. Here, the rolling triple feel is emphasized within the duple measure by the ensemble's first- and third-beat triplets. The movement from the first to the second part, like all sectional divisions in the piece, is abrupt and unmediated, no common temporal value rationalizing the break. This short section (seventeen seconds long) is followed by a choppy, grinding 4/4 unit (♩ = 150), even eighth-note chords emphasizing each primary beat. The angular, duple regularity of verse 3 breaks down fifteen seconds later with a measure of unpulsed, high-speed tremolo thrash. Verse 4 then commences with a blast-beat measure of eighth notes (♩ = 108) followed by a second measure of unpulsed thrash (a subtle guitar-bass surge on the first and third beats, however, introducing an incipient temporal organization within the tremolo unit). The alternation in verse 4 of blast beat and thrash, of hyperactive rush and catatonic collapse, gives way after seventeen seconds to a twelve-second instrumental section, a sixteenth-note guitar-bass-kick-drum tremolo drone on the dominant, the 4/4 (♩ = 162) organization of the drone being established primarily by a slow cymbal rhythm (♩ ♩| ♩ ♩ +). After a brief reprise of the thrash-blast beat material (eight seconds), verse five begins with full power chords in E, all instruments articulating what initially feels like the quarter-note values of a regular 3/4 meter. A half-bar of rapid sixteenth notes in 4/4 (♩ = 134) reveals, however, that the massive 3/4 chords are to be understood as hemiolas, triple figures against a duple beat. The implicit three-against-two syncopation of the power chords is emphasized when the next set of six power chords is followed by a full bar of galloping sixteenth notes in 4/4. Although verse 5 betrays an underlying

Rhythmic Structure of Sinister's "Sadistic Intent"

Time	Section	Tempo	Rhythm
0:00	introduction	♩ = 156	
0:22	verse 1	♩ = 156	
0:41	verse 2	♩. = 102	
0:58	verse 3	♩ = 150	
1:13	verse 4	♩ = 108	(blast beat)
1:30	break 1	♩ = 162	
1:42	verse 5	♩ = 108	
1:50	verse 6	♩ = 134	
2:04	break 2	♩ = 134	
2:18	verse 7 (repeat verse 4)		
2:32	silence		
2:33	repeat verses 1-4		
4:07-4:10	coda		

eight-bar, 4/4 regularity, the effect of the section is that of a discontinuous succession of spasmodic stutters (3/4) and manic rushes (4/4) in a pattern of 3-1-2-2 (three units in 3/4, one in 4/4, two in 3/4, and two in 4/4). A four-bar instrumental repetition of the 4/4 sixteenth-note motif in verse 5 separates that verse from verse 6, which simply provides new lyrics for a reprise of the musical material of verse 5. After a final four bars of the galloping 4/4 figure of verse 5, the first half of the song comes to a sudden halt, two minutes and thirty-two seconds into the tune. Following one second of silence, the band repeats the first five sections (verses 1 through 4 and the first instrumental section), adding a twelve-second guitar solo above the tremolo drone on B in the instrumental passage. A three-second coda of unison power chords in a staccato 4/4 ($\jmath = 108$) brings the piece to a sudden close.

Words

While death metal in certain respects represents an intensification of elements of rock, in many ways it is an antipop music, and no more so than in its lyrics. Formally, death metal lyrics largely avoid rhyme and seldom follow rock's traditional alternation of verse and chorus. Occasional refrains are repeated, but for the most part the songs are structured as a sequence of autonomous verses of varying meters and numbers of lines. In terms of content, the lyrics transgress most pop norms. Just as the music rejects anything that might sound pretty, tender, or cheerful, so the lyrics shun all expressions of hope, optimism, or romantic love. Even themes common in heavy metal in general are abandoned in death metal. Weinstein usefully classifies heavy metal lyrics as either Dionysian or chaotic (Weinstein 35–43), noting that virtually all mainstream metal bands sing the praises of sexual ecstasy, intoxication, and loud music. Seldom, however, do death groups celebrate alcohol, drugs, or sex (save in connection with death), and hymns to the power of death music are relatively uncommon. While ignoring heavy metal's Dionysian themes, death bands specialize instead in metal's traditional dark side, themes of chaos, death, violence, and destruction.

Often death lyrics offer vague atmospheric images of physical decay, pain, and torment (as in the songs of Suffocation's *Pierced from Within*) or ghoulish invocations of infernal suffering (Sinister's *Diabolical Summoning*). Many albums evoke splatter film images of mayhem and disembowelment, perhaps the most insistently gruesome example being General Surgery's *Necrology,* with such songs as "The Succulent Aftermath of a Subdural Hemorrhage" and "Slithering Maceration of Ulcerous Facial Tissue." Frequent as well are psycho killer songs, first-person expressions of sadistic pleasures, and tormented obsessions (much of Cannibal Corpse's *The Bleeding* falling within this category), or third-person accounts of the deeds of mass murderers (Macabre's *Sinister Slaughter* being a particularly extreme example). Still others simply enunciate abstract feelings of anger, hopelessness, or psychic numbness (Napalm Death's *Fear, Emptiness, Despair*). It is important to note, however, that the songs are seldom laments of self-pitying Angst, the tone of the lyrics generally ranging from icy detachment to manic exuberance.

Satanic references abound in death lyrics, and some groups make Satanism their central message. Perhaps the most strident of Satanists is Deicide's lyricist and lead singer, Glen Benton, whose forehead bears the branded imprint of an inverted cross. An avowed believer in the supernatural and servant of Satan,[11] Benton insistently attacks Christianity in album after album, Deicide's 1995 CD, *Once Upon the Cross*, featuring such titles as "Christ Denied," "When Satan Rules His World," and "Kill the Christian." Many death metal Satanists, however, are atheistic materialists who find inspiration in Anton Szandor LaVey, founder of the Church of Satan and author of *The Satanic Bible* (1969). Preaching hedonistic indulgence and enlightened self-worship, LaVey adopts the language of Satanism merely to shock the sanctimonious and conducts Satanic rituals only to satisfy what he sees as humankind's stubborn craving for mystery and wonder.[12] Morbid Angel's former lead singer, David Vincent, once one of death metal's most prominent LaVey adherents, echoes LaVey's atmospheric incantations in his lyrics, espousing in many of his songs, such as "Dominate," "Dawn of the Angry," and "This Means War!" (from Morbid Angel's 1995 *Domination*), individual strength and angry resistance to conventional Christian morality.[13]

Politics

For the most part, death metal restricts its social critique to attacks on religious fundamentalism (except, perhaps, for the occasional ecological protest, such as one finds in Exit-13's *Ethos Musick* and Napalm Death's *Utopia Banished*). But the genre's potential for wider political commentary is suggested by a few groups whose music, though somewhat outside the mainstream of the form, has close ties to death metal. For example, Brazil's Sepultura, whose *Beneath the Remains* (1989) is often listed as one of death metal's all-time great albums, is a band with pronounced death metal tendencies that has consistently treated political issues in its music, especially in their 1995 CD *Chaos A.D.* "Refuse/Resist," for instance, decries the global proliferation of armed conflict ("Chaos A.D. / Tanks on the streets / Confronting police / Bleeding the Plebs / Raging crowd / Burning cars"), while "Territory" protests the racist propaganda of dictators who foster "War for territory / War for territory." Other targets include censorship ("Slave New World"), propaganda ("Propaganda") and Amazon strip mining ("Biotech is Godzilla"). The instrumental "Kiowas," according to the liner notes, is inspired by a rain forest tribe that "committed mass suicide as a protest against the government," and "Manifest" is written in memory of the hundreds of inmates of "'Carandiru,' the biggest penitentiary complex in South America," shot by police "in a holocaust method of annihilation."

Another particularly interesting political use of death metal textures is that of Brujeria, again, not strictly a death metal group but one with close affinities with the genre. According to Roadrunner Records' tongue-in-cheek press release, Brujeria is a Mexican outlaw band with ties to the Medellin cartel, inside information about the O. J. Simpson murder weapon, and a fleet of submarines used to smuggle drugs into the United States. Identified only by names such as Juan Brujo (Juan Sorcerer) and Asesino (Assassin), Brujeria in its first album (1993) combines death metal Satanism ("Sacrificio" [Sacrifice] and "Seis Seis Seis" [Six Six Six]) with songs about drugs ("Cristo de la Roca" [Christ of the Rock]), dealers ("Leyes Narcos" [Drug Dealer Laws]) and drug executions ("Matando Güeros" [Killing White Guys]). In *Raza Odiada* [Hated Race, 1995], Brujeria's second release, the politics of race and ethnic identity implicit in their first offering are more explicitly delineated.[14] Bold letters on the back of the CD declare in Spanish, "MEXICANS! . . . WE ARE NOT LATINOS. Latinos are the white people of Latin America. WE ARE NOT HISPANICS. Hispanics are the people of Spain, Europeans." The first song, "Raza Odiada," opens with excerpts from a speech by California governor Pete Wilson accusing Mexicans of laziness, followed by sounds of machine gun fire. The chorus declares, "Pito Wilson—El Rey de Racistas / Pito Wilson—sera presidente / Pito Wilson—te quiere ver muerto / Pito Wilson—el Cristo de ódio" (Pete Wilson—King of the Racists / Pete Wilson—will be president / Pete Wilson—wants to see you dead / Pete Wilson—the Christ of Hate [with a play on the slang *pito* = penis]). "Revolución" celebrates the Chiapas rebellion and its masked leader Subcomandante Insurgente Marcos (whose photograph is on the album cover). Following shouts of "Viva Zapata, Viva Chiapas / Viva Mexico, Viva la

Revolución," the song concludes with the suggestive line, "Comunismo, Satanismo, P.R.I. [Partido Revolucionario Institucional]—es lo mismo" (Communism, Satanism, P.R.I.—is the same). Several of the songs speak of the violence and destruction of the drug trade, but the frequent association of drug dealers with Satanists, Zapatistas, and Pancho Villa-style outlaws suggests as well that the group views the border war on drugs as a cultural war of decidedly ambiguous significance.

Bodies

One can easily regard death metal lyrics as simple variations on the perennial theme of rock 'n' roll rebellion, songs of transgression and largely unfocused resistance that vent the discontent of disaffected youth. There can be no doubt that the imagery of death, putrefaction, and dismemberment, of psychotic violence and perverse desire, is meant to shock. Yet death musicians often insist they are simply reflecting the mayhem and destruction all around them, and audiences seem to value the music for its honesty and truth.[15] In this view, the horrific visions of death metal are simply verbal collages, ready-mades constructed from the clippings and footage of daily carnage and abuse. But beyond transgression, reportage, and critique, the most fundamental motive in death metal lyrics is to evoke an experience of the body, a libidinal dissolution of the self and of the organism as integrated system. As Deleuze and Guattari argue in *Anti-Oedipus,* "The body without organs is the model of death" (AO 393/329), the catatonic body's zero intensity rather than the body's physical demise serving as desire's primary experience of death. The body without organs is not opposed to the organs as such, but to the regulated organism: "There is no real opposition between the body without organs and the organs as partial objects; the only real opposition is to the molar organism that is their common enemy" (AO 393/329). Death metal's recurrent images of bodies without organs and organs without bodies are so many efforts to invoke an intensive, acentered, prepersonal, and preindividual affective continuum, an ecstatic, disorganized body of fluxes and flows. Death metal, in short, is appropriately named. There is in its lyrics an obsession with death—not with nothingness and negation, but with the death at the heart of life, the desire/death of zero intensity, which is figured as life in death or after death, the living death of zombies, vampires, ghouls, and devils, the undead, the already dead, the living dead: a becoming-death in the lyrics to accompany the becoming-metal of the sound.

Becoming-woman

All becomings, we are told, "commence with and pass through becoming-woman" (MP 340/277). But is there a becoming-woman in death metal? I don't think so. The music is produced almost exclusively by men,[16] and its audience, if one judges from concert attendance, is predominantly male. The dress, appearance, and gestures of the performers are never "feminine" but often aggressively macho—the clothes plain and grungy, the bodies heavily tattooed, the expressions tough, mean, and angry. Death metal lyrics seldom question conventional gender roles, and when sexual violence is described, it is almost always imagined as violence by men against women. The music, too, with its deep-voiced, growling vocals, its power chords, emphatic, pulse, and aggressive tempos, no doubt should be culturally coded as "male."[18]

Yet death metal can undergo a genuine becoming, primarily through an ascetic concentration on and intensification of certain possibilities inherent in rock music. Its characteristic sound is the product of an interactive process of becoming-metal, a synthetic, nonhuman, electrical-industrial noise meant to rip, shred, and grind time. Its manipulations of volume, timbre, frequency, tempo, rhythm, accent, and pulse create a sonic plane of consistency, one composed exclusively of affective intensities and qualitative as well as quantitative speeds. Its lyrics of corporeal disaggregation and charnal eroticism evoke the body without organs, the verbal counterpart of the sonic plane of consistency, for "the plane of consistency is the body without organs" (MP 330/270). Musical elements that might be considered masculine are denatured, but through exaggeration rather than elimination. The orgasmic rise to a musical climax becomes in death metal a plateau of constant orgasm, and hence a plateau devoid of climax in the usual sense. The dominant, powerful pulse of heavy metal, which "could be called phallic" (Walser 49), is accelerated at times until it runs out of control. The insistent emphasis of the tonic in each motivic block and the relative absence of conventional chord progressions ensure a hyperstable tonality, yet the paratactic sequence of blocks generally admits of no organizational principle other than sheer juxtaposition; if, as McClary argues, the compositional "plot" of classical music is to move from a dominant male center to a distant female Other and eventually conquer that Other upon return to the center (McClary 68–69), then death metal is all male in its tonality, but curiously plotless and floating in its structure, its movement devoid of conquest or return. The death vocal, finally, deepens and hence hypermasculinizes the voice, but to the point that it ceases to sound human, its groans and growls resembling those of some unspecifiable animal or machine.

One might argue that by definition there can be no becoming here because there is no becoming-woman, or conversely, that there must be an incipient becoming-woman because there is a true becoming. But such an argument simply dismisses the problem, which finally is tied to the nature of music. Deleuze and Guattari remark that "the properly musical content of music is traversed by becomings-woman, becomings-child, becomings-animal, but it tends, under all sorts of influences, including those related to instruments, to become more and more molecular, in a kind of cosmic lapping in which the inaudible makes itself heard and the imperceptible appears as such: no longer the songbird, but the sonorous molecule" (MP 304/248). They also state that music, when compared to painting, "seems to have a much greater deterritorializing force, at once much more intense and collective" (MP 371/302).

Music, I believe, is fundamentally molecular, a highly deterritorialized medium susceptible to various becomings through a direct experimentation with abstract sound. Music is created within a complex network of social institutions and practices, and once created it is appropriated for a variety of uses. Among the contextual elements enmeshed in death metal culture are the multiple codes associated historically with rock in general and heavy metal in particular, the technological developments that have made possible the death metal sound, the communicative circuits of the commercial recording industry and the marginal fanzine press, and the various conventions of performance and audience participation that prevail in live concerts. Lyrics are a mode of action within the music, at once a component of the composition and a separate stratum of semantic elements interacting with the sonic material, giving the sound a voice and providing it with an index of possible uses.

Each death metal group appropriates the genre for its own purposes, finding in the sound and the musical conventions material receptive to various semantic manipulations—horror film visions, psycho-killer ravings, blasphemous fantasies or Satanic chants. But the musical elements of death are available as well for the social protests of a Sepultura or the minor politics of a Brujeria. The sonic material's high level of deterritorialization opens it to various becomings, a becoming-animal, a becoming-metal, a becoming-imperceptible, no one of which has precedence over the other. The sounds are socially coded in a variety of ways, it is true, but they are underdetermined. Each group's lyric appropriation of the sound contributes to its encoding, but that appropriation also constitutes an experimentation with the music, a testing of the genre's possibilities for new uses. Death metal's musical material has not yet been plied by a becoming-woman, but there is nothing inherent in the sound to preclude such an event in the future.[18]

Deleuze and Guattari warn that there are dangers in the construction of a body without organs (BwO), the possibility of a suicidal collapse into an empty black hole or the formation of a cancerous totalitarian node. "How do we fabricate a BwO without its being the cancerous BwO of a fascist inside us, or the empty BwO of a drug addict, of a paranoiac, or of a hypochondriac?" (MP 202/163). Music's high level of deterritorialization gives it an affinity with death, and hence with the dangers of black holes and fascist cancers. "Music has a thirst for destruction, all kinds of destruction, extinction, breakage, dislocation. Is that not its potential 'fascism'?" (MP 367–68/299). Death metal lyrics thematize this danger, the images of corporeal fragmentation and dissolution figuring the collapse of the body without organs into suicidal black holes, the fantasies of psycho-killers and Satanists often exemplifying the formation of cancerous fascistic cysts. There is much to object to in death metal lyrics, much that lends itself to nihilistic destruction or reactionary thought. It is not always easy to tell whether the lyrics critique, parody, or promote the violence and aggression they detail. But on one level, at least, they provide a semantic corollary for a musical becoming, a becoming-metal that at times makes possible the formation of a sonic plane of consistency of affective intensities and differential speeds.

❖ 6

Word, Image, and Sound: Deleuze and Semiosis

Throughout his career, Gilles Deleuze was intent on articulating a philosophy of difference. From *Nietzsche and Philosophy* (1962) through *Difference and Repetition* (1969) and *A Thousand Plateaus* (1980) to *Essays Critical and Clinical* (1993), he sought to overturn Platonism, to wrest difference from its subordinate position as a deviation from the Same and to theorize it as a positive force from which the Same issues as a secondary effect. This effort entailed an abandonment of the logic of representation, which dictates that difference be thought only *"in relation to a conceived identity, a judged analogy, an imagined opposition, a perceived similitude"* (DR 180/138), never in itself. Deleuze's philosophy of difference in this sense may be said to be essentially antimimetic.

In *A Thousand Plateaus*, *Foucault*, and his two books on cinema, Deleuze develops what might be called a nonrepresentational semiotics of the *énonçable* and the *visible*, of "that which can be stated" and "that which can be seen." His effort in analyzing the linguistic sign is to uncover the conditions of possibility of signification, the relations of power that shape the elements of a level of expression and a separable but interrelated level of content. Referentiality and representation, he argues, do not ground linguistic semiosis, but emerge as the residual products of interacting and nonsignifying forces. In *Cinema 1: The Movement-Image* (1983) and *Cinema 2: The Time-Image* (1985), Deleuze continues to stress the secondary nature of mimetic relations, but in these volumes he also develops an elaborate taxonomy of nonlinguistic signs that is less an analysis of the social forces that shape the visible than a description of the matter that may be so shaped. My aim here is first to offer an account of Deleuze's approach to the linguistic sign and then to map out the basic elements of his nonrepresentational semiotics of cinema. In a concluding section I will consider how the strata of the *énonçable* and the *visible* are treated in Deleuze's history of the interrelation of sound and images in film.

Linguisitic Signs

In *A Thousand Plateaus,* Deleuze provides his most complete account of the nature and function of the linguistic sign. The Saussurian approach to the sign Deleuze regards as inadequate for at least three reasons: the problem of reference is either subsumed within a logic of representation or simply bracketed, and hence ignored; the signifier dominates the signified and ultimately effaces the sign as an object of analysis; and the reign of the signifier encourages a textualism that either makes the real coextensive with language or closes language in on itself, thereby assigning pragmatics a secondary function outside linguistics.[1] Instead of the Saussurian schema of signifier and signified, Deleuze adopts a Hjelmslevian model, which isolates a level of expression and a level of content, each level having its own form and substance. Hjelmslev envisions the formation of a given level as the imposition of a grid on an undifferentiated surface, the amorphous surface being a shapeless matter, the square shape of each grid determining the form of the level, and the matter shaped by that form constituting the substance of the level. This model emphasizes both the materiality of expression and content and the separability of the two levels, each with its own substance and its own provenance of formation. The relation between the level of expression and the level of content is neither natural nor fixed, and the designation of one level rather than the other as expression or content is arbitrary.[2] What Deleuze focuses on in his analysis is the ways in which the levels of expression and content are formed and the forces that put those levels in relation to one another.

According to Deleuze, the basic linguistic unit is not the phoneme but the statement *(énoncé)*, or speech act, and the primary function of language is not to inform or to communicate but to transmit commands and enforce a given order.[3] Language is a mode of action that is fundamentally social, a coding that imposes power relations. The statement may be enunciated by an individual, but it is collective in origin and formation. Its basic purpose is to establish a social obligation, and it does so by effecting "incorporeal transformations" (MP 102/80) of the bodies of a given society: "We can give the word 'body' the most general sense (there are moral bodies, souls are bodies, etc.); we must nevertheless distinguish the actions and passions which affect these bodies and the acts which are only noncorporeal attributes, or which are 'the expressed' of a statement" (MP 102/80). We may describe peace and war strictly in terms of the interaction of bodies, but a peace treaty or a declaration of war "expresses an incorporeal and instantaneous transformation of bodies" (MP 102/81). In the doctrine of transubstantiation we have perhaps the purest example of an incorporeal transformation: "To eat bread and drink wine are mixtures of bodies; to commune with Christ is also a mixture of bodies that are properly spiritual yet no less 'real.' But the transformation of bread and wine into the body and blood of Christ is the pure expressed of a statement, which is attributed to bodies" (MP 103/81).

The aggregate of incorporeal transformations permissible in a given society constitutes a *"regime of signs or semiotic machine"* (MP 106/83), a configuration of forces that shape, legitimate and stabilize the pragmatic variables internal to language. A regime of signs determines the form of a particular level of expression (whatever its substance, whether sonic, lexical, electronic, and so on) and puts that level in relation to a level of content. The level of content itself is shaped by nonlinguistic forces that constitute a social technological machine. Between the two levels there is interaction, but no relation of representation and no unified process of formation: "In expressing a noncorporeal attribute, and at the same time in attributing it to a body, one does not represent, one does not refer, one *intervenes* in a fashion, and that is an act of language" (MP 110/86). The independence of the form of expression and the form of content founds neither a relation of correspondence nor one of causality, but "a cutting up and parceling out of the two, a means whereby expressions are inserted in contents, whereby one leaps continuously from one register to the other, whereby signs work on things themselves, at the same time that things are extended and unfolded across signs" (MP 110/87).

Perhaps the clearest example of what Deleuze means by expression and content, regimes of signs and social technological machines, is to be found in *Foucault,* Deleuze's 1986 tribute to his late friend and fellow philosopher. In *Discipline and Punish* (1975), Foucault tells of the emergence in the nineteenth century of the prison as modernity's dominant form of punishment and of a discourse of delinquency as our reigning juridical idiom. Foucault argues that the prison is an embodiment of a general disciplinary function that becomes established in the West by 1830 and that finds its clearest articulation in Bentham's 1787 "Panopticon; or, the Inspection House," a proposal for the design of an ideal prison. A central watch tower surrounded by a ring of prison cells, the Panopticon is constructed in such a way that the prisoners can never see into the tower but the guards can always observe the prisoners and thereby put into action a general disciplinary function of "seeing without being seen." Concomitant with the prison's rise is the formation of a discourse of delinquency, in which the object of juridical inquiry is not the action of a felon who implicitly wages war on the sovereign (as in the *ancien régime*) but the soul of the delinquent whose recalcitrant nature constitutes a continuing danger to society. In Deleuze's analysis, the panoptic prison is a form of content (the content-substance being the prisoners shaped by the panoptic institution), and the statements made possible by the discourse of delinquency make up its related form of expression. The prison and the discourse of delinquency each have their separate histories and their separate constituting forces. It is true that the levels of content and expression interact: judges perform incorporeal transformations on delinquent prisoners, just as prisons produce delinquents; supplementary discourses arise within the prison, just as nondiscursive institutions reinforce the juridical regime of signs. Nevertheless, even though there is "a reciprocal presupposition between the two forms," there is "no common form, there is no conformity, not even correspondence" (F 41/33).

Deleuze sees throughout Foucault's works similar analyses of content and expression, organized around the themes of *le visible* and *l'énonçable*, of that which can be seen and that which can be stated. What Foucault discloses in these studies are the strata of historic formations of knowledge: "'sedimentary layers,' they are made up of things and words, of seeing and speaking, of the visible and the sayable, of plains of visibility and fields of readability, of contents and expressions" (F 55/47). In *Madness and Civilization* (1961), Foucault shows how in the seventeenth century "the asylum arises as a new means of seeing the mad and making them visible, a means very different from that of the Middle Ages and that of the Renaissance; and medicine in its turn—but also law, regulations, literature, etc.—invents a regime of statements that bears on unreason as a new concept" (F 56/48). In *The Birth of the Clinic* (1963), Foucault tells of the formation of a new medical discourse in the early nineteenth century, but also of the autonomous emergence of a new spatialization of the body that brings to light hitherto unseeable objects of observation. And in volume 1 of *The History of Sexuality,* (1976), the regime of signs that produces the modern discourse of sexual confession is detailed, as well as the forms of visibility that make possible the regulation of populations.

What Deleuze means by "statements" and "regimes of signs" is clear, but what "forms of visibility" might signify deserves further consideration.

Visible entities, which Deleuze calls "visibilities," are not "forms of objects, nor even forms which would be revealed upon the contact of light and things, but forms of luminosity, created by light itself and allowing things or objects to exist only as flashes, mirrorings, scintillations" (F 60/52). Deleuze states that "just as statements are inseparable from regimes, so visibilities are inseparable from machines" (F 65/58), but this remark requires careful interpretation. One can see how insane asylums or prisons might be regarded as machines, but "they are not simply figures of stone, that is arrangements of things and combinations of qualities, but first of all forms of light which distribute the clear and the obscure, the opaque and the transparent, the seen and the not-seen, etc." (F 64/57). Forms of visibility, in fact, need not be produced by such obviously machinelike physical objects at all. Foucault's *Birth of the Clinic* details a history of medicine in terms of successive spaces of visibility of illness, but no single configuration of things makes the body appear at one moment as a collection of two-dimensional surfaces and at another as a three-dimensional depth. In *The Order of Things*, Foucault uses Velázquez's *Las Meninas* as a figure for the general form of visibility of the seventeenth and eighteenth centuries, the painting disclosing "a regime of light that opens the space of classical representation and distributes that which is seen and those who see, exchanges and reflections, including the place of the king which can only be inferred as outside of the painting" (F 64–65/57–58). A machine, in short, must be understood not simply as an object, but as "an assemblage of organs and functions that cause something to be seen, and that bring things to light and put them in evidence" (F 65/58). As John Rajchman aptly puts it, visibility for Deleuze "is a matter of a positive, material, anonymous body of practice" (93).[4] The machine that brings entities to light and puts them in evidence is a collectively produced configuration of heterogeneous objects, organs (including the positions from which subjects are able to perceive objects), institutions, and ways of doing things, which, when regulated and coordinated with other machines, forms part of a general "regime of light."

If one concludes, as I do, that this analysis of the *enonçable* and the *visible* in Foucault is above all an elaboration of Deleuze's own thought, especially of the concepts of regimes of signs and social technological machines developed in *A Thousand Plateaus,* then one can say that for Deleuze linguistic semiosis has as its condition of possibility two interacting but separate configurations of material, anonymous practices: a *regime of signs,* a regulated set of socially authorized and legitimated speech acts that perform incorporeal transformations of bodies; and a *regime of light*, a conglomeration of arrangements of entities, organs, and functions that allow a world of things to become visible. The relations of signifier to signified and of sign to referent do not have their origin in a logic of resemblance or representation, but in the play of forces that generate the forms of the visible and the sayable, of that which can be seen and that which can be stated. If, then, by semiosis we mean the process of the production of signs, we may say that for Deleuze representational mimesis is a secondary effect of semiosis.

Cinematic Signs

It would seem from this account that Deleuze would have little interest in conventional semiotic analysis, that is, in the classification of signs and the formalization of the workings of sign systems, since his attention is drawn principally to the conditions that make possible the emergence of such signs and sign systems. Yet in his two-volume study of film Deleuze writes a work that in his words is "not a history of cinema" but "a taxonomy, an essay in the classification of images and of signs" (IM 7/xiv). What Deleuze does, however, is not so much to abandon his investigation of the power relations inherent in semiosis as to redefine the sign in such a way that the semiotics of cinema becomes less a categorization of actual film images than an examination of the conditions of possibility for producing such images. The domain of cinematic visibility (and "aurability"), though, does introduce a new element in Deleuze's thought on signs, for this domain is not characterized as a set of practices but as "a plastic mass, an asignifying and asyntactic matter, a nonlinguistically formed matter, even though it is not amorphous and is formed semiotically, esthetically, and pragmatically" (IT 44/29). What relation this semiotic matter may have to the dimension of practices that allow visibilities to emerge must await a more detailed specification of what Deleuze means by "signs" and "images."

Deleuze finds fault with the dominant approach to cinematic signs in France—the Saussurian semiological orientation of critics like Christian Metz—because it subordinates the cinematic sign to the linguistic signifier and it assumes that narrative is fundamental to film. In both ways it ties cinema to a logic of representation: first, by substituting for the visual image an analogous statement governed by linguistic laws, and second, by insisting on a constitutive resemblance between the cinematic image and a represented action (IT 38–42/25–28). Deleuze argues that the image must be conceived independently of linguistic models and that "narration is only a consequence of visible images themselves and of their direct combinations, never a given" (IT 40/26).

Deleuze approaches the cinematic sign along two axes, the first of which he labels an axis of differentiation. It is along this axis that the problem of movement is addressed, the terms of the analysis being the immobile cut *(coupe immobile)* and the set *(l'ensemble),* and the mobile cut *(coupe mobile)* and the Whole *(le Tout).* Among the Ancients, movement was conceived of as a synthesis of ideal poses or privileged instants, a regulated passage from one ideal form to another. During the scientific revolution, movement was rethought in terms of a homogeneous space and a sequence of equal and interchangeable immobile instants, time and motion being treated as independent variables. The mechanics of cinema provide an apt illustration of this conceptual model: just as twenty-four still photographs projected at a constant speed produce moving pictures, so a sequence of immobile instants in an object's trajectory synthesized at a given rate account for the movement of that object. But according to Bergson (Deleuze's primary inspiration throughout his study of film), if movement is to be understood properly it must not be conceived of as something separate from the object that moves or the space that is traversed. The movement of an object involves a translation in space, but one in which the relations between the object and all surrounding objects are changed. When the tortoise passes the hare, for example, there is a qualitative change in all elements of the situation. And there is no logical limit to the number of relations changed by a given object's movement—indeed, every movement is part of the flux of the Whole. The Whole is the sum of the relations between objects, and that sum may be defined as duration *(la durée)* or time (IM 21/10). Any specific movement, therefore, must be regarded as a mobile section or cut of duration, a slice of a qualitative and indivisible Whole. (The Whole constantly changes, but as it changes so do its qualities, and were it to be divided, its qualities would also be altered and it would thus no longer be the same qualitative Whole.) Deleuze does not regard the scientific approach to movement as entirely illusory, but as a spatial perspective made possible by the establishment of provisionally closed sets *(ensembles)* of elements. The Whole, by contrast, is essentially open and hence never given. "The whole creates itself, and never ceases to create itself in another dimension without parts, as that which draws the set from one qualitative state to another, as the pure unhalting becoming that passes through these states" (IM 21/10). Hence the world is open to two different readings, one in terms of immobile cuts and closed sets, and the other in terms of mobile cuts and open wholes: "Sets are in space, and the whole or wholes are in duration, they are duration itself in that it never ceases to change" (IM 21/11).

In Deleuze's view, cinema gives us a concrete image of Bergsonian movement, a movement-image that indirectly expresses a whole. The shot is at once a delimitation of a closed set of elements and a mobile cut or slice of duration. The shot is "the concrete intermediary between a whole which has changes and a set which has parts, and it never ceases to convert one into the other along its two faces" (IM 36/22). What allows this conversion is the extraction of a pure movement from bodies via camera movement and montage. The consciousness of film is not that of the director or the spectator, but that of the camera, "now human, now inhuman or superhuman" (IM 34/20). Whatever the supposed objectivity or subjectivity of camera angles or movements, the camera consciousness releases a pure movement from things and establishes the shot as a *"temporal perspective or a modulation"* (IM 39/24) of things. Likewise, montage creates between shots, no matter how static they may be, a pure mobility subsumable within no single point of view. Although the shot and montage are interdependent and ultimately inseparable, the two may be assigned different functions, the shot converting a closed set into a mobile cut, and montage revealing the existence of an open whole. Each mobile cut is an expression of the whole, but it is primarily through montage that one gains an indirect image of the whole as the sum of relations and that one understands the various mobile cuts as so many differentiations of the whole.

The second axis of Deleuze's analysis is that of specification, or the determination of specific kinds of images and signs. Deleuze introduces this portion of his examination by noting that at the end of the nineteenth century a crisis arose in the relation of images to movement, images being conceived of generally as qualitative and unextended aspects of consciousness, movements as quantitative, extended aspects of space: "What appeared without solution, finally, was the confrontation of materialism and idealism, the one wanting to reconstitute the order of consciousness with pure material movements, the other, the order of the universe with the pure images of consciousness. It was necessary above all that this duality of image and movement, of consciousness and the thing, be overcome" (IM 83/56). Husserl tried to solve the problem through the doctrine of intentionality, but Bergson approached it in another way, arguing for the fundamental identity of movement and image, consciousness and matter.

In Bergson's view, the limited and fixed perspective of human perception distorts movement, thereby encouraging its theorization as either a synthesis of ideal poses (the Ancient model) or a synthesis of immobile instants (the scientific model). If one is to free movement from the distortions of consciousness and conceive of it as it is in itself, one must adopt as a model "a state of things which would ceaselessly change, a matter-flow in which no anchoring point or center of reference would be assignable" (IM 85/57). From this matter-flow, consciousness must then in a sense be deduced as a specific center or anchoring point formed out of this flux. So Bergson posits a primal "world of universal variation, universal undulation, universal rippling: no axes, no center, neither right nor left, neither up nor down" (IM 86/58–59). This world "constitutes a sort of plane of immanence" (IM 86/58–59) in which things are indistinguishable from their movements and even from each other, a molecular, gaseous realm of fluxes. But if it is a world of gaseous matter, it is also a world of images-in-motion or movement-images, for "the *movement-image* and the *matter-flow* are strictly speaking the same thing" (IM 87/59). The reason for this is that "the plane of immanence in its entirety is Light. The totality of movements, of actions and reactions is light which diffuses, which spreads" (IM 88/60). In this plane of immanence, then, matter=light=image=movement.

Images on the plane of immanence are so many "prehensions," total perceptions of the whole in that they are responsive to all surrounding images. In this sense consciousness "is immanent within matter" (IM 90/61). The eye "is in things, in luminous images in themselves" (IM 89/60), and the plane of immanence "is the universe as cinema in itself, a metacinema" (IM 88/59). Consciousness and perception in the more limited and conventional sense come into existence with the formation of animate beings, which are points of image/matter that create an interval in the flux of universal variation. When viewed as matter, such points mark a break in the universal interaction of things, a hiatus between a received action and a subsequent reaction. When viewed as images, such points function as blank screens on which other images are projected. Perception, then, is an "image reflected by a living image" (IM 92/62). Unlike an image on the luminous plane of immanence that receives actions on all sides and responds in all directions, a living image (animate being) develops a specialized surface that receives only those actions that serve its needs and interests, that is, that correspond to its perceptual capacities and its reactive capabilities. Such an image is a partial prehension, a point of limited receptivity.

A living image, in selectively receiving other images, frames the world as a camera does. From this framing arises the first subdivision of the movement-image, the perception-image. But a living image not only frames other images. It also induces a curvature of the world around it, an organization of space in terms of its future actions. Through this curvature of the world, "perceived things offer me their usable face, at the same time that my delayed reaction, become action, learns to use them" (IM 95/64).

All perception is sensorimotor, an inseparable complex of reception and possible action. Hence, if there is a movement-image that frames the world, there is a second movement-image, the action-image, that gives the world a center and surrounding horizon and that shapes it according to "the virtual action of things on us and our possible action on things" (IM 95/65). Finally, between perception and reaction, a third subjective function of the living image must be located, from which arises a third type of movement-image. In the gap between perception and delayed reaction is affection, which "is a coincidence of subject and object, or the way in which the subject perceives itself, or rather undergoes or senses an 'inside.' . . ." It relates movement "to a 'quality' as lived state" (IM 96/65). This affective center is an affection image, an expression of affect that "marks the coincidence of the subject and the object in a pure quality" (IM 96/65).

Thus, when the movement-image is related to a center of indetermination, or an animate being, three species of image arise: the perception-image, the action-image and the affection-image. To these three basic images Deleuze adds three more: the relation-image, a mental image that *"takes as its object, relations*, symbolic acts, intellectual sentiments" (IM 268/198), and two "intermediary" images, the impulse-image *(l'image-pulsion),* halfway between affection and action, and the reflection-image, midway between action and relation (IT 48/32–33). On the basis of these six images Deleuze forms his classification of signs, defining the sign as "a particular image that represents a type of image, either from the point of view of its composition, or from the point of view of its genesis or its formation" (IM 102/69). The perception-image, for example, has two compositional signs, the *dicisign* and the *reume*. The dicisign is a perception of perception, in which the camera "sees" someone who is seeing something; the reume is a fluid or liquid perception which flows across the frame. The genetic sign of the perception-image is the *engramme,* "or the gaseous state of perception, molecular perception, which the other two presuppose" (IT 48/32). Each of the other images has a similar array of compositional and genetic signs associated with it, bringing the number of signs associated with the movement-image to roughly eighteen.[5]

The movement-image is matter itself, but matter semiotically (non-linguistically) formed by the six species of images, "and signs themselves are the expressive units that compose these images, combine them and ceaselessly recreate them, carried or conveyed by matter in movement" (IT 49/33). Narrative, far from forming the basis of cinematic semiosis, is a secondary organization of this "asignifying and asyntactic matter" (IT 44/29); this matter constitutes the condition of possibility of all film narrative. What makes conventional, rational narratives possible is that the six species of movement-image are coordinated by a sensorimotor schema that necessarily accompanies the fixed and centered perspective of a living image. Perception, affect, action, and relations are interconnected when structured around a single point. They presume what Kurt Lewin calls a "hodological space," a "field of forces, of oppositions and tensions between forces, of resolutions of these tensions according to a distribution of goals, obstacles, means, detours . . ." (IT 167/127–28). A conventional narrative unfolds within such a space and consists of a "development of sensorimotor schemas within which the characters react to situations or act in such a way as to disguise the situation" (IT 167/127), the veridical, unified form of the narration deriving from these schemas.

Every film, however, has at most a partial and intermittent link to the sensorimotor schema. Shifting camera angles, camera movements and the juxtaposition of different visual perspectives through montage ensure that even the most conventional of films is in touch with a luminous plane of immanence in which ubiquitous "eyes" are scattered across space, a plane of "universal variation, total perception, objective and diffused" (IM 94/64). And in every shot, in every montage, immobile cuts and closed sets are converted into mobile cuts that express open wholes in which objects and their movements fuse in a single qualitative flux of duration. The sensorimotor schema regulates the movement-image, coordinates relations between the six species of movement-images and their constitutive signs, and makes possible conventional narratives. Yet in a way the sensorimotor schema is always on the verge of collapse, always being reconstituted as it is being undermined.

But when the sensorimotor schema does completely break down, something unexpected takes place. A new type of image appears, one that is qualitatively different from all forms of the movement-image: the time-image. According to Deleuze, in Italian neorealism and the French New Wave one can see the collapse of the sensorimotor schema and the advent of a modern cinema that decisively breaks with the classic cinema of the movement-image. Duration is expressed in the mobile cut and given an indirect image in the movement-image, but with the breakdown of the sensorimotor schema time is no longer subjugated to movement, but given a direct image and made preeminent over movement. The time-image has as its basic signs the *opsign* and the *sonsign,* pure optic and sonic images that open directly onto time.[6]

A brief example should suffice to indicate what the time-image is and what the ramifications of its emergence are. In Resnais and Robbe-Grillet's

Last Year at Marienbad, Deleuze finds two kinds of time-images, *peaks of the present* and *sheets of the past*. Peaks of the present, on one hand, are alternative moments that coexist in a Leibnizian incompossibility, a time of multiple present moments in which A knows X, A does not know X, A and X have returned to Marienbad, A and X have never been to Marienbad before, and so on. Sheets of the past, on the other hand, are part of a single, virtual past, a dimension of commingling past moments that have never been present but have coexisted with their various corresponding present instants as virtual doubles of those moments. *Last Year at Marienbad* shuttles between these two time-images, offering direct images of incompossible presents and a pure, virtual past. With the appearance of these time-images come multiple consequences. The virtual and the actual are rendered indistinguishable. Imagination, dream, fantasy, hallucination, memory, and waking consciousness become undecidable categories. No longer is the goal the recounting of a single story, but the activation of a "power of the false" *(puissance du faux)* as generative force of multiple, splintered narratives. The cut no longer functions as a link between images, but as a nonrational gap with its own value that dictates a new kind of montage, one in which relations unallied with the sensorimotor schema are invented to link independent images in new sequences.

Cinema, then, has as its condition of possibility a luminous plane of immanence, which when organized in accordance with a sensorimotor schema forms six species of movement-image, the most basic of which are the perception-image, the action-image and the affection-image. Each species of movement-image may be further characterized by the compositional or genetic signs that constitute it and function as particular points of view of the given image. The various signs of the movement-image are embedded in closed sets constructed as series of immobile cuts, but at every moment they also are converted into mobile cuts that express open wholes, qualitative fluxes of duration identical with the plane of immanence. As long as the sensorimotor schema is intact, the movement-image and its signs dominate cinema, but with the collapse of the schema a new image and new signs emerge: the time-image and the opsign and sonsign. The narratives of classic film do not ground cinematic semiosis but come into being as secondary effects. Signs, rather than representing action or activating social and narrative codes, are units of image-matter that the director works and shapes as a sculptor does marble or wood. And when the image-matter consists of opsigns and sonsigns, multiple, nontotalizable narratives take form and time itself finds a direct image.

Sight and Sound

For Deleuze, as for many analysts of film, the medium is essentially visual. As a result, most of Deleuze's time in *Cinema 1* and *Cinema 2* is spent delineating a dimension of cinematic visibility, a domain of movement-images and time-images that directors take as the matter from which they shape their compositions. Yet from its inception film has had a linguistic component, and from the advent of sound it has had a variety of sonic constituents. It might seem that the sonic aspect of cinema is beyond Deleuze's model, since he bases his analysis of the movement-image on the concept of a plane of immanence in which matter equals light. But this represents no essentialist ontology, simply a heuristic means of envisioning what cinema presupposes and brings into existence: the cosmos as acentered flux of image-matter. It would be equally possible to construct a model of the cosmos as sound-matter filled with immanent, virtual "ears," and even to treat the cosmos of light-matter and the cosmos of sound-matter as parallel, compossible worlds. Deleuze proposes no such theory, but he does suggest that the sonic and the visual components of film function as separate, interacting layers whose interrelationship is parallel to that of the *énonçable* and the *visible* in Deleuze's reading of Foucault.

In silent films, the word is visual, either directly presented in titles or indirectly indicated through the action shown on the screen (the open mouths of the screaming crowd, the jet of steam from a whistle blast). The words on the titles are read and they function as indirect speech, the title "I love you," for example, being interpreted as "He says he loves her." The visual image in silent films has a kind of innocence and naturalness, says Deleuze. It presents the structure of a society, its functions, sites, roles, and attitudes, a "social physics of actions and reactions" (IT 293/226). In silent film in general, "the visual image is as if naturalized, in that it gives us the natural being of man in History or in society, whereas the other element, the other plane which is distinguished both from History and from Nature, takes form as a 'discourse' that is necessarily written, that is read, and framed in an indirect style" (IT 293–94/226).

With the introduction of sound into cinema, the word instead of being read is heard, and as a result the visual image of silent film becomes denaturalized. Speech and sound become new dimensions of the visual image itself; in this manner, something that earlier could not be seen is made visible in the image. If in silent films a speech act is visually evident, it is as a function of initial physical situations and consequent actions, and reactions. In films with sound, by contrast, the speech act is not determined by social structures, actions, and reactions; instead, "through its autonomous circulation, propagation, and evolution," the speech act "creates the interaction between distant, dispersed individuals or groups, indifferent to one another" (IT 295/227). The extreme instance of such a speech act is the rumor, which passes from mouth to mouth across a heterogeneous group of individuals and classes, the enunciation of all and yet the product and property of none. Its most contracted manifestation is the conversation, the pure form of sociability that allows interactions outside "natural" and structured relations, in "encounters with the other, the other sex, the other class, the other region, the other nation, the other civilization" (IT 299/230). The conversation, with its schizophrenic nonlogic of aleatory topics and its anonymous ad hoc rules of formation, has a life of its own that goes beyond the individuals involved and that can only enter film with the advent of sound. Once such speech acts are given voice, the visual image is directly affected. The possibility of lies, deceptions, misunderstandings, and unintentional remarks that haunt conversation inscribes the images with hints of hidden motives and unrecognized thoughts. The voice-off and the voice-over provide a concrete extension to the framed shot. The subjective shot plus voice function as a "seeing voice" that, in being heard, "is itself seen, as if itself tracing a path in the visual image" (IT 303/233). Thus, with the coming of sound, "instead of a seen image *and* a read speech, the speech act becomes visible at the same time that it makes itself heard, but also the visual image becomes readable, as such, as the visual image in which the speech act as component is inserted" (IT 303/233–34).

Of course, the advent of sound meant the presence in film not only of speech but also of music and various sound effects. Indeed, Deleuze argues, speech should be considered only as one part of an indivisible sonic continuum whose components constitute a "fourth dimension of the visual image" (IT 305/235). Like the speech acts of Deleuze's linguistic theory, which intervene in bodies, the elements of the sonic continuum do not represent or signify but interact with images, tracing "a path full of obstacles within the visual space" (IT 305/235). Although indivisible, the sonic continuum differentiates itself in two ways that parallel the division of the movement-image into the mobile cut and the open whole. Sounds and speech acts fill the off-camera space, giving us the noise of an approaching truck, the words of an unseen speaker, the sound of breaking glass in the next room. But besides this relative off-camera space, which parallels the mobile cut, the sonic continuum is in touch with an absolute off-camera field, with a Whole that it expresses in music and in the disembodied voice-over of a reflective consciousness commenting on the film. Among the great directors of the classic cinema, the relative off-camera space is not simply a redundant doubling of the visual field, but an active force that impinges on images, and the absolute off-camera domain does more than echo the Whole of the movement-image. In great films, movement-images and music "express the whole in two incommensurable, noncorresponding ways" (IT 311/239), movement-images indirectly offering an image of duration as a Whole that changes, music directly presenting the Whole as qualitative temporal flux but solely in a musical, nonanalogous form.

The introduction of sound marks an important moment in the development of film, but Deleuze believes that the breakdown of the sensorimotor schema in the modern cinema represents an even more decisive watershed in the medium's history. With sound, the silent film's naturalized social images and indirect, legible speech acts (titles) give way to direct speech acts that denaturalize images and a sonic continuum that directly presents the whole; yet in essentials, classic sound films merely extend and develop tendencies and possibilities already present in silent films. In the modern cinema, however, a much more fundamental change takes place, one that renders cinema for the first time "truly audio-visual" (IT 316/243). Sound and visual images become autonomous strata that test the limits of the audible and the visible, and as a result induce basic transformations of the sonic continuum and visual images.

If in silent films speech is indirect and read, and in classic sound films it is direct and heard, in modern films it is "free indirect" and overheard, speech foreign to the characters who enunciate it, floating and folded back upon itself. In Flaubert one finds a liberal use of free indirect speech, the voice of the objective narrator subtly adopting the inflections of a character's voice, enunciating his or her sentiments, and then imperceptibly regaining its ironic, distanced tone. Rather than representing a hybrid of direct and indirect speech, however, free indirect speech according to Deleuze is a qualitatively distinct mode of collective speech that hovers between speakers, invades them, and possesses them. And such is the speech that one finds in the modern cinema. In Rohmer's films, for example, a text written in indirect style is given direct, dialogic form, "but under such conditions that the direct style retains the marks of an indirect origin and does not allow itself to be fixed to a first person" (IT 315/242). In the films of Bresson, the actors are instructed by the director to deliver their lines as if they were simultaneously hearing their words being reported by someone else. In these works, as in many other modern films, the speech act "folds in on itself, it is no longer dependent on or ancillary to the visual image; it becomes a sonic image completely apart, it takes on a cinematographic autonomy" (IT 316/243).

With the breakdown of the sensorimotor schema, the visual image as well becomes autonomous, the space it reveals no longer being organized by characters' projects, conflicts, struggles, and movements, but becoming fragmented and defamiliarized, thereby assuming a disconnected, anonymous character, as if it were the desert site of an enigmatic archeological dig (for example, Wenders, Antonioni, and Straub/Huillet). Such visual images must be read, but in a different way than the visual images in classic sound films. In modern films, the director reconnects disjointed images, invents links that compel an audience to discover what it is they are seeing, what strata of a given archeological site are being unearthed, what unconventional assemblages of heterogeneous visibilities are being constructed. Unlike the classic image, which is legible because speech and sound are components of the visible image, the modern image is legible because it is problematic yet suggestive, a disjointed shard whose relations with other shards are in need of constant interrogation, exploration, and reconceptualization.

Although sounds and visual images are separate in modern films, a relation does hold between the two, "an incommensurable or 'irrational' relation which ties them to one another, without forming a whole, without proposing the slightest 'whole'" (IT 334/256). Deleuze offers as examples of this incommensurable relation the connection between sound and image in the films of Marguerite Duras. *The Woman of the Ganges* according to Duras consists of a film of images and a film of voices that touch at an infinite point, and in Deleuze's view all her cinematic works show an equal autonomy of visual images and sounds. Throughout her cinema, Duras extracts a pure speech act from the sound continuum that aspires at its extreme to statements of "total love or absolute desire" (IT 337/258), and in the visual continuum she discloses a universe of primary liquidity, a becoming-fluid of the world in which "the legibility proper to the visual image becomes oceanographic" (IT 338/259). Speech is denaturalized and pushed to its limit, to the cry or song, to that which "is at once seemingly unsayable and yet something that can only be said" (IT 339/260). Seeing too is defamiliarized "and carried to a limit which is at once something invisible and yet something that can only be seen" (IT 340/260), a new form of seeing in which the empirical world is dissolved and reformed as matter-flows.[7] In both cases, what is being made speakable and visible are the unsayable and unseeable forces that play through the *énonçable* and the *visible*.[8]

And what determines the relation between the two layers of sounds and images is the limit proper to each layer: "it is the limit of each that relates it to the other" (IT 340/261).

Intervening Strata

In Deleuze's history of cinema, speech acts and images (the sonic continuum and the plane of visual signs) are treated as interacting and intermingling but essentially separable elements. In this, they resemble the linguistic planes of expression and content and the Foucauldian domains of the *énonçable* and the *visible*. Words are visual components of silent films, and speech acts impinge on the images of classic sound films, just as linguistic speech acts perform incorporeal transformations of bodies and juridical statements intervene in penal visibilities. But always Deleuze insists that the various levels have distinct modes of formation and heterogeneous histories of emergence. What Deleuze opposes is the adoption of language as a ground, either for a universal semiology or for a more restricted self-referential linguistics. To see is not to speak, any more than speaking is itself an exclusively linguistic activity. The visual is shaped by nonlinguistic forces, and language has as its condition of possibility interconnected regimes of signs and regimes of light.

Yet if Deleuze consistently opposes the visual and the verbal, it would seem that he offers two different accounts of the visible itself—as a collectively produced configuration of objects, organs, institutions, and practices, and as an asignifying and asyntactic matter. In large part, the differences in the accounts arise from differences in the objects of analysis and the purposes of the arguments. Deleuze's treatment of linguistic semiosis takes as its object linguistic regularities and conventions, just as Foucault's studies focus on the regularities of disciplines (medicine, historical philology, political economy, biology) and institutions (insane asylums, prisons, schools, armies). For both Deleuze and Foucault the goal is to demonstrate that the apparently natural regularity of a given domain is actually the result of a play of forces and the product of relations of power. In the cinema Deleuze is not confronting a comparable disciplinary regularity, and his purpose is primarily to develop a set of concepts that allow him to talk about cinematic images in nonlinguistic terms. The great directors do not enforce the conventions of the *énonçable* and the *visible* but explore those dimensions, experiment with them and push them to their limits. They do what Deleuze and Foucault themselves do: they uncover regimes of signs and light, they separate planes of statements and visibilities, and they invent new ways of articulating their differences. Rossellini's *The Rise to Power of Louis XIV*, says Deleuze, reveals in its handling of words and things "an 'archeological' conception almost in the sense of Michel Foucault" (IT 323/248), and Foucault's handling of the relation between the *énonçable* and the *visible* parallels the treatment of sound and image in the films of Syberberg, Straub/Huillet, and Duras (F 71–72/64–65).

Yet there is nothing inherent in film to stop Deleuze from writing a history of cinema in terms of the configurations of power that enforce cinematic regularities. Such a history would be one of machines, architecture, institutions, disciplines, codes, practices, and bodies, of the unimaginative films that confirm dominant power configurations as well as the creative films that unsettle them. Such a history would show how cinematic hacks take the asignifying and asyntactic matter of cinema and fashion it in conformity with ruling conventions, and it would show how that nonlinguistically formed matter only comes into existence through the practices of good and bad directors alike within the regimes of signs and regimes of light that organize twentieth-century industrial societies.[9] Finally, such a history would disclose the historical nature of cinematic visibility, a particular mode of seeing that emerges in our century and only finds its Deleuzian formulation after the breakdown of the sensorimotor schema.

Deleuze does say at one point that the cinematic sign "represents" an image (IM 102/69), but it is clear that no relation of imitation, referentiality, or adequation is intended by this remark. The cinematic sign is itself an image, a particular component of a given image that is part of a plastic image-matter. Forces shape that matter, and traditional mimetic relations are produced as secondary effects. In this regard cinematic and linguistic semiosis are the same. In his treatment of language Deleuze undermines the conventional notion of the linguistic sign by revealing its permeability to action and power structures. In his analysis of cinema he defines the sign in such a way that the traditional problems of representation are avoided. In one case, conventional linguistic signs are shown to be units produced by forces, in the other asignifying and asyntactic signs are revealed as the cinematic matter that forces shape in various ways. And in both instances semiosis—the process of sign production—is fundamentally nonrepresentational.

❖ 7

Deleuze and the Invention of Images: From Beckett's Television Plays to Noh Drama

In 1992, Minuit published a volume of four of Samuel Beckett's television plays *(Quad, Ghost Trio, . . . but the clouds . . .* and *Nacht und Träume),* accompanied by an essay on Beckett by Deleuze, titled "L'Epuisé" ("The Exhausted"). In his comments on *. . . but the clouds . . .,* Deleuze remarks briefly on the lines from Yeats's "The Tower" that give the play its title and then suggests a general affinity between drama and Beckett's television plays, one that Deleuze links to Yeats's fascination with Japanese Noh drama, which directly and significantly influenced Yeats's theater. Though Beckett nowhere acknowledges any indebtedness to Noh drama in his own works, Deleuze senses a convergence of interests and sensibilities in Noh drama, theater, and Beckett's television plays, one centered on the concept of drama as a "visual poem"—a theater of the mind and spirit, limited in plot, rich in images, with puppetlike characters and spare, ascetic sets. Deleuze argues that the object of Beckett's television plays is to produce an *espace quelconque,* an "any-space-whatever," in which "pure" visual and sonic "images" at the limits of language may arise, and that it is especially in the medium of television that Beckett is able to meet this object. The curious implication of this argument is that there is an essential affinity between Noh drama and television—or at least between Noh drama and television as Deleuze sees it used by Beckett. My object is to explore this hypothesis and in the process determine precisely the characteristics of the medium of television as Beckett exploits it and Deleuze understands it.

Yeats and Noh

The widow of Ernest Fenollosa, a pioneer in Western scholarship dedicated to Chinese and Japanese culture, had long been seeking a writer to whom she could entrust her husband's manuscripts following his death in 1908. She had been told that Ezra Pound would be an ideal choice, and in 1913 Pound agreed to edit the papers and develop aesthetically polished versions of Fenollosa's translations, which included renditions of several Noh dramas. Thus began Pound's lifelong fascination with Chinese and Japanese literature, with the concrete fruits of his labor being the 1916 publication of *Certain Noble Plays of Japan,* "from the manuscripts of Ernest Fenollosa. Chosen and finished by Ezra Pound."[1] When Pound began work on the Fenollosa manuscripts, he had just moved to Stone Cottage in Sussex, where he was serving as Yeats's secretary. During the three years Pound spent on the Fenollosa papers, he was in regular contact with Yeats, who was quite taken with Pound's project and with Noh drama in general. Yeats eventually wrote an introduction to *Certain Noble Plays of Japan,* in which he praised Noh theater and indicated the important influence Noh was coming to have on his own dramaturgy. In 1917, Yeats staged *At the Hawk's Well,* the first of several of his plays to be shaped by the conventions of Noh drama.[2]

For some time Yeats had been seeking a theatrical mode that would be conducive to poetry and spiritual themes, and while completing *At the Hawk's Well* in 1916, he told Lady Gregory, "I believe I have at last found a dramatic form that suits me" (Tuohy 156). In his introduction to the Fenollosa volume (*Essays),* Yeats noted that "the human voice can only become louder by becoming less articulate, by discovering some new musical sort of roar or scream" (223), and in Western drama the size of the theater had tended to encourage in actors the development of such a musical roar, to the detriment of true poetry. Movement had also grown "less expressive, more declamatory" (223), and Yeats saw the only antidote to these tendencies to lie in the restoration to the theater of intimacy, "the measure of all arts' greatness" (224). To create this intimacy required distance, he argued, "firmly held against a pushing world" (224), such that "a group of figures, images, symbols, enable us to pass for a few moments into a deep of the mind that had hitherto been too subtle for our habitation" (225). Whereas "realism" was "created for the common people" (227), newly developed theater, "distinguished, indirect, and symbolic," was "an aristocratic form" (221) that emphasized poetic subtlety and a refined aesthetic of suggestion and contemplation. In Noh he had found a model for his own practice. Despite its popular origins, Yeats remarked, Noh had developed into an aristocratic form whose conventions were patently nonrealistic. The paucity of scenery, the presence of musicians on the stage, and the stylized delivery and movements of the actors all contributed to this effect. "The players wear masks and found their movements upon those of puppets," such conventions highlighting both the word and the expressiveness of the body's movements as a whole. The actors "sing as much as they speak," and "at the climax, instead of the disordered passion of nature, there is a dance" (230). By ignoring the development of character, so central to realistic drama, Noh dramatists "made possible a hundred lovely intricacies" (235) in poetic imagery, and by concentrating on the entire body and its moments of muscular tension, they focused not on the human form per se but on "the rhythm to which it moves, and the triumph of their art is to express the rhythm in its intensity" (231).

The elements of Noh drama are immediately evident in *At the Hawk's Well*. The two speaking actors, an Old Man and a Young Man (Cuchulain), wear masks, and the three musicians and Guardian of the Well have "faces made up to resemble masks" (*Plays* 207). The setting "is any bare space before a wall against which stands a patterned screen" (*Plays* 207). The musicians are onstage throughout, providing musical accompaniment to the action and poetic commentary on the events. The action is minimal: an Old Man at a well is joined by the young Cuchulain, who has heard that a drink from the well's water will make one immortal. The Old Man confirms this fact, indicating that he has been waiting fifty years for the water to rise from the dry well; only three times has it risen during that period, and each time he has been asleep. At the play's climax, the water rises, but the Old Man sleeps while Cuchulain is lured away from the well by the dance of the Guardian, a female spirit who takes the form of a hawk. In the play's premiere performance, the climactic dance consisted of three movements lasting two minutes each, the role of the Guardian being played by Michio Ito, a traditional Japanese dancer.[3] The emphasis throughout the play is on poetry, music, and dance, with setting, character, and action reduced to a minimum. Thematically, the play echoes many Noh dramas as well, the stage representing a space in which the natural and supernatural come together and the characters seek reconciliation of these domains.[4] We should note, however, that Yeats does not emphasize the Shite character (the hawk spirit Guardian), which often in Noh is the spirit of a ghost haunting a locale, but the Waki, or secondary figure (usually a traveling priest, and here represented by both Cuchulain and the Old Man), and that the attempt at reconciliation of the physical and spiritual ends in failure. In this regard, Yeats clearly modifies Noh conventions to meet his own artistic aims.

Beckett, Noh, and Language

Beckett seems to have had little awareness of Noh drama, but he certainly knew and appreciated *At the Hawk's Well*. In 1956, he responded to a request for a tribute to George Bernard Shaw by saying, "I wouldn't suggest that G. B. S. is not a great play-wright. . . . What I would do is give the whole unupsettable apple-cart for a sup of the Hawk's Well, or [Synge's The Well of] the Saint, or a whiff of [O'Casey's] Juno [and the Paycock], to go no further" (cited in Pountney 2). He saw *At the Hawk's Well* among "other Yeats's plays" at the Abbey Theatre while a student at Trinity College in the 1920s (Pountney 28), and in *Happy Days* he has Winnie cite the opening line of Yeats's play, "I call to the eye of the mind" (*Dramatic Works* 164).[5] Many have noted the "Beckettian" sensibility of *At the Hawk's Well*, and some have suggested that Beckett's appreciation of the play exhibits a general affinity between Beckett and Noh drama. Takahashi has systematically investigated this hypothesis, delineating thematic and structural parallels between Noh and several of Beckett's dramatic works. Takahashi concentrates on the "so-called Fukushiki Mugen-Noh (dream-noh in two parts)," in which "the Shite (protagonist) first appears as an ordinary village woman and then, after an exit, reappears as a veritable ghost to enact her life story before the eye of the Waki (secondary character), a traveling priest, who finally manages to pacify her agonized soul by the power of his prayer. Noh in this light could be regarded as theatrical transformation of a ritual of exorcism of the demonic power of the dead" (Takahashi 100).

The dream-noh is "a 'minimalist' art," a "form of 'holy theater' whose ultimate aim lies in making an epiphany possible, that is, in preparing a space, a kind of 'void,' so that this empty space may be filled in by the arrival of a strange guest, a sacred spirit in a human form, a god incarnate" (Takahashi 101). Didi and Gogo, he observes, are like Wakis in a minimalist Noh setting, awaiting the epiphanic appearance of the Shite Godot. In *Krapp's Last Tape* (1958), Krapp is Waki to his own tape-recorded Shite; here, we see "the first unmistakable emergence in Beckett's canon of an essentially Noh-like structure: the voice (Shite) arriving out of an alien time-space dimension versus the character (Waki) listening to that voice" (Takahashi 103). The purest example of this alliance of Shite-Voice and Waki-Character Takahashi finds in *Not I* (1972), with the Shite "Mouth" (a spot-lit bare outline of an actress's mouth) recounting a woman's life and the Waki "Auditor" facing "Mouth." In other plays, such as *Eh Joe* (1965), *That Time* (1976), *Rockaby* (1981), and *Ohio Impromptu* (1981), the roles of Shite and Waki are less clearly separated, and sometimes doubled within a single character, but the basic structure, Takahashi shows, remains the same. An intriguing variant of this structure, as we shall see, occurs in the television play . . . *but the clouds*. . . .

It seems plausible, therefore, that, as Deleuze asserts, "the convergences of Beckett with Noh, even unintentional, presuppose perhaps the theater of Yeats" (E 98/CC 170), though what Yeats's theatrical example and Noh drama might have to do with television requires a rather extended consideration of Deleuze's understanding of Beckett's use of the medium. Deleuze sees Beckett's television plays as an effort to overcome the limitations of words by nonlinguistic means, through the exhaustion of space and above all through the creation of visual and sonic images. Over the years, Deleuze observes, "Beckett was less and less able to put up with words" (E 103/CC 172), though this was not a newfound intolerance. Indeed, Deleuze sees Beckett's entire oeuvre as dominated by a struggle with language, first enunciated in critical remarks from the 1930s. In a key 1937 letter to which Deleuze makes frequent reference, Beckett expresses his impatience with "official English," stating that "more and more my own language appears to me like a veil that must be torn apart in order to get at the things (or the Nothingness) behind it" (*Disjecta* 171).[6] Language cannot be eliminated "all at once," he says, but it should be torn apart and riddled with holes. "To bore one hole after another in it, until what lurks behind it—be it something or nothing—begins to seep through; I cannot imagine a higher goal for a writer today" (*Disjecta* 171).

Beckett laments that literature adheres to practices "long ago abandoned by music and painting," and then asks, "Is there any reason why that terrible materiality of the word surface should not be capable of being dissolved, like for example the sound surface, torn by enormous pauses, of Beethoven's seventh Symphony, so that through whole pages we can perceive nothing but a path of sounds suspended in giddy heights, linking unfathomable abysses of silence?" (*Disjecta* 172). Beethoven creates music that emphasizes the silence between sounds, and by implication literature should likewise reveal the "something or nothing" between words.

Beckett in fact says as much in the 1932 fragment *Dream of Fair to Middling Women* (another seminal text to which Deleuze often alludes), in which the character Belacqua voices his desire to write a book such that "the experience of my reader shall be between the phrases, in the silence, communicated by the intervals, not the terms, of the statement" (*Disjecta* 49). This literary project puts Belacqua in mind of "the dehiscing, the dynamic décousu of a Rembrandt, the implication lurking behind the pictorial pretext threatening to invade pigment and oscuro." In Rembrandt he discerns "a disfaction, a désuni, an Ungebund, a flottement, a tremblement, a tremor, a tremolo, a disaggregating, a disintegrating, an efflorescence, a breaking down and multiplication of tissue, the corrosive ground-swell of Art," and in Beethoven he notes a similar "punctuation of dehiscence, flottements, the coherence gone to pieces" such that the compositions are "eaten away with terrible silences" (*Disjecta* 49).

In these early critical texts, a parallel is established among painting, music, and literature as so many efforts to penetrate a surface to a "something or nothing" beneath. In Rembrandt the various pictorial figures and objects separate from one another, become disunited, and make visible the empty space between them, just as in Beethoven the phrases disaggregate and make audible the silences between sounds. Yet empty space, it seems, is not simply the space between, but the entire expanse beneath the surface of the painting, the background depths from which the painting arises ("the corrosive ground-swell of Art"), just as the "unfathomable abysses of silence" form the background dimension beneath the surface of the music. Hence, to tear apart the veil of language, to bore holes in words, to dissolve the word surface, is in an analogous fashion to reveal whatever background nonlinguistic element may lurk behind words, whatever counterpart to the visible void or sonic silence might function as language's underlying depths.

It might seem that Beckett's aesthetic project is essentially negative, that what lurks behind the art work's surface is much more a "nothing" than a "something," but Deleuze reads Beckett otherwise. Deleuze comments that when one bores holes "in the surface of the painted canvas, as does Rembrandt, Cézanne, or Van Velde, in the surface of sound, as does Beethoven or Schubert," it is in order that "the void or the visible in itself, silence or the audible in itself, may surge forth" (E 103/CC 173). What these painters and composers do is to create a "pure intensity that pierces the surface" (E 104/CC 173), a pure visual or sonic image that reveals *the visible in itself, the audible in itself*—that is, the invisible or inaudible forces that play through the visible or the audible. In Deleuze's reading, painting's void and music's silence are not empty but full, and what Beckett's favored painters and composers bring to the fore is the virtual plenum of forces that make actual forms possible and from which they arise.

The problem for writers is that language's surface is more difficult to tear apart than are the surfaces of visibilities or sounds: "It is not simply that words are liars; they are so laden with calculations and significations, and also with intentions and personal memories, with old habits that cement them together, that scarcely has their surface been broached when it closes over again. The surface sticks. It imprisons us and suffocates us"

(E 103/CC 173). When painters or composers manage to undo the narratives and codes that organize and regularize sights or sounds, they are then able to create pure images, indefinite entities that are neither general nor particular. "Music manages to transform the death of this young girl into *a young girl dies*; music brings about this extreme determination of the indefinite as pure intensity that pierces the surface" (E 103–04/CC 173). No longer "the young girl" as universal, nor Jane Marie Jones, a specifically identified subject, she is the locus of a process of becoming, "a young girl." Music and painting have a facility for creating such indefinite images that pierce the surface, but not so words, "with their adhesions that maintain them in the general or in the particular. They lack that 'punctuation of dehiscence,' that 'disconnection' that comes from a groundswell proper to art" (E 104/CC 173).

Beckett's Three Languages

Deleuze frames his analysis of Beckett's television plays in terms of exhausting the possible. (In the French text of *Quad,* the first of the four television plays Deleuze examines, Beckett insistently repeats the phrase "all possible combinations thus exhausted" [E10–13] when detailing the movements of the characters, the lighting, percussion sounds, and costumes.) To realize the possible is to pursue "certain goals, projects and preferences: I put on my shoes in order to go out and slippers in order to stay in" (E 58/CC 152). But the pursuit of goals, projects, and preferences has no ending, for whatever choices one makes, there are always others that remain possible. To exhaust the possible requires an abandonment of preferences, aims, and plans, a disconnection of elements from the endless sequence of wants and desires, such that a closed set of limited terms may undergo a thorough and exhaustive permutation of combinations. Murphy's calculation of the five biscuits' "total permutability, edible in a hundred and twenty ways" (*Murphy* 96–97), Watt's list of "twelve possibilities regarding Mr. Knott and his eating habits" (*Watt* 89–90), Molloy's description of the "sucking-stones" and all their possible placements in his pockets and mouth (*Three Novels* 69–74) are well-known instances from Beckett's fiction of this exhaustion of the possible, and in *Quad* a similar operation takes place, as four indistinguishable actors traverse all possible paths connecting the four corners of a square in all combinations of performers (solos, duos, trios, quartet), lighting, percussion, and costumes. What is crucial in all these instances is that the elements to be combined be stripped of all preference, all purpose and all signification, such that they form a closed set of terms whose permutations are finite. To disconnect these elements is to cut them off from the normal function of language, for "language enunciates the possible, but in preparing it for a realization" (E 58/CC 153). Language articulates all the codes, conventions, narratives, and representations of human wants and needs, whose continuations, connections, and combinations are open and inexhaustible. The purpose of exhausting the possible is finally that of undoing language, of dissolving the glue of calculations, significations, intentions, personal memories, and old habits that cement words together.

Deleuze identifies three means whereby Beckett undoes ordinary language and exhausts the possible. The first is through the creation of a metalanguage, "a very special language such that the relations between objects are identical to those between words" (E 66/CC 156). This metalanguage Deleuze calls *language I (langue I)*, a language that is "atomic, disjunctive, cut up, chopped, in which enumeration replaces propositions, and combinatory relations replace syntactic relations: a language of nouns" (E 66/CC 156). Such a language is that of Watt's and Molloy's lists of permutations, a collection of words severed from their usual networks of linguistic connotations, asignifying save in their one-to-one correspondence to the objects undergoing permutation. But if one exhausts the possible with words through language I, there is also a need to exhaust words themselves, and "hence the necessity of another metalanguage, of a *language II*, which is no longer one of nouns, but one of voices" (E 66/CC 156). If the words of language I are disconnected particles, the voices of language II are "waves or flows that pilot and distribute the linguistic corpuscles" (E 66/CC 156). The purpose of language II is to dry up the flows, to put an end to the surrounding din of incessant voices, each of which is an Other articulating a possible world, narrating an endless stream of stories with all their significations, preferences and goals. The problem, however, is that even when voices cease, they soon start again, and when one speaks of those voices, one risks continuing their stories. Thus the need of a *language III*, "which no longer relates language to enumerable or combinable objects, nor to emitting voices, but to immanent limits that are ceaselessly displaced, hiatuses, holes or rips" (E 69/CC 158). Language III involves "something that comes from outside or elsewhere" (E 70/CC 158), and that something is an "Image, visual or sonorous" (E 70/CC 158).

The image of language III, however, is an image in a very specific sense. It is a pure image, a sight or sound that "surges forth in all its singularity, without retaining anything of the personal, or the rational, acceding to the indefinite as to a celestial state" (E 71/CC 158). A language III image is disconnected from the narratives and codes of normal language and conventional representation. It is defined by "its 'internal tension,' or by the force that it mobilizes in order to create the void or bore holes, to loosen the grasp of words, dry up the oozing of voices, in order to disengage itself from memory and reason, a small alogical, amnesic, almost aphasic image, now standing in the void, now shivering in the open" (E 72/CC 159). Such images possess a "mad energy . . . ready to explode," but they are "like ultimate [i.e., subatomic] particles, they never last long" (E 76/CC 160-61). Their energy is "dissipative," for they "capture all the possible in order to make it explode" (E 77/CC 161), dissipating themselves as they put an end to the world of inexhaustible possibilities, that world of language, "weighed down with calculations, memories and stories" (E 73/CC 159).

Pure images form the outside of language, but that outside includes as well "the 'vastitude' of space" (E 74/CC 160), for which reason language III consists of both images and *un espace quelconque*, an any-space-whatever, "deconsecrated and put to another use *{désaffecté}*, unalloted *{inaffecté}*, although it is geometrically completely determined (a square, with such and such sides and diagonals, a circle with such and such zones, a cylinder 'sixty meters round and sixteen high')" (E 74/CC 160). In such a disconnected, "indefinite" any-space-whatever, all the potentialities of space may be exhausted, all the permutations of movement between the specified points of a closed area may be enacted, and it is within this *espace quelconque* that visual and sonic images may arise, explosive events tearing apart the surface of words and dissipating into the background expanse beneath.

Deleuze thus identifies four means of exhausting the possible: "forming exhaustive series of things" (language I), "drying up flows of voices" (language II), "extenuating the potentialities of space" (language III), and "dissipating the power *{puissance}* of the image" (also language III) (E 78/CC 161). The first two means (language I and language II) dominate in Beckett's novels, dramas, and radio plays, but the latter two, the twin elements of language III, only come to the fore in the television plays. In . . . *but the clouds* . . . (written 1976, televised 1977), all four means are present, though the emphasis is primarily on the emergence and dissipation of the image.

The Creation of Images: . . . *but the clouds* . . .

The play . . . *but the clouds* . . . consists of a series of dissolves between three immobile camera shots: M, "near shot from behind of man sitting on invisible stool bowed over invisible table"; W, "close-up of woman's face reduced as far as possible to eyes and mouth"; and M1, long shot of a blank circle of light, "about 5 m. in diameter, surrounded by deep shadow" (*Dramatic Works* 417–18). The man traverses M1 several times, the man's voice (V) identifying the shadowed area to the left as "roads" (designated "West" in Beckett's script), the shadows to the right as "closet" (East), and those directly in front of the camera as "sanctum" (North), the camera occupying the South position. V tells of the man's returning from walking the roads, entering his closet to change clothes, exiting to walk the roads again, or going into "my little sanctum, in the dark, where none could see me" (*Dramatic Works* 420). The man's movements through M1 correspond to those described by V, with the man changing his costume from the greatcoat and hat of the roads to the robe and skullcap of the sanctum (and vice versa) in the East shadows of the closet. As V eventually makes clear, M is a shot of the man in his sanctum. V's narration may be read as an allegory of the creative process of writing,[7] the man repeatedly roaming the outside world, retreating to his sanctum, and there trying again and again to summon up his muse, in this case, the memory image of an unidentified woman reciting lines from "The Tower." Only once or twice in a thousand tries does her image appear, according to V, and in those few instances, an even fewer tries bring with them the recited lines. Thus, V distinguishes four "cases" for the appearance of her image: "case nought," the 998 or 999 instances when no image comes; case one: "she appeared and— . . . In the same breath was gone"; case two: "she appeared and— . . . Lingered"; case three: "she appeared and— . . . After a moment— . . ." fragments of the verse began to be recited (*Dramatic Works* 420–21). As cases one, two, and three are described, the image of the woman's eyes and mouth appears, for two seconds in case one, for five seconds in case two. In case three, the lips initially mouth words inaudibly, and then V's murmuring of verse fragments synchronizes with the lip movements. Twice the lips synchronize with V's recitation of the fragments. In a final appearance of the woman's face, the lips do not move and V recites the complete lines: ". . . but the clouds of the sky . . . when the horizon fades . . . or a bird's sleepy cry . . . among the deepening shades . . ." (*Dramatic Works* 422).

Deleuze's language I is evident in the play's verbal repetition, especially in the reiterative enumeration of the articles of clothing, V punctuating reprises with such comments as "Right," "Let us now make sure we have got it right," and "Let us now run through it again." The words delimit a closed set of things, places, and actions, and then exhaust their possible combinations. V is the voice flow that carries the word particles, and the eventual evocation of an image leads to the dissipation of the voice, and hence functions as the means of exhaustion Deleuze labels "language II." The space of M1 is clearly an *espace quelconque*, a precisely circumscribed site with arbitrarily demarcated coordinates, through which the man traces a finite set of movements. The close-ups are likewise located in an indeterminate space, M (the image of the man on an invisible stool over an invisible table) and W (the image of the woman's eyes and mouth) both surrounded by black shadow. Deleuze asserts as well that the east-west axis of M1 constitutes a physical dimension, whereas the north-south traces a primarily mental domain (which, significantly, includes the camera), M and W also belonging to that realm of mental images. M1 may be seen, then, as both the *espace quelconque* within which the man exhausts all possible trajectories (first aspect of language III) and as the intersection of physical and mental space that allows for the appearance and dissipation of an image (second aspect of language III).

Clearly, the dramaturgy of . . . *but the clouds* . . . bears some resemblance to that of Noh theater. The set is minimal; the only image of a human face, the close-up of the woman's eyes and mouth, is a televisual version of a mask; the man's repeated movements through M1 form a kind of dance; his costume and spare, stylized gestures give him the appearance of a marionette. The parallels Takahashi establishes between the dream noh and Beckett are also evident. The circular area of M1 is "a kind of 'void'" (Takahashi 101) that makes possible an epiphany. Like the dream noh set, it marks the intersection of the physical and nonphysical, and after its own fashion it may be seen as the stage of a "ritual exorcism of the demonic power of the dead" (Takahashi 101), the man's memory image (W) being a haunting female spirit from the past, the verses cited from "The Tower" coming from a poem focused explicitly on old age and the imminence of death. The Shite is the woman's face, the Waki the man, represented here in three guises, as the near-shot hunched form (M), as the figure walking through M1, and as V. The eventual alignment of V with the movements of the woman's mouth marks the resurrection of the dead and, perhaps, the temporary exorcism of this ghost—a variation of the "Noh-like structure" of "the voice (Shite) arriving out of an alien time-space dimension versus the character (Waki) listening to that voice" (Takahashi 103).

Like Yeats, Beckett uses the minimalist techniques found in Noh to create a nonrealistic, "mental" stage of ideas. *At the Hawk's Well* is a symbolic drama of the human quest for immortality, but also an allegory about the related quest of the poet for inspiration. The play . . . *but the clouds* . . . cites Yeats's meditation in "The Tower" on "Decrepit age" and the poet's power through memory and language to transform "the wreck of body" into art, and Beckett's play may easily be read as a parallel meditation on poetic creativity. Deleuze argues, however, that Beckett's meditation is much more specific. It concerns the creation of an image—or rather, several images. To create an image requires both erasure and invention (in the word's dual etymological sense of creation and discovery). We see the world in terms of our desires, fears, plans, and predictions, imposing on things a host of associations, codes, and narratives. We also ignore those characteristics of things that are of no use to us, subtracting qualities from objects that do not concern our actions (just as our eyes filter out infrared and ultraviolet rays). To create a visual image is in part to strip the object of all its cultural accretions, to erase everything that is not really there. But it is also to discover and bring into visibility whatever we habitually ignore, to make present what is actually there. The visual image created by a great painter is an appearance, stripped of personal, individual associations, an apersonal appearance-in-itself. It is also a rendering visible of what is habitually invisible, but more importantly, a rendering visible of the invisible forces that give rise to things and inform their genesis and becoming. The sonic images of music perform a parallel function, rendering audible the inaudible forces that play through things.

Language, too, renders forces palpable, and in a way that conjoins the ends of poetry, painting, and music. Great writers, claims Deleuze, through the medium of language create "visions" and "auditions," visual and sonic images that form the outside limit of language. Language's limit "is made of visions and auditions that are nonlinguistic, but that language alone makes possible," and hence there is "a painting and a music proper to writing, like effects of colors and sonorities that rise above the words" (CC 9/lv). Visions and auditions are appearances that form the *between* of words and things, like hazy clouds that emanate from words and seem to haunt the surfaces of things.[8] To create linguistic visions and auditions one must divest language of all its conventional uses and habitual narratives, render it strange so that its untapped sonic and visual potential may be realized in the actual sounds and images of poetry.

What we witness in . . . *but the clouds* . . . is the emergence of three pure images. By stripping words of their complex of personal associations (language I), by exhausting voices and their interminable histories (language II), and by extracting from the coordinates of our spatiotemporal habits an adimensional *espace quelconque* (language III), a site is prepared for the appearance of a visual image (a depersonalized face), a sonic image (a disembodied voice), and a poetic image (lines from Yeats's "The Tower"). The initial silence of the mouth's movements and the subsequent synchronization of voice and mouth induce a ventriloquistic depersonalization of the face and voice, but only in order that face and voice may become autonomous visual and audio components—hence the absence of lip movements when the lines are recited in their entirety. Those lines are a distillation of poetry's essence: a vision of "the clouds of the sky/ When the horizon fades," and an audition of "a bird's sleepy cry/ Among the deepening shades" (ll. 191–95). And all these pure images, visual, sonic and poetic, are like fading clouds and vanishing cries, ephemeral appearances whose evanescent manifestation are one with their dissipation.

Deleuze regards television as a medium that lends itself especially well to the creation of such pure images, despite the fact that its commercial exploitation has had an almost universally stultifying and oppressive effect.[9] He concurs in large part with the video artist Nam June Paik that "the difference between film and television resides in the fact that film concerns the image and space, whereas with television, there is no space, there is no image, but only lines, electronic lines. The essential concept, in regard to television, is time" (Fargier 10). The television image, explains Paik, is "an electronic image, an interwoven image, recomposed from an extremely rapid scanning of a certain number of lines by a beam of electrons" (10). If, as Godard claims, film is "truth twenty-four times a second," in television "there is no truth at all. And no matter what you do, there is no longer any image. Everything is pure invention, everything is produced starting from an electronic and artificial interweaving" (Fargier 12). Implicit in Paik's contrast of film image/space and television lines/time is an opposition between an essentially photographic registration of the world, in which a spatially determinate object is converted into a frozen celluloid image by an equally spatially determinate camera, and an electronic simulation of an ephemeral appearance world of uncertain provenance, produced through a constant temporal scanning of lines. One might argue that television cameras and the objects they record are also located in a concrete space, but Paik's point is that the television image itself, as a temporal flow of impermanent light beam oscillations, generates temporary image events that by their very nature tend to become disconnected from their origins and "float" in a decontextualized, self-referential world of appearances.

Unlike Paik, Deleuze continues to use the terms "space" and "image" to talk about television, but he agrees that television's space and images are different from those of film. Television space tends toward an *espace quelconque*, and television images tend to relate primarily to one another rather than to external objects. This is because television, in its conversion of real-world objects into electronic impulses rapidly and constantly scanned across a grid of horizontal and vertical lines, is a harbinger of digital images. Digital images are simple configurations of numerical data, capable of alignment in various pixel grids, that may be metamorphosed through diverse statistical permutations. They may or may not have a real counterpart, since they may be generated directly by computational means as well as by mechanical means of reproduction. For this reason, argues Edmond Couchot, digital images must be regarded as transformable emissions of "immedia," without ultimate origin or final destination.[10] Their use tends to be interactive rather than passive, to encourage a "conversational" manipulation of images, such that no image is a stable referent in relation to an altered image, but each is an image in process of metamorphosis into a succeeding one, for which reason Couchot suggests that we speak of "'diamorphosis' in order to insist on this passage, not from one form to another, but between *(dia)* two forms which are neither origins nor terms" (Couchot 128). One consequence of this essentially "diamorphic" malleability, Deleuze asserts, is that television images ultimately have no genuine "out-of-field," or off-camera space, as do classical cinematic images, but rather "a right side and a reverse [a recto and verso], reversible and nonsuperimposable, like a power to turn back on themselves" (IT 347/265). Any image may be transformed into any other image, each image subject to a "perpetual reorganization" (IT 347/265) and recombination. The mutable nature of the television image also renders arbitrary the dimensions of up and down, right and left, the screen functioning not as a window but as a table of information, an inscription of data capable of various manifestations. If in cinema the screen is like the image of an eye framing nature, in television it is that of a brain displaying information, film's opposition of a mental subject eye and a physical object nature giving way to a brain information amalgam that makes subject/object and mental/physical distinctions undecideable. Finally, television makes possible a mutability of sound equal to that of visual images, and even more important, it grants sound autonomy from sight, thereby allowing for both a separation of audio and visual and a creative conjunction of the two as independent yet interacting strata.

Television, in short, produces an *espace quelconque* as well as a succession of images without clear origin or destination, floating appearances in a brain information world of undecideably mental/physical, subject/object ephemera. Its transformable, reversible, adimensional images invite a division and reconnection of the visual and the sonic as autonomous flows. But to render visible and audible such an *espace quelconque* and such autonomous, pure images requires an ascetic elimination of all the regular, habitual, conventional patterns of our seeing, hearing, and speaking, all the clichés of our practical, commonsense quotidian existence. Only by the careful erasure of both the personal and the universal, both the individualizing details and the conventional categories through which we organize existence, can an apersonal yet concrete image-in-itself arise, a pure appearance that makes visible invisible forces, audible inaudible forces, or articulable inarticulable forces. Television invites such a creative subtraction of clichés and lends itself to the emergence into direct visibility and audibility of such images—though without the inventive manipulations of the medium by a genuine artist, its potential remains dormant and unrealized.

Pure Images

Yeats discovered an ascetic, refined sensibility in Noh drama, one that stripped the world of particularizing, realistic details and made of it a mental space of poetry, song, and dance. In *At the Hawk's Well,* he fashioned his own version of Noh, reducing plot, décor, and characterization to a minimum. Beckett, in Deleuze's analysis, simply carried this ascetic tendency to an extreme, subtracting from space and time virtually all determinable markers, exhausting the permutations of action and characters that might constitute a plot, and focusing his play on the appearance of the simplest of images—*a* face, *a* voice, *a* poetic vision/audition. And in television Beckett found the optimal medium for producing such images within an *espace quelconque*. What Deleuze sees in Noh drama, Yeats's theater, and the television plays of Beckett, then, is a common ascetic sensibility whose goal is the creation of aesthetic images through the elimination of the particularizing details of conventional realism.

Though the thread tying Noh to Beckett's television plays may seem slender, the connection is real, if indirect. We must of course be cautious in comparing such heterogeneous cultural traditions as the contemporary Western theater and Noh drama, but finally there is at least some affinity between the aesthetic predilections of Beckett and the practitioners of Noh. When Zeami (1362–1441), the great playwright, performer, and theorist of Noh, says that "it is the fundamental Non-Being that gives rise to the outward sense of Being {in the *no}*" (Zeami 118); when he epitomizes the actor's art with the words from the Heart of Wisdom Sutra, "Form is no other than Emptiness, Emptiness is no other than Form" (Zeami 115); and when he characterizes the moment of Peerless Charm, the highest flower of Noh, as "an appearance that transcends any specific form" (Zeami 98), and as something that "surpasses any explanation in words and lies beyond the workings of consciousness" (Zeami 120), it is difficult not to hear a premonitory echo of Beckett's call for a literature that tears the veil of language apart "in order to get at the things (or the Nothingness) behind it," that bores holes in words "until what lurks behind it—be it something or nothing—begins to seep through" (*Disjecta* 171).

The pure image, for Beckett, is like "the clouds of the sky/ when the horizon fades;/ Or a bird's sleepy cry/ Among the deepening shades." The flower of Peerless Charm, says Zeami, is expressed in the phrase, "In Silla, in the dead of the night, the sun shines brightly" (Zeami 120). Perhaps the distance between television and Noh drama is not as great as we might initially think.

❖ 8

The Betrayal of God

In *A Thousand Plateaus,* Deleuze and Guattari delineate four "regimes of signs," or regular patterns of power relations that organize sign production: the primitive, presignifying regime; the despotic, signifying regime; the nomadic, countersignifying regime; and the passional, postsignifying regime. The postsignifying regime they identify as "the regime of betrayal, universal betrayal, in which the true man never ceases to betray God just as God betrays man, in a wrath of God that defines the new positivity." In this regime, God and prophet turn away from one another, averting their faces, and in so doing draw "a positive line of flight." God invents "the reprieve, existence in reprieve, *indefinite postponement,*" but also "the positivity of alliance as the new relation with the deity, since the subject remains still alive" (MP 154–55/123). What I wish to explore is the logic of this mutual betrayal of God and prophet, this aversion of faces that draws a line of flight, this existence in reprieve that signals a new relation. To accomplish this task, two rather lengthy divagations are necessary, one through Jérôme Lindon's *Jonas,* in order to clarify Deleuze and Guattari's account of Jewish prophetism, the other through Jean Beaufret's "Hölderlin et Sophocle," in order to explain the connection Deleuze and Guattari draw between the Jewish prophets and Oedipus. The mutual betrayal of the passional, postsignifying regime entails a positive alliance of the human and the divine, but betrayal itself, I shall argue, finally provides a means of subverting what Deleuze refers to as the "doctrine of judgment," and thereby of breaking free from the God of judgment.[1]

Jonah

Deleuze and Guattari cite Jérôme Lindon as "the first to analyze the relation between Jewish prophetism and betrayal, in the exemplary case of Jonah" (MP 155/529), and in fact they rely heavily on Lindon's 1955 commentary and translation of the Book of Jonah for their exposition of the postsignifying regime of betrayal. At first glance one might understand how Jonah's flight from Nineveh could represent a betrayal of God, and perhaps how God's refusal to destroy Nineveh could stand as a betrayal of Jonah, but the exemplary nature of this complex and enigmatic tale only becomes apparent after one traces the contours of Lindon's ingenious and rather idiosyncratic reading of the biblical text.

Most frequently, the Book of Jonah is taken to be the story of a reluctant prophet who preaches doom to the heathens but finally learns of God's universal mercy, which extends even to Israel's enemies. Many have objected to this unflattering reading of a petulant and vindictive Jonah manipulated by a condescending God, but in offering alternative interpretations, they, like all commentators, have had to grapple with several puzzling features of the story. Why, after all, does Jonah flee Nineveh when he knows full well there is no escaping the Lord on the face of the earth? Why does Jonah sleep during the storm at sea? What is the significance of his hymn of praise from the belly of the whale? Why does he seem crestfallen at the salvation of Nineveh? And what lesson is taught through the mysterious *qîqayôn* plant, which flourishes and dies in a day?

Lindon's answers to these questions spring from his interpretation of Jonah in terms of the scapegoat motif, suggested first by the association of Jonah with Yom Kippur, the Day of Atonement. Traditional readings on this tenth day of the seventh month open with Leviticus 16, in which Aaron is instructed in the proper sacrifice of the goat of the Lord and in the ritual expulsion of the goat of Azazel. After recitations of Isaiah 57:14–58:14 concerning humility and contrition and Leviticus 18 on sexual purity, Yom Kippur closes with a reading of the four chapters of Jonah. According to Lindon, the scapegoat's function is to "cover and isolate," to take divine punishment upon itself and thereby shield the community from God's wrath. He points out that the unvocalized consonants of *kapper,* "he covered," are the same as the *kippur* of the Day of Atonement,[2] and that a series of related verbal associations plays through texts connected with Jonah. In Leviticus 16, for example, Aaron is instructed to sacrifice the goat of the Lord and sprinkle its blood "on the *kapporeth* [the cover that is over the Ark of the Covenant; King James: "mercy seat"] and in front of the *kapporeth;* he will thus make a *kapparah* [purgation, cleansing] of the uncleanness of the children of Israel and their sins and their transgressions" (Lindon's translation 35). And in the narrative of the Flood, God instructs Noah, "Make an ark of gopher wood. You will make the ark in cells and you will cover it with *kapper,* an isolating cover, on the inside and on the outside."[3] Among those covered and protected from the storm is the dove, *yônâ* (the name Jonah means literally "dove"), the one designated by Noah "to recognize the dry land amidst the sea, the terrain of men amidst the space of God, to be at the same time the sign that separates and the messenger that connects" (Lindon 25–26).

Thus, in Lindon's reading, when Jonah hears God's summons to Nineveh and proceeds instead to Tarsis, he deliberately assumes the role of the scapegoat, that which "covers and isolates." He knows he cannot flee God's presence; by his flight he takes on the guilt of Nineveh, thereby anticipating God's action and awaiting his punishment. Jonah's sleep during the raging storm is indeed the sleep of the just, for his response to God's call is a voluntary acceptance of God's will, not a rejection of it.[4] The sailors want Jonah to join them and pray to his god, but he thinks to himself, "Safety {*salut*} is theirs, on the contrary, if I cut the ties between us, if I take their affair on myself alone. I will separate them as the *kapper* covers and isolates the ark of men from the waves of God" (Lindon 30). The helmsman asks Jonah where he comes from and who his people are, to which he replies, "I am a Hebrew" (Jonah 1:9). In this response is the essence of Jewish identity, says Lindon, for there is no physiological, ethnic, cultural, or linguistic characteristic that unequivocally differentiates Jews from Gentiles, other than the willingness to say, "I am a Jew." When the Nazis gather Jews to be registered, and eventually interred and exterminated, each individual is summoned to say, "I am a Jew," to accept an imposed separation from others and an unmerited suffering. It is not surprising, then, that Jonah's declaration of his identity is followed by his sacrifice. Indeed, he suggests to the sailors that they throw him overboard (Jonah 1:12), and they fear lest his blood will be on their hands (Jonah 1:14). Only after appealing to YHWH do they cast Jonah into the sea. When the waves subside, a powerful fear of YHWH overcomes them and they offer sacrifices and vows to the Lord (Jonah 1:16).

Yet Jonah does not die. Like the goat of Azazel, the scapegoat of Leviticus, he is allowed to live. The great fish saves Jonah, and he praises God's mercy, for he knew from the beginning that God was merciful, that through his assumption of guilt Nineveh would be spared, just as the sailors were kept from drowning. But if God wants him to remain alive, he concludes, he will go to Nineveh and proclaim God's warning, "Forty days and Nineveh will be turned upside down" (Jonah 3:4).[5] Jonah proceeds to the city, and his prophecy leads to Nineveh's penance and God's decision to spare the city. Then "un mal vient sur Jonas, un grand mal, et cela le brûle" ("a trouble comes over Jonah, a great trouble, and it burns him") (Jonah 4:1). As Lindon notes, the word *ra'â*, which he translates as *mal,* can mean "sin," "catastrophe," "punishment," "bitterness," or "error" (Lindon 14). (Sasson adds to the list "iniquity," "distress," "misery of body or mind" [272].) But Lindon insists that the line does not mean that "this greatly displeased Jonah and he was angered," as many translators render the phrase.[6] Rather, Jonah believes that the evil has been placed on him, that he is the covering and isolating scapegoat upon whom the sins of Nineveh have fallen, and the burden of this evil affects him deeply. He prays to God, saying that he knew God was compassionate and good when he fled to Tarsis, and that God would relent from bringing disaster:[7] "I knew that You would save Niniveh and that You needed someone to assume their evil. It was their evil that I purchased at Jaffa" (Lindon 44). He therefore accepts his role and asks God, "Take my spirit from me, for my death is worth more than my life" (Jonah 4:3). His death, in other words, is "le mal de Ninive anéanti, c'est Ninive définitivement sauvée" ["the evil of Nineveh wiped out, it is Nineveh definitively saved" (Lindon 45)].

Yet once again God spares Jonah. Unsure of the significance of God's action, Jonah reasons that in any case he must not remain among the Ninevites, since he has taken the evil upon himself and become "an object of opprobrium and terror" (Lindon 46). He therefore isolates himself and leaves the city. At this juncture, God offers Jonah an allegorical lesson (Jonah 4:6–11). God causes a *qîqayôn* plant to grow over Jonah and give him shade from the sun. The next day, however, the *qîqayôn* plant dries up and Jonah is so distraught over the plant's demise that he cries out once again for death (Jonah 4:8). God's point is that Jonah has covered Nineveh and shielded it from God's punishment just as the *qîqayôn* plant covered Jonah and shielded him from the sun; yet Nineveh can no more endure Jonah's death than Jonah can support the death of the plant. God requires that Jonah survive and that he bear the mark of his expiatory role. The *qîqayôn* plant, says Lindon, is the "tree of Cain," and Jonah the Cain of Nineveh.[8] Cain, like Jonah, thought his punishment was greater than he could bear (Genesis 4:13), but "the Lord set a mark upon Cain, lest any finding him should kill him" (Genesis 4:15). Likewise, Jonah must continue to live. He must be marked and separated, set aside to wander in the wilderness like the goat of Azazel.[9]

Lindon concludes his translation and study of Jonah with a brief narrative. The Flood marked the failure of Cain. To save His creation, God made a covenant with Noah and subsequently "invented the Jews" (Lindon 54), a people distinguished only by God's choice of them as the people before whom he would appear. For centuries, the goat of the Lord was sacrificed, and a second goat, as if a living replacement for the first, was sent forth to Azazel. In this way, the "rupture in the equilibrium of Creation" caused by Cain's bloodshed was overcome, and "the knife of Aaron, making the goat untouchable, forced God Himself to assume the impurity of Israel" (Lindon 56). One day, however, Israel rejected God's commandments; sacrifices ceased and the Temple was destroyed. Thereafter a new mode of salvation was necessary. The people themselves assumed the evil that befell them, yet in their misery they cried to the Lord, "Why hast thou forsaken me?" (Psalms 22:1; Matthew 27:46; Mark 15:34). And God remembered His covenant and protected His people, though thenceforth they would be eternal scapegoats condemned like Cain to live with the burden of their woe. In this sense Jonah, "irremediably isolated in his turpitude, justly condemned to death and each day resuscitated," proved the exemplar of his people, "the one called Israel, 'wrestling with God' and with men" (Lindon 58). The covenant of Noah was sustained, though it "no longer rested on anything but its betrayal" (Lindon 59).

Lindon speaks of the son of Amittai as "the absurd and criminal Jonah, traitor to that for which he dies and living his continual death" (Lindon 61), but in what regard is he a traitor? Only, it would seem, in his decision to go to Tarsis, to flee the Lord and his command. Yet for Lindon, this betrayal is actually an act of faith, not its breach. True betrayal would only arise if Jonah were to say, "I am not a Hebrew, I am like you," if he were to refuse to say, "let misfortune befall me." Lindon's primary concern is with the scapegoat, and betrayal is but another name for the assumption of that role. Time and again throughout the Pentateuch, of course, God's "stiff-necked people" break His covenant, and in this sense they betray God and incur guilt, but Jonah's betrayal has little to do with renegade crime and just punishment. Rather, it concerns the willingness to "cover and protect," to be the scapegoat, already condemned yet marked for survival.

What Deleuze and Guattari see in this story, however, is something else. They treat the scapegoat as the link between two regimes of signs. In the despotic, signifying regime, signs are centered on the frontal face of the omnipotent despot, from whom all signification emanates; he is surrounded by ever-widening circles of priests, officials, and bureaucrats interpreting his pronouncements; and at the limits of the system, at the walls of the city, the path of escape is blocked, the faceless, accursed scapegoat being the only creature allowed to wander outside the sphere of despotic control. The scapegoat "incarnates finally and above all the line of flight that the signifying regime cannot tolerate, that is, an absolute deterritorialization.... Anything that risks putting the system to flight will be killed or put to flight itself. Anything that exceeds the excess of the signifier or passes beneath it will be marked with a negative value" (MP 146/116). In the passional, postsignifying regime, however, the scapegoat is transformed. What was purely negative becomes a positive source of semiotic organization. Rather than tracing a line of absolute deterritorialization, the scapegoat marks discrete stages whereby an unoriented wandering is momentarily coded, then set adrift, only to be fixed and coded again. At each stage, an obsessive point of subjectification (such as God) defines a subject of enunciation (in this case, the prophet) and a subject of the statement (the people), the signs of a given stage functioning in terms of this limited, temporary, tripartite structure.[10]

For Deleuze and Guattari, then, it is this positive encoding of the wandering scapegoat that defines the regime of signs of Jewish prophetism: "'Let misfortune fall upon us' is the formula that punctuates Jewish history; it is we who must follow the most deterritorialized line, the line of the scapegoat, but while changing its sign, in converting it into the positive line of our subjectivity, of our Passion, of our trial *{procès}* or grievance. We will be our own scapegoat" (MP 153/122). In their elaboration of this history, Deleuze and Guattari recapitulate the phases of Lindon's account while stressing the theme of betrayal. Cain, "the true man," "turns away from the God who turns away from him"; he "already follows the line of deterritorialization, protected by the sign that allows him to escape death" (MP 154–55/123). The dove of Noah's ark occupies "the limit of separation or line of flight" between land and water. Moses, before his death, "receives the great cantical of betrayal" (this phase Lindon does not mention). And Jonah betrays God in all the ways detailed in Lindon's reading (MP 155/123). The final figure in Deleuze and Guattari's narrative, Jesus, "pushes to the universal the system of betrayal: betraying the God of the Jews, betraying the Jews, betrayed by God ('Why hast thou forsaken me?'), betrayed by Judas, the true man" (MP 155/124).

If for Lindon, then, betrayal is a way of being faithful to God and assuming the scapegoat's role, for Deleuze and Guattari, betrayal is the moment of flight, the break in the order of things. The scapegoat is first and foremost the wanderer in the desert, and the history of Jewish prophetism is that of a continual departure from any prescribed course and a continual remapping and recoding of that errant path. Crucial to Jonah's betrayal is his anticipation of God's actions, his orientation toward the future: "But Jonah, in fleeing from the face of God, did precisely what God had wanted: he took the evil of Nineveh upon himself; and he did it even more effectively than God had wanted, he anticipated God" (MP 155/123–24). Though he travels toward Tarsis, his flight is uncharted, his destination unknown—or at any rate, insignificant, since his orientation is his point of departure, not his point of arrival. Like other prophets, "his relation to God is passional and authoritative rather than despotic and signifying; he anticipates and detects the powers *{puissances}* of the future rather than applying present and past powers *{pouvoirs}*" (MP 156/124). Jonah's flight is an underdetermined movement whose sense God will determine through his response. God's reaction, however, is not a betrayal, at least not in the same sense as Jonah's. God stops Jonah's wandering and returns him to Nineveh, thereby reinstating him within a regulated order. If God betrays the prophet, it is in the general sense that He seems to forsake him, to abandon him in his position of scapegoat. But the relation between prophet and God is one of only partial and limited betrayal, for God preserves the prophet in a state of "reprieve, existence in reprieve, *indefinite postponement*" (MP 154/123). Each betrayal is a brief rupture in the order of God's reason, which then serves as the beginning of a new order, a new disclosure of the divine will and plan. Betrayal is subsumed within a *regime* of signs, a systematic organization of practices that produces regulated speech acts. But in itself, betrayal stands outside the semiotic realm, a gap in the fabric of signs.

Oedipus

In Lindon's reading of Jonah, the prophet betrays God, but only in a partial sense, and God's betrayal—if such there is—is even more limited than the prophet's. Deleuze and Guattari by contrast stress the mutuality of human and divine betrayal in the history of Jewish prophetism, a motif they see culminating in the narrative of the life of Jesus. But Deleuze and Guattari cite another narrative that provides the best model of the mutual betrayal of man and God, one outside the Judaic tradition—that of Oedipus. Deleuze and Guattari note that the first part of Oedipus's story is "imperial, despotic, paranoid, interpretive, divinatory" and hence best understood in terms of the despotic, signifying regime of signs, but that the second part, detailed in *Oedipus at Colonus,* concerns "Oedipus's wandering, his line of flight in a double turning away of his own face and that of God" (MP 156/124). Oedipus's name "is *atheos:* he invents something worse than death or exile, he takes the strangely positive line of separation or deterritorialization where he wanders and survives. Hölderlin and Heidegger see this as the birth of the *double turning away,* the change of the face, and the birth of modern tragedy, for which they bizarrely credit the Greeks: the result is no longer murder or sudden death but survival under reprieve, unlimited postponement" (MP 156/124–25). The full sense of this observation depends on a familiarity with Jean Beaufret's essay "Hölderlin et Sophocle," a brilliant Heideggerian explication of Hölderlin's abstruse "Remarks on Oedipus" and "Remarks on Antigone." A brief summary of Beaufret's exegesis should help clarify the nature of Oedipus's relationship to the divine and the extent to which it may be seen as one of mutual betrayal.

Beaufret begins with an analysis of Hölderlin's conception of art, which is framed in terms of an Aristotelian opposition of *techne* (art) and *physis* (nature). Aristotle speaks of art imitating nature, but also of art surpassing nature and thereby completing it. Hölderlin distinguishes clearly between nature—the native, the natural, the innate—and culture, regarding culture's proper task as that of separating itself as much as possible from nature and thereby bringing to completion what nature could not achieve on its own. Yet when culture reaches its highest goal, it reunites with the essence of nature through what Hölderlin refers to as a *vaterländische Umkehre,* a return to one's native land, "the turnabout *{volte}* which comes back to the very essence of the native" (Beaufret 8).[11] Hence, art may be said both to oppose nature and to imitate it, to distance itself from nature but eventually to reveal nature's essence through a *vaterländische Umkehre.*

Hölderlin regards the ancient Greeks as "sons of fire," by nature passionate, ecstatic, "aorgic."[12] Thus, the proper task of Greek artists is to go beyond their "oriental" nature and attain lucidity, sobriety, and clarity of exposition, yet eventually to return to their aorgic nature (though very few are successful in reaching this highest aim). Conversely, Hölderlin sees Germans (and modern Europeans in general) as naturally lucid and therefore faced with the cultural task of creating passionate, ecstatic art, with the modern artist's eventual (and hitherto unachieved) goal that of returning from the ecstatic to become again *knowingly* what one is *naturally*—that is, clear and composed (Beaufret 11). It is in this context that Hölderlin approaches Sophocles's *Oedipus the King,* viewing the play as a model of the lucid tragedy modernity should seek to create as its highest *vaterländische Umkehre.*

Hölderlin finds the essence of Sophocles's tragedy in "the retreat or the distancing of the divine" (Beaufret 12). One may say that Greek tragedy as a whole is concerned with the limit or the border between humans and the gods. Yet in Aeschylus, for example, if humans transgress the limit of the divine (one thinks especially of Agamemnon and Prometheus), the limit itself remains clearly demarcated, the mortal's crime being that of a patent exceeding of limits. In Sophocles, by contrast, the limit qua limit is in question, and the hero falls into a dangerous gap in which the divine and human are undifferentiated. Thus in his "Remarks on Oedipus," Hölderlin speaks of the tragic moment in which "God and man couple *{sich paart}*, and without limits *{grenzenlos}* natural force *{Naturmacht}* and man's innermost *{des Menschen Innerstes}* become one in wrath." "The presentation of the tragic rests primarily on this," he says, "that the unlimited becoming-one *{das grenzenlose Eineswerden}* purifies itself through unlimited separation *{durch grenzenloses Scheiden}*" (SWB, II, 395–96).

What Hölderlin means by the "unlimited becoming-one" of man and god is suggested in the second section of his "Remarks on Oedipus." The intelligibility of *Oedipus the King,* says Hölderlin, rests on a proper understanding of Oedipus's response to the oracle reported by Creon. The oracle charges the Thebans to purify the city and drive the corruption from the land, but Oedipus *"interprets too infinitely"* (SWB, II, 391). Though the oracle might simply call for a rigorous trial and the maintenance of "good civil order" *{gute bürgerliche Ordnung}*, Oedipus goes beyond his civic, human role and speaks in a "priestly" fashion of the need for rites of purification. He also asks for particular details (of whom is the oracle speaking?) and leads Creon's thoughts to the murder of Laius. In this manner, Oedipus links the oracle and Laius's death, "which are not necessarily connected to one another." At this point, Oedipus enters a realm in which the human order of the state and the divine order of the oracle interpenetrate, and the subsequent scenes of the drama are so many demonstrations of the suffering, mad furor of man-and-god's "endless becoming one": the "wonderful angry curiosity" (SWB, II, 392) of Oedipus before Tiresias, as his knowledge, "after it has broken its barriers," seeks that which it cannot bear or contain; the "joyous destruction" of his words to Creon as his "unbound" thought rages under the weight of "tragic secrets"; the "imbecility" and "pathetic naive error of the powerful man" as he tells Jocasta of his efforts to avoid killing Polybus and marrying Merope; the "desperate struggle" to "come to himself" in the second half of the play, the "foolishly wild search for a consciousness" *{das närrischwilde Nachsuchen nach einem Bewußtsein}* (SWB, II, 393); and the "insane questioning for a consciousness" *{das geisteskranke Fragen nach einem Bewußtsein}* (SWB, II, 394) evident in his final interrogation of the messenger.

The tragedy of *Oedipus* thus dramatizes the unlimited becoming-one of man and god, but that becoming-one also "purifies itself through unlimited separation *{durch grenzenloses Scheiden}*" (SWB, II, 396). By purification Hölderlin clearly refers to tragic catharsis, but what he means by "unlimited separation" is less evident. Beaufret finds a clue in Hölderlin's reference later in the Remarks to the "categorical turn/reversal" *{kategorischen Umkehr}* whereby man responds to the moment when the god "categorically turns" *{sich kategorisch wendet}* (SWB, II, 396). He argues that Hölderlin's "categorical turn" echoes the categorical imperative of Kant, whom Hölderlin in a letter calls "the Moses of our nation, who has led us out of Egyptian torpidity into the free desert of his speculation, and who has brought back from the sacred mountain the vigorous law."[13] Kant's categorical law, in Hölderlin's view, is a sobering force that returns moderns to their native lucidity and disabuses them of their pretensions to understand the divine language of intuitive reason. Kantian morality is devoid of theophany, and hence "it is no longer a vision of God, but already the retreat of the divine. The law is the most proper document of such a *retreat*. If God is presence, it is to the exclusion of any 'intuitive representation'" (Beaufret 14–15).

The categorical turn, then, is the moment of divine abandonment, "When the Father turned his face from men" ("Brot und Wein," stanza 8, l.127, SWB, I, 313), but also the moment when humans must assume the burden of the law and "endure this *lack of God* that is the most essential figure of his presence" (Beaufret 15). Although Oedipus is seized by an "unlimited becoming-one" with God, he is also *atheos* (Sophocles, *Oedipus the King,* 1. 661), "not *atheist,* but deserted as much as possible by the god who separates himself and turns away from him" (Beaufret 16). Even when Oedipus's crime is revealed, the heavens remain silent. Oedipus exacts his own punishment, but then embarks on an extended terrestrial wandering that only concludes in *Oedipus at Colonus.* This second life of Oedipus is that of the "categorical turn of the divine," in which Oedipus must "learn to lead a life of death in postponement" (or "in reprieve," *une vie de mort en sursis)* (Beaufret 17). As the drama of maximum separation of the human and the divine, *Oedipus* represents the furthest cultural distancing of Greek art from its native aorgic roots. As a "tragedy of slow death" (Beaufret 17), it serves as a model for modern tragedy, which should go beyond its culturally created enthusiasm and ecstasy and aim at a higher lucidity through a *vaterländische Umkehr* or return to the native land of modern clarity.

Oedipus is the exemplary drama of the categorical turn, and this turn Hölderlin associates with infidelity and betrayal. In the "frighteningly festive forms" of the drama, which is "like a heresy trial *{wie eines Ketzergerichtes}*," God and man *"express themselves in the all-forgetting form of infidelity" {in der allvergessenden Form der Untreue sich mitteilt}*. They do so in order that "the memory of the Heavenly ones *{der Himmlischen}* not fade," for "divine infidelity is the best to retain" *{göttliche Untreue ist am besten zu behalten}*. In the moment of such a turn, "man forgets himself and forgets god, and turns around, indeed in a holy manner, like a traitor" (SWB, II, 396). This mutual betrayal entails a mutual forgetting, which Hölderlin describes in a passage that Beaufret declares as dense as any written *"depuis que le monde est monde"*: "Inside it [the moment of the utmost limits of suffering], man forgets himself, because he is entirely in the moment *{weil er ganz im Moment ist}*; god [forgets himself], because he is nothing but time *{weil er nichts als Zeit ist}*; and each is unfaithful [*untreu*], time, because at such a moment it turns categorically, and beginning and end no longer rhyme at all; man, because within this moment he must follow the categorical turn, and thus cannot at all equal the beginning in what follows" (SWB, II, 396).

Man forgets himself in the sense that at the height of his tragic suffering he ceases to focus on past and future, to orient himself in terms of memories and projected plans, and instead exists solely within the present moment. But he also forgets in that he "decisively liberates himself from *dead customs and opinions, devoid of spirit or sense*" (Beaufret 19), as Hölderlin puts it in a letter of 1799 (SWB, II, 798). The tragic moment is a caesura in the rhythm of man's life, a break that makes past and future incommensurable from that instant on. Continuity is ruptured; beginning and end no longer rhyme; the beginning cannot equal what follows.[14]

God forgets himself in that he "is nothing but time," a phrase that is clarified somewhat by Hölderlin's comment in the preceding paragraph that in the moment of the utmost limit of suffering, nothing remains but "the conditions of time or space" (SWB, II, 396). The reference to Kant is evident, as Beaufret points out: "The *conditions* of time or space signify in Kantian language that by which time and space are essentially themselves, an abstraction made of 'affections' that alone give them a content" (Beaufret 21). Kant also speaks of the condition of time or space as the pure and empty form of time or space. Hence, argues Beaufret, "the god *who is nothing but time,* time being itself reduced to that in it which is a pure 'condition,' that is, its pure and empty form, isn't this indeed the retreat or the turning-away of god, such that he leaves man faced with the empty immensity of the endless sky?" (Beaufret 21).

God's infidelity, then, is in the manner of his revelation. No longer a father, a friend, or even an enemy, He manifests himself solely as the pure and empty form of time, a blank and featureless sky. Man's infidelity is in his separation from God, his voluntary assumption of the task of living in this pure and empty form of time. Man turns from God as a traitor, but he does so in a holy manner. His effort is to be adequate to God's manifestation and thereby preserve "the memory of the Heavenly ones." That memory is one of divine infidelity, which is "the best to retain," a memory of God's forgetting of man in that moment in which man forgets himself by entering into an unoriented time devoid of past and future coordinates. Man's turn from God is a "categorical turn," and hence one that leaves him without divine intuition in the determination of his ethical judgments. His turn entails fidelity to a separation of the divine and the human, a discrete differentiation of what Kant calls the "noumenal" and the "phenomenal."

The God of Judgment

Lindon's Jonah betrays God in fleeing toward Tarsis, but God betrays Jonah only to the extent to which He abandons the prophet to the role of scapegoat. In Hölderlin's account of Oedipus, by contrast, the betrayal of man and God is much more decidedly mutual: if Oedipus is a saintly traitor who turns from God, it is simply because "the Father has turned his face from men" and set them adrift in the pure and empty form of time. In both Lindon's Jonah and Hölderlin's Oedipus, Deleuze and Guattari find the themes of the scapegoat and betrayal, but in Hölderlin alone does the turn from God take on an explicitly temporal dimension. For Deleuze and Guattari, I have argued, Jonah's betrayal per se rests in his flight toward an unknown future, and hence in his entrance into an uncharted and uncoded space and time. The precise nature of that time of betrayal now requires our attention.

Deleuze expands on this theme of the pure and empty form of time in his essay "On Four Poetic Formulas That Might Summarize the Kantian Philosophy" (CC 40–49/27–35), citing specifically Hölderlin's Oedipus (and Beaufret's commentary). Before Kant, says Deleuze, time is traditionally subordinated to movement. The world is seen as a great revolving door, spinning in an eternal circle, and time is conceived of as the measure of the passage between discrete and fixed points. With Kant, however, "time is no longer related to the movement it measures, but rather movement to the time that conditions it" (CC 41/28). Time is the condition of possibility of movement, that within which movement can appear. Thus time itself proves to be a form whose content is unspecified. No longer can time be thought of in terms of succession, for "things succeed one another in diverse times, but they are also simultaneous in the same time, and they reside in an indeterminate time *{un temps quelconque}*" (CC 42/28). That indeterminate time is neither eternal (time-less) nor changing (a qualitatively different time now than at some other moment): "It is the form of everything that changes and moves, but it is an immutable form and one that does not change. Not an eternal form, but precisely the form of that which is not eternal, the immutable form of change and of movement" (CC 42/29). And this new time has a theological dimension, for in it "time ceases to be curved by a God who makes it depend on movement" (CC 41/28).

Time, then, is a pure and empty form, "the immutable form of change and movement," which is not subordinate to an organizing God. Nor is it subsumable within some unifying Self, which, as Deleuze often comments, is but a substitute for God.[15] In Deleuze's analysis, Kant revolutionizes the Cartesian formula *cogito, ergo sum* by showing that the Self is forever doubled—*fêlé*, split, or fractured—and precisely through the pure and empty form of time. The Self (the *ego sum*) exists in time as something changing; it passively receives impressions and experiences itself through those changing impressions. The *cogito,* or thinking "I," is an act, a determining activity, itself undetermined; it determines its existence only as something existing in time. Thus, the active I *(cogito)* and the passive Self *(ego sum)* are "separated by the line of time, which relates each to the other under the condition of a fundamental difference. My existence can never be determined as that of an active and spontaneous being, but only as a passive 'self' that represents to itself the 'I'—in other words, the spontaneity of the determination, as an Other that affects it" (CC 43/29–30). Though time is the form of interiority, time is not within us but we are within it: "Interiority ceaselessly hollows us out, bifurcates us, doubles us, even though our unity subsists" (CC 45/31). The I and the Self are a two-in-one, a *"Je fêlé,"* or constitutively split I/Self, and it is this split that Hölderlin identifies when he speaks of the caesura that separates the no-longer-rhyming beginning and end. Hölderlin, Deleuze says in *Difference and Repetition,* "discovers the emptiness *{le vide}* of pure time, and in this emptiness, simultaneously the continued turning away *{détournement}* of the divine, the prolonged fracture of the I *{Je}* and the constitutive passion of the Self *{Moi}*" (DR 118/87).

One might think that this discovery of the split self in the pure and empty form of time would be an emancipating event, yet Hölderlin treats it as "the essence of the tragic," a kind of "death instinct" (DR 118/87) whereby Oedipus is condemned to the "slow death" of a "life of death in postponement *{une vie de mort en sursis}*" (Beaufret 17). Oedipus and God's mutual betrayal takes place in a "categorical turn," which both Beaufret and Deleuze identify with the categorical imperative of Kant's *Critique of Practical Judgment*. As Beaufret argues, the turn of God and man is categorical for Hölderlin since it reflects the Kantian absence of theophany in ethical judgments, the end of any "intuitive representative" of the divine. Deleuze adds that the categorical imperative implies a new relationship between Law and the Good, a reversal whereby Law no longer derives from the Good, but the Good issues from the Law as "a pure form that has no object, either sensible or intelligible. It does not tell us what we must do, but what subjective rule we must obey whatever our action might be" (CC 46/32). Kant's ascetic insistence that ethical action be devoid of interest and based solely on the principle of the categorical imperative leads to the curious resemblance of Kant's Law to Kafka's—blank, featureless, implacable. It is a law that never acquits us, "neither of our virtues nor of our vices or our faults: at each moment there is only an apparent acquittal, and the moral conscience, far from appeasing itself, is strengthened by all our renunciations and beats us even more harshly" (CC 46/32). As Titorelli informs K. in *The Trial*, there is no possibility of acquittal before the Law, only "ostensible acquittal" or "indefinite postponement" (Kafka 201). The application of the Law is unending, but its process is never concluded. Rather than announcing immortality, "it distills a 'slow death,' and never ceases to *defer the judgment of the law*" (CC 47/33).

Hölderlin's categorical turn, then, far from emancipating human beings, condemns them to an endless judgment without release or execution. In this regard, Deleuze and Guattari see a basic continuity between Jewish prophetism as traced by Lindon and Hölderlin's lineage of Oedipal abandonment that eventuates in the modern Kantian Law as "pure form that has no object" (CC 46/32). In both, betrayal leads to the perpetual judgment of God, albeit in different guises. The passional, postsignifying regime of signs, we will recall, is a regime of the mutual betrayal of man and God, but one that involves as well a positive relation between the two. It would seem that this relation is based on a perpetual yet endlessly deferred judgment. How, then, is judgment related to betrayal?

In "To Have Done with Judgment" *(Essays Critical and Clinical)*, Deleuze offers a brief genealogy of judgment based largely on Nietzsche's remarks on debt in *The Genealogy of Morals* and his analysis of the "doctrine of judgment" in *The Antichrist*. All exchange has its origin in debt, and debt itself first comes into existence when individuals make promises but do not fulfill them. The debt owed the creditors is paid through the extraction of pain from the debtors, that pain giving the creditors pleasure. Tribal rites in which initiates are marked or scarred are merely extensions of the creditor-debtor relation, the elders extracting a measure of pleasure from the unit of communal debt inscribed in the bodies of the debtor initiates. The creditor-debtor relationship is a cruel system of justice, but one devoid of judgment, and it is exclusively human, the gods at most serving as passive witnesses or advocates for one of the parties involved. Gradually, however, debt is transferred to the gods, as humans and gods begin to judge. Judgment presupposes "that the gods give *lots* to men, and that men, depending on their lots, are fit for this or that *form*, for this or that organic *end*" (CC 161/128). Humans stake claims to certain lots, and the legitimacy of their claims is judged by mortals and gods. Human actions are measured according to the higher standard of divine forms, judgment assessing the extent to which an ideal form is realized. Thus, judgment initially appears "in the form of the false judgment that leads to delirium, to madness, when man is mistaken about his lot; and in the form of the judgment of God, when the form imposes another lot" (CC 161/129). In Christianity, says Deleuze, "a final bifurcation is produced: there are no longer any lots, for it is our judgments that make up our only lot; and there is no longer any form, for it is the judgment of God that constitutes the infinite form" (CC 161–62/129).[16] The Christian's only role is that of perpetual self-judge, and the sole form against which that role is measured is the infinite form of the deity, that form being one with an all-pervasive judgment. Ultimately, this form of judgment culminates in Kafka's blank law of perpetual postponement and in the tragic destiny of Hölderlin's Oedipus living a death in continual reprieve: "At the limit, dividing oneself into lots and punishing oneself become the characteristics of the new judgment or modern tragedy" (CC 162/129).

The "doctrine of judgment," as Nietzsche outlines it, requires a debt to the deity that is infinite and thus unpayable. But an infinite and endless debt requires an infinite and endlessly indebted debtor—hence the necessity of the doctrine of the soul's immortality. "The debtor must survive if his debt is to be infinite" (CC 159/126–27). The debtor's debt can never be discharged, and in this sense judgment, as final judgment (or Last Judgment), is perpetually deferred. Judging, then, as an endless and forever uncompleted process, is directly related to deferral: "it is the act of deferring, of carrying to infinity, that makes judgment possible" (CC 159/127). Judgment's condition of possibility is a relation between existence and "the infinite according to an order of time: the existing being as having a debt to God" (CC 159/127). Thus, an infinite debt to God entails not only the immortality of the soul but also a specific conception of time and the relationship between existence and the infinite. Deferral is the act whereby existence is put in relation to the infinite, "carried to infinity," and this act takes place within an order of time, an infinite straight line of moments extending toward a perpetually receding end point. Judgment, then, does not create but instead presupposes this relation between existence and infinity and this order of time: "to anyone who stands in this relation is given the power to judge and to be judged" (CC 159/127).

If we return to Hölderlin's Oedipus, we can perhaps see more clearly how betrayal is related to judgment and its condition of possibility. When man and God turn from one another, man forgets himself in time and God reveals himself as time. This temporal turn Deleuze identifies with Kant's reversal of the relation between movement and time, an unbending of the divine circle of time. Time ceases to be organized around the hinge {cardo} of a revolving door and becomes a straight line: "It ceases to be cardinal and becomes ordinal, the order of empty time" (CC 41/28). The order of empty time is a simple but terrifying labyrinth, an infinite, inexorable, incessantly extending line, and it is this line that Deleuze finds in Hölderlin's Oedipus: "Hölderlin saw Oedipus as already engaged in this strict march of the slow death, following an order of time that had ceased to 'rhyme'" (CC 41/28). Hölderlin calls the mutual betrayal of God and man a "categorical turn," and hence ties it to the judgment of Kant's categorical imperative. Deleuze sees Kant's law as an opaque, self-enclosed principle, which imposes a perpetual and endless judging without final judgment. But that process of continual judging itself has as its condition the act of deferring, which puts existence in relation to the infinite in an order of time. In the turn of mutual betrayal, then, when time becomes a straight line, "we have to renounce the ancient cycle of faults and expiations in order to follow the infinite route of the slow death, of the deferred judgment, or of the infinite debt" (CC 47/33).

It would seem, then, that the betrayal of God, in which man and God turn away from one another, has the peculiar effect of confirming a moral and theological relationship—that presupposed by the doctrine of judgment. In the turn of mutual betrayal, time may no longer be "curved by a God," but the disclosure of a time that is "unilinear and rectilinear" (CC 41/28) leads finally to an endless connection between the human and the divine, one based on the act of deferral and infinite debt. Yet once again we must question whether betrayal per se brings the human and the divine into a relation of perpetual deferral, since the mutual aversion of man and God does not necessarily issue in a regime of endless judgment. Kant's "rectification of time" (CC 41/28) unbends the divine temporal circle, but it also discloses the condition of time as a pure and empty form. Further, time as the "form of interiority," as the "Affect of self by itself" (CC 44/31), is that which creates the *"Je fêlé,"* which "ceaselessly hollows us out, bifurcates us, doubles us, even though our unity subsists" (CC 45/31). The pure and empty form of time need not issue in the straight line of an "order of time." The determining action of the I need not be joined with the passive determinable Self in a regulated constitution of knowledge. This, says Deleuze, is the surprising discovery Kant makes late in life in the *Critique of Judgment*. What Kant discloses is a "pathos beyond all logic," an aesthetic "which will grasp time in its gushing forth *{dans son jaillissement}*, at the very origin of its thread and its vertigo. This is no longer the Affect of the *Critique of Pure Reason,* which related the Self to the I in a relationship that was still regulated by the order of time; it is a Pathos that lets them evolve freely in order to form strange combinations as sources of time, 'arbitrary forms of possible intuitions'" (CC 48/34). The possibility exists, therefore, that the categorical turn of mutual betrayal need not inaugurate the "form of judgment," that act of deferral that puts existence in relation to the infinite through an order of time and an unpayable debt. Nor need the "universal betrayal" of the passional, postsignifying regime of signs necessarily inaugurate a process of subject formation, whereby a point of subjectification determines a *sujet d'énonciation* and a *sujet d'énoncé*. With a deregulation of the senses and a disordering of time, the *"Je fêlé"* may escape reconstitution and enter into asubjective relations, apersonal and anindividual, "strange combinations as sources of time, 'arbitrary forms of possible intuitions.'"

Beyond Judgment

The passional, postsignifying regime of signs is a regime of universal betrayal, in which God averts His face as man turns away from God. It is a regime that territorializes the wandering of the scapegoat, submits the wanderer to a process of subjectification, and surrenders the subjected subject to the slow death of an indefinite postponement and perpetual reprieve. Lindon's reading of the Book of Jonah provides Deleuze and Guattari with an account of Jewish prophetism that makes it readily assimilable to the passional, postsignifying regime. Not only does Lindon transform what is often regarded as a tale of human disobedience and universal divine mercy into a story of faithful betrayal, showing Jonah to be a willing scapegoat who "covers and protects," but he also relates Jonah to Cain, who is marked for a life in perpetual reprieve, to Noah's dove, which separates earth and heaven while assuring their mutual relation, and to

Jesus, who reiterates the Psalmist's cry, "Why hast thou forsaken me"? In Hölderlin's Oedipus, Deleuze and Guattari find a continuation of the themes of Jewish prophetism—betrayal, the scapegoat, indefinite postponement. The betrayal of man and God, though, is much more clearly mutual in Hölderlin than in Lindon; the turn of God discloses the divine solely as the pure and empty form of time, and man's turn from God is but a means of preserving the memory of God's forgetfulness. In that categorical turn of man and God, a fundamental connection is established between betrayal and indefinite postponement. The infinite and unpayable debt to God is structured by a form of judgment, an act of deferral that puts existence in relation to the infinite in an order of time. Yet the turn also makes possible a disordering of time, a form of interiority that desubjectifies and shatters the *Je fêlé*.

What, then, is meant by "the betrayal of God"? The passional, postsignifying regime may involve universal betrayal, but the moment of betrayal itself is a break in the regime, an uncoded and unmapped gap that is then recoded and remapped in terms of a specific configuration of power relations. The mutual betrayal of Hölderlin's categorical turn is likewise a rupture, an opening in time and a split in the subject, albeit one that can initiate the "hell here below" (CC 47/33) of slow death and the indefinite deferral of the law. The God who is betrayed is the God of Judgment, whose principle is that of a ubiquitous evaluation of life by otherwordly standards. Everywhere life is judged guilty, and everywhere people are invited to judge others and themselves, to engage in an endless judgment that has as its aim a world of total social control and conformity to a dominant, homogeneous order. In the passional, postsignifying regime, the betrayal of God is fed back into the semiotic machine, made a part of a regular order of signs. In the modern form of tragedy outlined in Hölderlin's categorical turn, betrayal leads to an inexorable order of time and an implacable, blank law that makes life a slow death in continual reprieve. Yet the moment of betrayal itself, that mutual aversion of the human and the divine, makes possible a break with the form of judgment. Ultimately, then, betrayal is a way of having done with the judgment of God, and thereby doing away with the God of Judgment.

Notes

Chapter 1: Deleuze's Style

1. I do not wish to ignore Guattari's contributions to Deleuze/Guattari's collaborative efforts or to Deleuze's thought and style. One could, perhaps, attempt to unravel the Guattarian warp from the Deleuzian woof, but this is antithetical to the spirit of their joint enterprise. My argument is that a Deleuze effect plays through everything that bears his name. A proper tribute to Guattari would be to show that likewise a "Guattari effect" is present in every work he signed, an effect with its own peculiar identity. But that would be the subject of another study.

2. Émile Bréhier makes a similar point when reflecting on the choice of subjects he made in his various studies in the history of philosophy: "What I sought above all in a philosopher, I will confess, was a virtuosity of thought, and by that above all I mean an art of correspondences, that art peculiar to philosophers, so poorly understood by pure literary critics, whose analogue may be found in music and in certain forms of painting, and which consists of seeing in an idea only a passage, a direction toward another, a vector rather than a simple line, an intention more than an accomplishment. For some time I have not believed that this virtuosity has its end in itself, but I remain convinced that it can be acquired; just like fugue and counterpoint for the musician, it is an apprenticeship that is indispensable for the philosopher" (2).

3. Deleuze also devotes a paragraph to insomnia in his discussion of Nietzsche, Lawrence, Kafka, and Artaud, "To Have Done with Judgment" (CC 162–63/129–30).

4. "The logic of a thought is the whole set of crises it traverses; it resembles more a volcanic chain than a stable system close to equilibrium" (PP 116/84).

5. "All of grammar, all of syllogistic logic, is a means of maintaining the subordination of conjunctions to the verb to be, of making them gravitate around

the verb to be. One must go further: make the encounter with relations penetrate and corrupt everything, undermine being, make it teeter. Substitute the AND for IS. A *and* B. . . . To think *with* AND, instead of thinking IS, instead of thinking *for* IS" (D 71/ 57).

6. "The art of constructing a problem is very important: you invent a problem, a position of a problem, before finding a solution. None of this takes place in an interview, in a conversation, in a discussion. Even reflection, whether alone, or between two or more, is not sufficient. Above all, not reflection. Objections are even worse. Every time someone puts an objection to me, I want to say: 'OK, OK, let's go on to something else'" (D 7/1). "Philosophy is not communicative, any more than it is contemplative or reflective: it is creative or even revolutionary, by nature, in that it is ceaselessly creating new concepts. . . . The concept is that which keeps thought from being a mere opinion, a view, a discussion, idle chatter" (PP 186–87/136).

7. "So is this it, to paint, to compose, or to write? It's all a question of line, there is no substantial difference between painting, music, and writing. These activities are distinguished by their respective substances, their codes and their territorialities, but not by the abstract line they trace, which darts between them and carries them towards a common destiny. When one comes to trace the line, one can say, 'It's philosophy.' Not at all because philosophy would be an ultimate discipline, a last root that would contain the truth of the others, on the contrary. Even less is it a popular wisdom. It is because philosophy is born or produced from the outside by the painter, the musician, the writer, each time that the melodic line draws along the sound, or the pure traced line, the color, or the written line, the articulated voice. There is no need for philosophy: it is necessarily produced where each activity gives rise to its line of deterritorialization. To get out of philosophy, to do no matter what, in order to produce it from the outside. Philosophers have always been something else, they were born from something else" (D 89/73-74).

Chapter 2: Is Deleuze a Postmodern Philosopher?

1. For early accounts of postmodern architecture, see Charles Jencks, *The Language of PostModern Architecture;* of postmodernism in the arts, see Stanley Trachtenberg, ed., *The Postmodern Moment: A Handbook of Contemporary Innovation in the Arts,* and Matei Calinescu, *Five Faces of Modernity;* of postmodern philosophy, see Richard Rorty, *Philosophy and the Mirror of Nature,* Richard Bernstein, *Philosophical Profiles: Essays in a Pragmatic Mode,* and Hugh J. Silverman and Donn Welton, eds., *Postmodernism and Continental Philosophy;* of postmodern science, see David Griffin, ed., *The Reenactment of Science: Postmodern Proposals;* of postmodern politics, see Jonathan Arac, ed., *Postmodernism and Politics.* For concise presentations of the social theories of Lyotard, Jameson, and Baudrillard, see Lyotard, *La condition postmoderne* and *Le postmoderne expliqué aux enfants;* Jameson, "Postmodernism, or The Cultural

Logic of Late Capitalism"; and Baudrillard, "The Precession of Simulacra." Among the host of more recent volumes dedicated to postmodernism, particularly useful are Taylor and Winquest, Natoli and Hutcheon, and Bertens and Fokkema.

2. Félix Guattari, with whom Deleuze collaborated on *Anti-Oedipus* and *A Thousand Plateaus*, has taken up the issue of postmodernism in his *Cartographies schizoanalytiques*, 53–61. Although he is critical of postmodernism, regarding it as a latent form of structuralism, his remarks do not entirely rule out some degree of rapprochement between schizoanalysis and postmodernism, since, as I hope to show, the Lyotardian sense of the concept, with which Guattari takes exception, is not the only one available.

3. David Couzens Hoy, who identifies periodization as "itself a modernist tool," makes precisely this point in regard to Foucault: "In contrast to Lyotard's stance, a Foucauldian postmodern would not need to be an advocate of postmodernism. I think that Foucault was a consistent postmodern in that he would never have called himself a postmodern" (Hoy 13, 38).

4. On the importance of *Nietzsche and Philosophy* as a break from the Hegelian orientation of earlier French phenomenological and existential philosophy, see Vincent Descombes, *Modern French Philosophy*, 156–167.

5. That other, less traditional Marxian usage may be made of *Anti-Oedipus* and its sequel *A Thousand Plateaus*, of course, has become evident in a number of works, most notably Hardt and Negri's *Empire*.

6. Despite the Kantian framework of this analysis, it should be clear that Deleuze adopts a playful stance toward Kant's theory of the faculties. Deleuze suggests that faculties should be determined experimentally, the number of faculties proliferating as various forms of difference are revealed in contradictory and paradoxical phenomena. See DR 169–217/129–67.

7. For a concise statement of Foucault's views on power, see *The History of Sexuality*, vol. 1, 92–102. I develop the parallels between Deleuze-Guattari's notion of desire and Foucaldian power in *Deleuze and Guattari* 105–106 and 130–145. See also Deleuze's *Foucault*, which presents a systematic review of Foucault's thought within the analytical framework developed in *A Thousand Plateaus*.

8. Deleuze first addresses this point in his 1967 essay "Renverser le platonisme," reprinted in LS 292–307/253–66, and develops the concept more extensively in *Difference and Repetition* and *The Logic of Sense*. Derrida, of course, touches on the same motif in Plato in his "Pharmacie de Platon," in *La dissemination*, 69–197, which appeared shortly after Deleuze's "Renverser le platonisme" in 1968.

9. There is a certain similarity between Deleuze's valorization of modern art's rejection of the conventional codes of representation and Roland Barthes' praise of the writerly text's subversion of readerly codes of narration. Barthes, however, tends

to align popular art with readerly texts and high art with writerly texts, whereas Deleuze makes no such distinction, allowing for the possibility that a popular work of art may just as well undermine as reinforce conventional codes of representation. In this sense, Barthes's stance is modern, Deleuze's postmodern.

Chapter 3: Deleuze, Foucault, and the Playful Fold of the Self

1. For a full exposition of the concept of *mimesis* and its relation to archaic and median mentalities in ancient Greek culture, see Mihai I. Spariosu, *God of Many Names*, especially ix–xiii and 1–98.

2. For a full explication of the parodic, dissociative, and sacrificial aspects of Nietzschean thought, see the final section of "Nietzsche, Genealogy and History," *Foucault Reader*, 93–99.

3. See, for example, Foucault's remarks in "On the Genealogy of Ethics: An Overview of Work in Progress," *Foucault Reader*, 344–51.

4. For an elaboration of Deleuze's interpretation of the Eternal Return, see NP 26–43/22–38, 77–82/68–72, and 207–222/180–94, and DR 128–153/96–116. See also my *Deleuze and Guattari*, 27–34.

Chapter 4: Minor Writing and Minor Literature

1. The term "Grand Theory" I am borrowing from Quentin Skinner's introduction to *The Return of Grand Theory in the Human Sciences*, a volume which includes studies of Althusser, Derrida, Foucault, Habermas, and Lévi-Strauss. The concept of posttheory is discussed at length in the winter 1995 special issue of *Symploke*. I have found particularly useful the essays of Paxson and Williams, as well as the "Posttheory Postscriptum" of Di Leo and Moraru.

2. I myself have generally treated Deleuze as a poststructural theorist, primarily as a shorthand method of identifying his broad affinities with other French philosophers. In *Deleuze and Guattari*, I argued that his work through *Difference and Repetition* and *The Logic of Sense* could be seen as a philosophy of difference, in some ways consonant with assumptions evident in Derrida, and that Deleuze's later work bears resemblances to the genealogical thought of Foucault. For a discussion of Deleuze's relationship to poststructuralism and postmodernism, see chapter 2, "Is Deleuze a Postmodern Philosopher?"

3. It is important to distinguish the functionalism common in sociological theory from Deleuze/Guattari's functionalism. Rather than studying the purposive, pragmatic function of institutions and practices within a molar social system,

Deleuze/Guattari detail the operations of molecular desiring machines, whose dysfunctions are as much a part of their workings as their functions. The question is not, "What purpose does it serve?," but "Irrespective of its possible purpose (or lack thereof), what does it do?"

4. Perhaps the aestheticist tendency in Deleuze's work is most evident in his sympathetic remarks on Foucault's ethics of "life as a work of art." See especially F 101–30/94–123 and PP 129–38/94–101, and chapter 3: "Deleuze, Foucault, and the Playful Fold of the Self." Lest one stress aesthetics too much, however, one should also recall that Deleuze identifies ethics with ethology in "Spinoza and Us" (S 164–75/122–30). See also Deleuze/Guattari's references to ethology in their study of the refrain, MP 381–433/310–50.

5. It should be evident that while Deleuze would be sympathetic to Bové's institutional genealogy of American criticism, he would no doubt adhere as well to a differentiation between the sociology of knowledge and the history of philosophy. He would also differ with Di Leo and Moraru in their conception of posttheory as a philosophical movement inextricably tied to its institutional context, since such a conception precludes the possibility of a genuine philosophical event, or what Deleuze would regard as genuine thought.

6. The concept of the "problem" Deleuze develops at length in *Difference and Repetition* (see especially chapter 4, "Ideas and the Synthesis of Difference," DR 218–85/168–221). The time of Aion is discussed in LS 174–79/148–53, 190–97/162–68 (see also DR 96–168/70–128 and MP 318–24/260–65). On the untimely, see DR 171/130, 312/242, LS 305–06/265, MP 363/295–96, QP 92/96.

7. For a survey of uses of the concept of minor literature in cultural studies, see the special issues of *Cultural Critique*, 6 and 7 (spring and fall 1987), on "The Nature and Context of Minority Discourse." See also Reizbaum, Hicks, and Lloyd.

8. Notable exceptions include the excellent studies of Bensmaïa and Lloyd.

9. There are exceptions, of course. See, for example, the illuminating treatments of becoming-woman of Braidotti, Griggers, Grosz, and Reizbaum, and the essays included in Buchanan and Colebrook.

Chapter 5: Becoming Metal, Becoming Death . . .

For their assistance with this project, I would like to thank Toni Eng at Roadrunner Records, Maria Abril at Metalblade Records, Mike at Ace's Records, Tampa, Florida, and Curtis Bogue, chief archivist and native informant.

1. Classifications of popular music are always shifting, primarily because they form such an important part of the discourse of musicians and fans about the music itself. Mark Hale, for example, in *HeadBangers. The Worldwide MegaBook of Heavy*

Metal Bands provides a useful and largely reliable taxonomy of metal music, but he lists "death metal" and "black metal" as synonymous terms. This was arguably the case when he was writing in 1989, but since then black metal has developed as a separate category. The black metal groups of the 1990s, many of them from Norway, combine death metal textures and harmonies with sustained melodic lines on guitar and organ, and infuse death metal Satanic lyrics with Viking and pagan themes. (For a detailed study of the bizarre and often violent Norwegian black metal scene, see Moynihan and Søderlind.) Obviously, in such an unstable field, all classifications, including my own, must be provisional at best.

2. The obvious exceptions would be Christian death metal bands, such as Pennsylvania's Believer and Australia's Mortification.

3. Thorough documentation for this contention is provided in Walser, 7–16. As he points out, the virtual absence of radio airplay and mainstream press coverage of much of this music has meant that its considerable popularity has gone largely unnoticed by those who don't listen to it.

4. Besides the general histories of heavy metal music in Walser and Weinstein, I have found particularly useful the histories of death metal provided by Shapiro and Sutherland in the special issues of *Guitar Magazine* and *RIP* devoted to the genre. Accompanying Shapiro's article is the following "aural primer of . . . classic death metal sides": Black Sabbath, *Paranoid* [1969], Venom, *Welcome to Hell* [1981], Hellhammer, *Apocalyptic Raids* [1984], Slayer, *Reign in Blood* [1986], Death, *Scream Bloody Gore* [1987], Celtic Frost, *To Megatherion* [1985], *Into the Pandemonium* [1987], Kreator, *Endless Pain* [1985], Obituary, *Slowly We Rot* [1989], Sepultura, *Beneath the Remains* [1989], Deicide, *Legion* [1992], Disincarnate, *Dreams of the Carrion Kind* [1993], Napalm Death, *Death by Manipulation* [1991]. *RIP Photo Special Presents: Death Lives* 6, no. 4 (1994) closes with the following list of "the 10 most deadly metal albums of all time" (p. 46): Venom, *Black Metal* (1982), Bathory, *Bathory* (1984), Celtic Frost, *Morbid Tales* (1984), Slayer, *Hell Awaits* (1985), Possessed, *Seven Churches* (1985), Death, *Leprosy* (1988), Sepultura, *Beneath the Remains* (1989), Obituary, *Slowly We Rot* (1989), Morbid Angel, *Altars of Madness* (1989), and Entombed, *Left Hand Path* (1990).

For insightful analyses of the musical vocabulary of death metal, see Harrell and Berger.

5. The reluctance of record labels to carry death metal is no doubt explained in large part by the censorship campaign of the Parents' Music Resource Center (PMRC), Tipper Gore's coalition that testified before Congress in September 1985. Details of PMRC's attack on metal are available in Weinstein (265–270) and Walser (137–145).

6. Weinstein notes that "the physical properties of sound are such that very low frequencies require far more amplification than higher frequencies to be

heard at the same level of volume" (24–25). Citing Stith Bennett, she points out that "to be heard at an equal volume with other instruments in actual playing conditions, the bass may have to be as much as 100,000 times as intense as a middle-range frequency" (288, n. 32).

7. The great artists of popular music, I would argue, are often the producers, engineers and arrangers who capture and in large part create the sound of a particular group. One thinks of Phil Spector's "wall of sound," or the brilliant play of textures that Quincy Jones fashioned on Michael Jackson's *Thriller*. In the world of death metal, Scott Burns is perhaps the producer who has had the greatest influence on the genre, with Tampa's Morrisound Recording serving as the studio of choice for a number of American groups, especially in the early to mid 1990s.

8. For a more detailed treatment of the relationship of Messiaen's music to Deleuze and Guattari's understanding of music, see Bogue, "Rhizomusicosmology."

9. A representative example of a death metal solo can be found in Slayer's "Angel of Death" (1986), a transcription of which appears in *Guitar Presents: Speed Demons of Metal*, 68–78.

10. The differentiation between movement and speed is not consistently maintained in *A Thousand Plateaus*. In this instance, movement refers to spatiotemporal displacements on the plane of organization, speed to relations between particles on the plane of consistency. Movement, however, is itself a problematic concept, one that Deleuze, following Bergson, discusses in various works—most fully in *Cinema 1: The Movement-Image,* especially IM 9–22/1–11. Common sense and Newtonian science treat movement as the measure of the displacement of discrete bodies within a fixed and uniform spatiotemporal container. Such a chronometric model reduces movement to a succession of static slices of time, and hence, in Bergson's critique, to no genuine movement at all. When adequately conceived, movement is a qualitative change of an open whole, the change in position of one entity altering the relations of all, and no frame of reference serving as an external, fixed measure of the motions of individual entities (hence the imprecision of even speaking of "the position" of one entity). In their most extended discussion of movement in *A Thousand Plateaus,* Deleuze and Guattari equate speed and movement, stating that "movement is in an essential relation with the imperceptible; it is by nature imperceptible. . . . Movements, and becomings, in other words, pure relations of speed and slowness, pure affects, are below or above the threshold of perception. . . . However, we must make an immediate correction: movement also 'must' be perceived, it cannot but be perceived, the imperceptible is also the *percipiendum*" (MP 344–45/280–81). The reference to the *percipiendum* recalls Deleuze's discussion in *Difference and Repetition* of the intensity as *sentiendum,* that which common sense, or the coordinated cofunctioning of the faculties, cannot experience, but which sensation alone can experience through a deregulation of the faculties and consequent dissolution of common sense. The import of their discussion of

movement/speed as the *percipiendum,* I believe, is that movement/speed escapes common sense and can only be experienced through a deregulation of our faculties on a plane of consistency.

11. In a 1995 interview, Benton was asked if he believes there is a God: "There is Jehovah, and then there's Gabriel. Gabriel is Satan, Jehovah is God." *Do you believe there is a real power in it?* "Of Course!" *What evidence do you have?* "Just look at me (laughs)! Don't look at my appearance, look at my soul. It doesn't belong to myself any more. I belong to my fucking boss, my god. That's who I answer to. That's who I serve" ("'I Don't Take'" 34).

12. A former assistant lion tamer, sideshow magician, and one-time police photographer, LaVey claimed to have had an affair with Marilyn Monroe in 1948, and in the mid 1960s was able to boast Jayne Mansfield as one of his most devoted followers. A 1950s, Playboy-style eroticism haunts *The Satanic Bible,* but this aspect of his work death metal musicians largely ignore. His cautious and somewhat inconsistent condemnation of cruelty and unjustified violence also has not been stressed by death metal followers. LaVey himself seems somewhat bemused by his popularity among metal musicians, claiming in a 1994 interview that "my six-month-old son can play better than most of these so-called 'musicians'! Most of today's musicians play just like they fuck or eat, just shoving in and out" (Moynihan, "Anton LaVey" 58).

13. For an exposition of Vincent's LaVey-inspired Satanism and its relation to his music, see Moynihan, "Morbid Angel."

14. Obviously, the relationship of race to death metal deserves greater elucidation than is possible here. Most death metal musicians are white. In the United States, only a few death metal groups have African-American, Hispanic, or Asian-American members. For an enlightened discussion of some of the complexities of race in heavy metal music, see Walser 17.

15. Cannibal Corpse's former lead vocalist Chris Barnes reacts to criticism of his violent lyrics by observing, "It's the same as if a newspaper or television did a story about a serial killer and someone saw it and then went out and killed people. Does that make the newspaper or television responsible? It's the same with music. You can't blame us. I'm just a person who writes what I see and what I feel" (Violanti 1). Audience reactions to death metal are more difficult to document, but Walser notes that in his surveys of heavy metal fans "there was a solid concurrence that the intensity and power of the music, its impressive guitar solos, the relevance of its lyrics, and its truth value were crucial" (Walser 19). Walser asked hundreds of fans to select statements that most aptly reflected their feelings about metal music, and among the responses chosen most frequently in his survey were "It deals with things nobody else will talk about" and "It's true to life; it's music about real important issues." My own informal interaction with death metal fans suggests that in this regard death metal and heavy metal audiences share common values.

16. To date, I have learned of only two all-female death metal groups: the obscure Mythic, whose three-song EP, *Mourning in the Winter Solstice,* appeared in March, 1992 (the trio disbanded in June of 1992), and the Canadian quartet November Grief, formed in 1993 and dissolved in 1997, whose CD *To Live . . . in This World of Chaos* appeared in 1995 on the SMDS Mur du Son label.

17. Given the frequency with which journalists and commentators associate death metal's "machining" of the voice with Linda Blair's possession in *The Exorcist,* perhaps one might argue that there is a becoming-Linda Blair in the death metal growl, and hence a becoming-woman and becoming-child of the voice. But of course this vocal becoming would be a becoming-Linda Blair-becoming-Satan, or a becoming-woman-becoming-man, Satan being decidedly male in the film. Her possession, I would argue, deterritorializes by perverting what the film codes as female sweetness and child innocence, but only to be reterritorialized in the voice and attitudes of the masculine Devil.

18. An indication of the possibility of a feminist appropriation of death metal may be found in the debut album of Crisis, *Deathshead Extermination* (Metalblade, 1996), a group fronted by lead singer Karyn Crisis. Although not a mainstream death metal band, Crisis uses many death motifs in its music, while its lyrics, penned by Karyn Crisis, articulate decidedly feminist concerns. I first learned of Crisis in a telephone conversation with Maria Abril of Metalblade Records shortly before the release of *Deathshead Extermination.* Noting that metal has traditionally been "a boy's club," Abril described Karyn Crisis as a "strong feminist" who finds extreme forms of music, such as death metal, conducive to the expression of her feelings and thoughts. For further discussion of Crisis and death metal, see my "Death and the Metal Maiden."

Chapter 6: Word, Image, and Sound: Deleuze and Semiosis

1. For an analysis of the dominance of the signifier and the disappearance of the sign in recent linguistic theory, see Oswald Ducrot and Tzvetan Todorov, *Encyclopedic Dictionary of the Sciences of Language,* 349–365. For an extended critique of textualism as the ultimate fulfillment of Western logocentrism, see Jean-François Lyotard, *Discours, figure,* especially 9–89.

2. On the arbitrary designation of levels of expression and content, see Louis Hjelmslev, *Prolegomena to a Theory of Language,* 60.

3. I simplify in identifying the *énoncé* as a speech act, whereas Deleuze sees the *énoncé* and the speech act as two components of the *mot d'ordre.* The distinction, however, is not crucial here. Deleuze takes the concept of the *énoncé* from Foucault and discusses it at length in his 1970 article "Un nouveau archiviste," reprinted in *Foucault* (F 11–30/1–22). Hubert Dreyfus and Paul Rabinow, in *Michel Foucault:*

Beyond Structuralism and Hermeneutics, conclude that Foucault's concept of the *énoncé* is best understood as a "serious speech act" (Dreyfus and Rabinow 48).

4. Whether or not Deleuze's reading of Foucault is a persuasive piece of Foucauldian criticism I have chosen not to consider here. Rajchman, however, in "Foucault's Art of Seeing" has shown in detail how useful Deleuze's emphasis on vision and the visible may be in understanding Foucault's works.

5. Deleuze is not greatly concerned with generating a definitive list of signs, and as a result his nomenclature shifts from time to time. Nor is it always clear whether two species of a particular sign are subdivisions of that sign or simply two different signs (e.g., figures of attraction and figures of inversion). My enumeration of signs here is based on Deleuze's recapitulation of images and signs in *Cinema 2,* 47–49. For a full discussion of these issues, see my *Deleuze on Cinema,* chapter 3.

6. What Deleuze means by a "sound image" is not entirely clear, nor do I find in his works on cinema a full explanation of the possible relationship of light to sound on the luminous plane of immanence. I assume that he is simply extending the sense of "image" beyond the visual sphere and that by "sound images" he means something like "sonic prehensions and apprehensions."

7. This logic of the unsayable that can only be said and the invisible that can only be seen is systematically developed in Deleuze's formulation of his "transcendental empiricism" in *Difference and Repetition.* There, he characterizes the various mental faculties—sensation, memory, imagination, reason—in terms of their function when dissociated from common sense, or the coordinated interrelation of the faculties, each faculty having as its proper object that which cannot be perceived through common sense but which can be perceived through that specific faculty. For a further discussion of Deleuze's transcendental empiricism, see my *Deleuze and Guattari,* 57–58.

8. Deleuze does not state that by "the unsayable" and "the invisible" he is referring to forces. In his study of the painter Francis Bacon, however, he suggests that the object of art is to make palpable and material the forces that play through things. "If one cries, it is always as prey to invisible and insensible forces which blur every spectacle, and which even go beyond pain and sensation. . . . Bacon paints the cry because he puts the visibility of the cry, the mouth open like a shadowy abyss, in relation with invisible forces which are no longer anything other than those of the future" (FB 41).

9. In *Kafka: Toward a Minor Literature,* Deleuze and Guattari differentiate between a major and a minor use of language, seeing in a major use a confirmation of a language's codes, beliefs, and power configurations, and in a minor use a systematic unsettling of its regularities. It seems that one could make a parallel distinction between major and minor film directors, with Deleuze's study of cinema being essentially an analysis of the sonic and visual matter discovered by minor directors.

Chapter 7: Deleuze and the Invention of Images: From Beckett's Television Plays to Noh Drama

1. The Fenollosa/Pound translations are included in *Ezra Pound: Translations*, 213–360.

2. Other Noh-influenced dramas are *The Dreaming of the Bones* (1919), *The Only Jealousy of Emer* (1919), *Calvary* (1920), and *The Cat and the Moon* (1926).

3. Ito was not familiar with Noh drama (Tuohy 156), but his training in traditional Japanese dance allowed him to perform in a manner that Yeats found fully satisfactory. He readied himself for the role of the hawk spirit by visiting the London Zoo, where he was seen daily, "flapping and prancing as he imitated the motions of hawks in preparation for his role; Yeats was often with him, watching in rapt admiration. People stared" (Norman 183).

4. Genet provides a thorough and insightful account of the thematic parallels between Noh drama and *At the Hawk's Well*, esp. 343–350.

5. Beckett explicitly notes the citation when providing a list of quotations in *Happy Days* for a production notebook used in a German staging of the play (reproduced in Pountney 251).

6. These observations come from the typescript of a letter written in German to Axel Kaun. I cite the English translation by Martin Esslin provided in the notes to *Disjecta*. The editor of *Disjecta* says that this letter Beckett "now dismisses as 'German bilge'" (170); nonetheless, Deleuze and several other commentators regard the document as a particularly lucid expression of the tenets of Beckett's art.

7. Homan provides such a reading in *Beckett's Theaters*, 218–23. He also offers illuminating commentary on . . . *but the clouds* . . . in *Filming Beckett's Television Plays: A Director's Experience,* one chapter of which details Homan's own production of a version of Beckett's script (67–86).

8. The surface between words and things Deleuze identifies as *sens*, "meaning" or "sense," something produced through language but never exhausted by language. To name the meaning produced by a sentence always requires an additional sentence, whose meaning in turn must be enunciated in a third sentence, and so on in an endless regress. That meaning itself transforms things, but without being an actual constituent of things. It is what the Stoics call an "incorporeal," a real but nonactual attribute of things. In Stoic logic, everything that is actual is a body, and when someone speaks, the actual words are sonic bodies. Greeks and barbarians hear the same sonic bodies when someone speaks Greek, but one group finds the words intelligible and the other finds them incoherent. The incorporeal known as a *lekton* is that immaterial "something" that is added to the sonic bodies to render them coherent. Deleuze suggests that *lekta* perform "incorporeal transformations" of bodies in much the same way that a speech act

transforms real-world entities, as when the preacher transforms a man and woman into husband and wife by saying, "I thee wed." It is in this sense that meaning, produced through language, also forms a "surface" of things. See Deleuze's *Logic of Sense* and my *Deleuze and Guattari*, 67–80.

9. In "L'Epuisé" Deleuze only hints at the specific characteristics of television, but in *Cinéma 2* he provides a somewhat more detailed analysis of the medium (IT 346–47/264–66).

10. Couchot uses as his model of the transformable digital image a sequence of prints produced by the artist Lillian Schwartz. An early example of "morphing," Schwartz's sequence uses a computer to transform a Rembrandt self-portrait into a photograph of Einstein, with six intermediary Rembrandt-Einstein meldings in between. Deleuze cites both Paik and Couchot in his commentary on the television image in *Cinéma 2*.

Chapter 8: The Betrayal of God

1. Deleuze and Guattari also associate betrayal with the warrior, a central figure in the nomadic, countersignifying regime. The warrior "is in the situation of betraying everything, including the military function" (MP 438/354); there is "a fundamental indiscipline of the warrior, a questioning of hierarchy, a perpetual blackmail by abandonment or betrayal, and a highly volatile sense of honor" (MP 443/358). Further, the nomadic is linked to the invention of "a people to come" (MP 467/377), a motif that Deleuze also ties to betrayal in an essay on T. E. Lawrence, who "betrays England as much as Arabia, in a nightmare-dream of betraying everything at the same time" (CC 147/117). Unfortunately, the issues raised by these passages—those of the relation between the postsignifying and countersignifying regimes, the passional and the nomadic, the mutual betrayal of God and prophet, the warrior's betrayal of everything, and the universal betrayal inherent in the invention of a people to come—are beyond the scope of this essay. My reading of "betrayal" as a break or gap in power relations, however, should suggest the lines I would follow in exploring these questions.

2. Bamberger comments that "In Scripture, this holy day is called the Day of the *Kippurim* (Lev. 23:27f., 25:9). The word probably comes from a root meaning "to cover up." It refers to the process by which guilt or impurity is canceled out, made nonexistent" (162).

3. Genesis 6:14. Lindon's French translation of the passage reads: "Fais-toi une arche d'arbres de gopher. Tu feras l'arche en cellules et tu la couvriras de *kapper*, d'une couverture isolante, au-dedans et au-dehors" (Lindon 23). The King James version of the verse is "Make thee an ark of gopher wood; rooms shalt thou make in the ark, and shalt pitch it within and without with pitch." In a note on the

word *kapper* at the conclusion of his translation, Lindon remarks, "Let us remember that *kapper*, which gives its name to the ark of the Covenant and to the day of *Kippur*, was, first, the *pitch* that covered-and-isolated the dove in the ark of Noah, and that it is represented here [in Jonah 4] by the *sap* that covers-and-isolates Jonah under the *qîqayôn* plant" (Lindon 61).

4. In his exhaustive Anchor Bible commentary on Jonah, Sasson reviews various interpretations of the significance of Jonah's puzzling sleep. In wisdom literature, "we do have a citation or two in which *radam* and *tardemâ* refer to the sleep of the irresponsible. . . . In stories about prophets, however, 'deep sleep' is said to overtake a prophet only *after* signs and wonders of God's presence become manifest." Sasson's own reading is that "prophets come to be *nirdamîm* when, upon recognizing signs of God's presence, they make themselves ready to receive the divine message. In this way, they readily accept divine control over their future behavior. Jonah's situation is not, however, similar to the abandoned prophets upon whom an angry God pours deep sleep (cf. Isa 29:10); rather, his condition is that of a prophet who realizes that there is no escaping God. It is at this juncture in our narrative, therefore, that Jonah capitulates and runs away no more" (101–02).

5. Lindon's translation is "Encore quarante jours et Ninive sera bouleversée" (Lindon 40). Lindon adds in a footnote: "As in French, the word [*nehpaket*, rendered as *bouleversée*] has a literal and a figurative sense (I Samuel 10:6: 'You will be changed into another man')." The King James versions reads, "Yet forty days, and Nineveh shall be overthrown." Sasson's wording is "Forty more days, and Nineveh overturns" (224). The sense of *nehpaket*, "overturns," says Sasson, "is crucial to the development of the plot" (Sasson 234) for it renders Jonah's proclamation fundamentally ambiguous. Jonah could mean that in forty days Nineveh will be destroyed, but he could mean as well that Nineveh will be transformed. Often Jonah is viewed as a disgruntled prophet who predicts the demise of Nineveh and then is angered that God's mercy makes him a liar (or worse yet, that God's mercy spares those whom Jonah wants dead). Sasson argues that Jonah thinks he is foretelling destruction but that God is announcing repentance through words whose true meaning Jonah (and the reader) will only understand later. What Lindon implies is that Jonah is aware of the double meaning of his prophecy and that he is therefore not disappointed at its fulfillment in God's mercy.

6. Sasson also rejects the attribution of anger to Jonah, arguing that 4:1 should be translated, "This outcome was so terribly upsetting to Jonah that he was dejected" (Sasson 270). In his comment on the verse, Sasson notes that the line refers literally to the heating sensation that accompanies emotion. He observes that though the Vulgate unequivocally identifies Jonah's emotion as anger (*iratus est* is Jerome's phrase), the Septuagint says that "Jonah was terribly saddened, and was confused/shaken up"; the Arabic translation renders the line, "He was very much grieved by all this"; the Targum reads, "Jonah felt extremely bad and it affected him severely"; and the Syriac translation says that "it distressed him exceedingly"

(Sasson 275). Sasson observes as well that the attribution of anger to Jonah, besides helping to shape a decidedly unappealing portrait of the prophet's character, has all too frequently been marshaled in anti-Semitic discourse: "Jonah's alleged incapacity to share God's love with anyone who is not a Hebrew has unfortunately become a metaphor by which to censure Judaism and Jewish attributes." Sasson's hope, he adds, is that "most heavy-handed manifestations of this repugnant disposition are behind us" (Sasson 274).

7. Sasson translates Jonah's prayer (4:1–3) as follows: "Please, Lord, this certainly was my opinion, while yet in my own homeland; accordingly, I planned to flee toward Tarshish because I realized then that you are a gracious and compassionate God, very patient and abundantly benevolent, who would also relent from bringing disaster. Now then, Lord, take away life from me, because for me death is better than life" (Sasson 270). As Sasson notes, commentators have struggled considerably with the logic of this passage. He himself concludes that Jonah is angrily saying, in effect, that he knew God would be merciful to Nineveh, so he ran away, but God made him come to Nineveh anyway and prophesy its destruction; and now that God has done as Jonah expected, Jonah is so humiliated he wants to die. Sasson also remarks, "It is not easy to offer a good reason for Jonah's feeling that only his own murder would adequately compensate for Nineveh's survival" (Sasson 296). Clearly, Lindon is arguing that the reasoning in question is that of the scapegoating mechanism, a line of thinking that must at times seem void of "good reason."

8. The word *qîqayôn* occurs only in Jonah, and there is considerable debate concerning its meaning. Most frequently it is said to be either a type of gourd or the *ricinus,* or castor oil plant. In his lengthy review of the debate, Robinson concludes that "if the choice is between the *ricinus* and the gourd (and there is not much to be said for the other traditional candidates), the gourd has perhaps the stronger case" (Robinson 402), though neither is a particularly suitable match for the plant described in Jonah. He suggests that perhaps the author had heard of a mythical Assyrian plant, the *kukkanitu(m),* and had included it to lend Assyrian authenticity to the story, or that it "may be a nonce-word, newly coined to give an exotic flavour to the story," in which case the coinage may be "derived from the root meaning 'to spew'" (Robinson 402), since the whale had "spewed" Jonah from its mouth. Robinson does not mention the possibility that *qîqayôn* might be a nonce word echoing the name of Cain.

9. Lindon notes that the same word denotes Abel, the "vanity of vanities" of Ecclesiastes, and the "mists" of the second chapter of Jonah. Conversely, "Cain" comes from "*kaniti,* 'I have acquired'" (Lindon 48). Hence, Lindon's conclusion that in God's eyes "Abel was nothing, it was Cain who was man" *{Abel n'était rien, c'était Kaïn, l'homme}* (Lindon 48).

10. The specific workings of the point of subjectification, the subject of enunciation *{sujet d'énonciation}* and subject of the statement *{sujet d'énoncé}* need not concern us here. I discuss these concepts in *Deleuze and Guattari,* 139–45.

11. The phrase *vaterländische Umkehre* occurs in Hölderlin's "Anmerkungen zur Antigone" {Remarks on Antigone}, section 3 (Hölderlin, *Sämtliche Werke und Briefe*, II, 454). Pfau translates the phrase as "patriotic reversal" (Pfau 114), a literal rendering that is potentially misleading, I believe. Fedier's French translation, *retournement natal* (Hölderlin, *Remarques* 83), though somewhat freer, conveys more clearly Hölderlin's point. Citations from Hölderlin's "Anmerkungen zum Ödipus" and "Anmerkungen zur Antigone" will be from Mieth's edition of the *Sämtliche Werke und Briefe* (abbreviated as SWB); all translations my own.

12. Pfau says of his translation of *aorgisch* that "Hölderlin's distinction [between *organisch* and *aorgisch*] must be understood in the context of Swabian Pietism and the energetically inspired concept of nature of German Romanticism. Unlike Schelling's distinction between *organisch* and *anorganisch*, Hölderlin's "organic" does not imply a natural organism or the like, but designates the organized, reflected principle of the spirit and of art. Similarly, the term *aorgisch*, subsequently translated as "aorgic," does not refer to the merely lifeless but designates, in the course of this translation, the unreflexive, unrepresented, disorganizing manifestation of nature" (Pfau 168). The *aorgisch* is close to what Nietzsche calls the Dionysian, though as Beaufret notes, Hölderlin associates it with Apollo, "not as the absolute contrary of Dionysus, but rather its highest accomplishment as the extreme of virile force" (Beaufret 9).

13. Letter to Karl Gock, January 1, 1799, SWB, II, 797; cited in Beaufret, 14.

14. Hölderlin speaks at length of the rhythm of the action of *Oedipus* and *Antigone*, seeing each as a single metrical structure divided by a caesura. In both dramas, the appearance of Tiresias marks the caesura of the action. The beginning and ending are of unequal length in the two works, he notes, the beginning shorter than the ending in *Oedipus*, and vice versa in *Antigone*. It would seem that by the inequality and disharmony of beginning and ending Hölderlin refers to a radical discontinuity in the action signaled by the caesura of the prophet's appearance. Deleuze makes extensive use of Hölderlin's remarks on the caesura and the lack of rhyme between beginning and end in DR 118–20/87–89.

15. "More generally, the supposed identity of the I has no other guarantee than the unity of God himself. This is why the substitution of the point of view of the 'I' for the point of view of 'God' has much less importance than is commonly thought, so long as the one conserves an identity that it owes precisely to the other. God continues to live as long as the I enjoys a subsistence, a simplicity and an identity which express all of its resemblance to the divine. Conversely, the death of God does not allow the identity of the I to subsist, but installs and interiorizes within it an essential dissemblance, a 'demarcation' in place of the mark or the seal of God" (DR 117/86–87).

16. Deleuze expands on the Christian "system of Judgment" in his study of D. H. Lawrence's *Apocalypse*, "Nietzsche and Saint Paul, Lawrence and John of Patmos" (CC 50–70/36–52). The Christian rage to judge is at once a will to

destruction and a will to penetrate every nook and cranny of the world and the soul with a conforming power. A collective Self seeks both the destruction of an unspecified enemy, defined as "anyone who does not conform to the order of God" (CC 61/45), and the creation of a New Jerusalem of total social control. The "postponed destiny" so central to Jewish prophetism is transformed from an open-ended expectation of an unforeseen future into a preprogrammed, destructive destiny, "'postferred,' placed *after* death, after the death of Christ and the death of each and everyone" (CC 56/41).

Works Cited

Abrams, M. H. *The Mirror and the Lamp*. Oxford: Oxford University Press, 1953.

Arac, Jonathan, ed. *Postmodernism and Politics*. Minneapolis: University of Minnesota Press, 1986.

Bamberger, Bernard J. *The Torah: A Modern Commentary. III: Leviticus*. New York: Union of American Hebrew Congregations, 1979.

Baudrillard, Jean. "The Precession of Simulacra." Trans. Paul Foss and Paul Patton. In *Art After Modernism: Rethinking Representation,* ed. Brian Wallis. New York: New Museum of Contemporary Art, 1984.

Beaufret, Jean. "Hölderlin et Sophocle." Preface to Hölderlin, *Remarques sur Oedipe/Remarques sur Antigone,* trans. François Fedier, 7–42. Paris: 10–18, 1965.

Beckett, Samuel. *The Complete Dramatic Works*. London: Faber and Faber, 1986.

———. *Disjecta. Miscellaneous Writings and a Dramatic Fragment*. Ed. Ruby Cohn. New York: Grove Press, 1984.

———. *L'Innomable*. Paris: Minuit, 1953.

———. *Murphy*. New York: Grove Press, 1958.

———. *Nouvelles et textes pour rien*. Paris: Minuit, 1958.

———. *Quad: et Trio du fantôme, . . . que les nuages . . . , Nacht and Träume*. Trans. Edith Fournier. Paris: Minuit, 1992.

———. *Stories and Texts for Nothing*. New York: Grove Press, 1967.

———. *Three Novels by Samuel Beckett: Molloy, Malone Dies, The Unnamable*. New York: Grove Press, 1965.

———. *Watt*. New York: Grove Press, 1953.

Benjamin, Walter. "The Work of Art in the Age of Mechanical Reproduction." In *Illuminations,* trans. Harry Zohn, ed. Hannah Arendt. New York: Schocken, 1969.

Bensmaïa, Réda. "On the Concept of Minor Literature. From Kafka to Kateb Yacine." In *Gilles Deleuze and the Theater of Philosophy,* ed. Constantin V. Boundas and Dorothea Olkowski, 213–228. New York: Routledge, 1994.

Bentham, Jeremy. "Panopticon; or, the Inspection House." In *The Works of Jeremy Bentham,* ed. John Bowring, v. 4, 36–66. New York: Russell and Russell, 1962.

Berger, Harris M. "Death Metal Tonality and the Act of Listening." *Popular Music* 18 (1999): 161–176.

Bernauer, James W. *Michel Foucault's Force of Flight: Toward an Ethics for Thought.* Atlantic Highlands, N.J.: Humanities Press, 1990.

Bernstein, Richard. *Philosophical Profiles: Essays in a Pragmatic Mode.* Cambridge: Cambridge University Press, 1985.

Bertens, Hans, and Douwe Fokkema, eds. *International Postmodernism: Theory and Literary Practice.* Amsterdam: John Benjamins, 1997.

Blanchot, Maurice. *L'Entretien infini.* Paris: Gallimard, 1969.

———. *L'Espace littéraire.* Paris: Gallimard, 1955.

Bogue, Ronald. "Death and the Metal Maiden." *American Book Review* 18 (Oct–Nov 1996): 3, 5.

———. *Deleuze and Guattari.* London: Routledge, 1989.

———. *Deleuze on Cinema.* New York: Routledge, 2003.

———. "Rhizomusicosmology." *SubStance* 66 (1991): 85–101.

Boulez, Pierre. *Boulez on Music Today.* Trans. Susan Bradshaw and Richard Rodney Bennett. Cambridge, Mass.: Harvard University Press, 1971.

Bové, Paul A. "The Foucault Phenomenon: the Problematics of Style." Foreword to *Foucault,* by Gilles Deleuze, trans. Seán Hand, vii–xl. Minneapolis: University of Minnesota Press, 1988.

———. *Intellectuals in Power: A Genealogy of Critical Humanism.* New York: Columbia University Press, 1986.

Braidotti, Rosi. "Discontinuing Becomings. Deleuze on the Becoming-Woman of Philosophy." *Journal of the British Society for Phenomenology* 24 (January 1993): 44–55.

Bréhier, Émile. "Comment je comprends l'histoire de la philosophie." In *Études de philosophie antique*, 1–9. Paris: Presses Universitaires de France, 1955.

Buchanan, Ian, and Claire Colebrook, eds. *Deleuze and Feminist Theory*. Edinburgh: Edinburgh University Press, 2000.

Calinescu, Matei. *Five Faces of Modernity: Modernism, Avant-Garde, Decadence, Kitsch, Postmodernism*. Durham: Duke University Press, 1987.

Couchot, Edmond. "Image puissance image." *Revue d'esthétique* new series 7 (1984): 123–33.

Derrida, Jacques. *La dissemination*. Paris: Seuil, 1972.

Descombes, Vincent. *Modern French Philosophy*. Trans. L. Scott-Fox and J. M. Harding. Cambridge: Cambridge University Press, 1980.

Di Leo, Jeffrey R., and Christian Moraru. "Posttheory Postscriptum." *Symploke* 3 (winter 1995): 119–122.

Dreyfus, Hubert, and Paul Rabinow. *Michel Foucault: Beyond Structuralism and Hermeneutics*. 2nd ed. Chicago: University of Chicago Press, 1983.

Ducrot, Oswald, and Tzvetan Todorov. *Encyclopedic Dictionary of the Sciences of Language*. Trans. Catherine Porter. Baltimore: Johns Hopkins University Press, 1979.

Fargier, Jean-Paul, Jean-Paul Cassagnac, and Silvia van der Steger. "Entretien avec Nam June Paik." *Cahiers du cinéma* 299 (April 1979): 10–15.

Foucault, Michel. *The Archaeology of Knowledge and the Discourse on Language*. Trans. A. M. Sheridan Smith. New York: Harper Colophon, 1972.

———. *The Birth of the Clinic: An Archaeology of Medical Perception*. Trans. A. M. Sheridan Smith. New York: Pantheon, 1973.

———. *Death and the Labyrinth: The World of Raymond Roussel*. Trans. Charles Ruas. Garden City, N.J.: Doubleday, 1986.

———. *Discipline and Punish: The Birth of the Prison*. Trans. Alan Sheridan. New York: Pantheon, 1976.

———. *The Foucault Reader*. Ed. Paul Rabinow. New York: Pantheon, 1984.

———. *The History of Sexuality. Vol. 1*. Trans. Robert Hurley. New York: Pantheon, 1978.

———. *Madness and Civilization: A History of Insanity in the Age of Reason*. Trans. Richard Howard. New York: Pantheon, 1965.

———. *The Order of Things: An Archaeology of the Human Sciences*. Trans. A. M. Sheridan Smith. New York: Vintage, 1971.

———. *The Use of Pleasure*. Vol. 2 of *The History of Sexuality*. Trans. Robert Hurley. New York: Vintage, 1985.

Genet, Jacqueline. "Yeats et le Nô: Au Puits de l'Épervier." In *William Butler Yeats*, ed. Jacqueline Genet, 336–353. Paris: Cahiers de l'Herne, 1981.

Griffin, David, ed. *The Reenactment of Science: Postmodern Proposals*. Albany: State University of New York Press, 1988.

Griggers, Camilla. *Becoming-Woman*. Minneapolis: University of Minnesota Press, 1997.

Grosz, Elizabeth. "A Thousand Tiny Sexes: Feminism and Rhizomatics." In *Gilles Deleuze and the Theater of Philosophy*, ed. Constantin V. Boundas and Dorothea Olkowski, 187–210. New York: Routledge, 1994.

Guattari, Félix. *Cartographies schizoanalytiques*. Paris: Galilée, 1989.

Habermas, Jürgen. "Modernity versus Postmodernity." *New German Critique* 33 (winter 1981): 3–14.

Hale, Mark. *HeadBangers: The Worldwide MegaBook of Heavy Metal Bands*. Ann Arbor, Mich.: Popular Culture, Ink., 1993.

Hardt, Michael, and Antonio Negri. *Empire*. Cambridge, Mass.: Harvard University Press, 2000.

Harrell, Jack. "The Poetics of Destruction: Death Metal Rock." *Popular Music and Society* 18 (1994): 91–104.

Hicks, D. Emily. *Border Writing: The Multidimensional Text*. Minneapolis: University of Minnesota Press, 1991.

Hjelmslev, Louis. *Prolegomena to a Theory of Language*. Trans. Francis J. Whitfield. Madison: University of Wisconsin Press, 1961.

Hölderlin, Friedrich. *Essays and Letters on Theory*. Ed. and trans. Thomas Pfau. Albany: State University of New York Press, 1988.

———. *Remarques sur Oedipe/Remarques sur Antigone*. Trans. François Fedier. Paris: 10–18, 1965.

———. *Sämtliche Werke und Briefe*. Ed. Günter Mieth. 2 vols. Munich: Carl Hanser, 1970.

Holland, Eugene W. "The Anti-Oedipus: Postmodernism in Theory; or the post-Lacanian Historical Contextualization of Psychoanalysis." *boundary 2* 14 (1985/1986): 291–307.

Homan, Sidney. *Beckett's Theaters: Interpretations for Performance*. Lewisburg, Penn.: Bucknell University Press, 1984.

———. *Filming Beckett's Television Plays: A Director's Experience*. Lewisberg, Penn.: Bucknell University Press, 1992.

Hoy, David Couzens. "Foucault: Modern or Postmodern?" In *After Foucault: Humanistic Knowledge, Postmodern Challenges*, ed. Jonathan Arac, 12–41. New Brunswick, N.J.: Rutgers University Press, 1988.

Hutcheon, Linda. "A Postmodern Problematics." In *Ethics/Aesthetics: Post-Modern Positions*, ed. Robert Merrill, 1–10. Washington, D.C.: Maisonneuve Press, 1988.

Huyssen, Andreas. *After the Great Divide: Modernism, Mass Culture, Postmodernism*. Bloomington: Indiana University Press, 1986.

"'I Don't Take Fucking Shit from Anybody!'" Interview with Deicide's Glen Benton. *Metal Hammer* (June 1995): 32–34.

Jameson, Fredric. "Postmodernism, or The Cultural Logic of Late Capitalism." *New Left Review* 146 (1984): 53–92.

Jencks, Charles. *The Language of Post-Modern Architecture*. New York: Rizzoli, 1977.

Kafka, Franz. *The Trial*. Trans. Willa and Edwin Muir, rev. by E. M. Butler. New York: Modern Library, 1956.

Kaplan, Caren. "Deterritorializations: The Rewriting of Home and Exile in Western Feminist Discourse." *Cultural Critique* 6 (spring 1987): 187–198.

Lawrence, A. W., ed. *Letters to T. E. Lawrence*. London: Jonathan Cape, 1962.

Lawrence, T. E. *Seven Pillars of Wisdom: A Triiumph*. New York: Dell, 1962.

LaVey, Anton Szandor. *The Satanic Bible*. New York: Avon, 1969.

Lindon, Jérôme. *Jonas*. Paris: Minuit, 1955.

Lloyd, David. "Genet's Genealogy: European Minorities and the Ends of the Canon." *Cultural Critique* 6 (spring 1987): 161–186.

———. *Nationalism and Minor Literature: James Clarence Mangan and the Emergence of Irish Cultural Nationalism*. Berkeley: University of California Press, 1987.

Lyotard, Jean-François. *La condition postmoderne*. Paris: Minuit, 1979.

———. *Discours, figure*. Paris: Klincksieck, 1971.

———. *Le postmoderne expliqué aux enfants*. Paris: Galilée, 1986.

———. "Energumen Capitalism." Trans. James Leigh. *Semiotext(e)* 2 (1977): 11–26.

McClary, Susan. *Feminine Endings: Music, Gender, and Sexuality*. Minneapolis: University of Minnesota Press, 1991.

Megill, Allan. *Prophets of Extremity: Nietzsche, Heidegger, Foucault, Derrida*. Berkeley: University of California Press, 1985.

Moynihan, Michael. "Anton LaVey: Shout at the Devil." *Seconds* 27 (1994): 56–60.

———. "Morbid Angel: Heaven Can Wait." *Seconds* 26 (1994): 64–67.

Moynihan, Michael, and Didrik Søderlind. *Lords of Chaos: The Bloody Rise of the Satanic Metal Underground*. Venice, Calif.: Feral House, 1998.

Natoli, Joseph, and Linda Hutcheon, eds. *A Postmodern Reader*. Albany, N.Y.: State University of New York Press, 1993.

Nietzsche, Friedrich. *Untimely Meditations*. Ed. Daniel Breazeale, trans. R. J. Hollingdale. Cambridge: Cambridge University Press, 1997.

Norman, Charles. *Ezra Pound*. New York: Macmillan, 1960.

Paxson, James. "Locating Theory's Next Generation." *Symploke* 3 (winter 1995): 101–118.

Pound, Ezra. *Ezra Pound: Translations*. Intro. by Hugh Kenner. New York: New Directions, 1963.

Pountney, Rosemary. *Theatre of Shadows: Samuel Beckett's Drama 1956–76. From "All that Falls" to "Footfalls" with commentaries on the latest plays*. Gerrards Cross, Buckinghamshire, England: Colin Smythe, 1988.

Rajchman, John. "Foucault's Art of Seeing." *October* 44 (spring 1988), 88–117.

Reizbaum, Marilyn. "Canonical Double Cross: Scottish and Irish Women's Writing." In *Decolonizing Tradition: New Views of Twentieth-Century "British" Literary Canons,* ed. Karen R. Lawrence, 165–190. Urbana: University of Illinois Press, 1992.

———. "The Minor Works of James Joyce." *James Joyce Quarterly* 30 (winter 1993): 177–189.

Renza, Louis A. *"A White Heron" and the Question of Minor Literature*. Madison: University of Wisconsin Press, 1984.

Ricoeur, Paul. "The History of Philosophy and Historicity." In *History and Truth,* trans. Charles A. Kelbley, 63–77. Evanston, Ill.: Northwestern University Press, 1965.

Robinson, Bernard P. "Jonah's Qiqayon Plant." *Zeitschrift für alttestamentliche Wissenschaft* 97 (1985): 390–403.

Rorty, Richard, ed. *The Linguistic Turn: Essays in Philosophical Method*. Chicago: University of Chicago Press, 1967.

———. *Philosophy and the Mirror of Nature*. Princeton, N.J.: Princeton University Press, 1979.

Rosset, Clément. "Sécheresse de Deleuze." *L'Arc* 49, new edition (1980): 89–91.

Samuel, Claude. *Olivier Messiaen: Music and Color. Conversations with Claude Samuel.* Trans. E. Thomas Glasow. Portland, Oreg.: Amadeus Press, 1994.

Sasson, Jack M. *Jonah: A New Translation, with Introduction, Commentary, and Interpretation {The Anchor Bible}.* New York: Doubleday, 1990.

Shapiro, Marc. "The Birth of Death: A Speed Demonology." *Guitar Presents: Speed Demons of Metal* (1993): 6–9, 23, 110–112.

Silverman, Hugh J., and Donn Welton, eds. *Postmodernism and Continental Philosophy.* Albany: State University of New York Press, 1988.

Skinner, Quentin, ed. *The Return of Grand Theory in the Human Sciences.* Cambridge: Cambridge University Press, 1985.

Sophocles. *Oedipus the King, Oedipus at Colonus, Antigone.* Trans. F. Storr. Loeb Classical Library. New York: G. P. Putnam's Sons, 1912.

Spariosu, Mihai. *God of Many Names: Play, Poetry, and Power in Hellenic Thought from Homer to Aristotle.* Durham, N. C.: Duke University Press, 1991.

Straus, Erwin. *The Primary World of Senses. A Vindication of Sensory Experience.* Trans. Jacob Needleman. 2nd ed. New York: Free Press, 1963.

Sutherland, Jon. "The Roots of Evil: Death Becomes Us." *RIP Photo Special Presents: Death Lives* 6 (1994): 4.

Sylvester, David, ed. *The Brutality of Fact: Interviews with Francis Bacon.* 3rd enlarged edition. London: Thames and Hudson, 1987.

Takahashi, Yasunari. "Qu'est-ce qui arrive? Some Structural Comparisons of Beckett's Plays and Noh." In *Samuel Beckett: Humanistic Perspectives,* ed. Morris Beja, S. E. Gontarski, and Pierre Astier, 99–106. Columbus: Ohio State University Press, 1983.

Taylor, Victor E., and Charles E. Winquest. *Encyclopedia of Postmodernism.* London: Routledge, 2001.

Trachtenberg, Stanley, ed. *The Postmodern Moment: A Handbook of Contemporary Innovation in the Arts.* Westport, Conn.: Greenwood, 1985.

Tuohy, Frank. *Yeats: An Illustrated Biography.* New York: New Amsterdam, 1976.

Violanti, Anthony. "Cannibal Corpse Shocks its Way to the Big Time." *Buffalo News,* February 28, 1994, Lifestyles, p. 1.

Walser, Robert. *Running with the Devil: Power, Gender, and Madness in Heavy Metal Music.* Hanover, Mass.: Wesleyan University Press, 1993.

Weinstein, Deena. *Heavy Metal: A Cultural Sociology.* New York: Lexington, 1991.

Williams, Jeffrey. "The Posttheory Generation." *Symploke* 3 (winter 1995): 55–76.

Yeats, William Butler. *The Collected Plays of W. B. Yeats*. London: Macmillan, 1952.

———. *Essays and Introductions*. New York: Macmillan, 1961.

Zappa, Frank. "The Oracle Has It All Psyched Out." *Life* 64 (June 28, 1968): 82–91.

Zeami. *On the Art of the No Drama. The Major Treatises of Zeami*. Trans. J. Thomas Rimer and Yamazaki Masakazu. Princeton, N.J.: Princeton University Press, 1984.

Index

Abrams, M. H., 77
absolute memory, 20–21, 55, 60
action-image, 118, 120
Aeschylus, 151
affection-image, 118, 120
affects, 1–2, 24–25, 76–79
Aion, 67, 74, 96–97, 165n. 6
aleatory point, 27–28
Alice in Wonderland, 26–27
Antigone, 175n. 11, 175n. 14
Antonioni, Michelangelo, 124
aorgic, the, 175n. 12
Aristotle, 45, 150
Artaud, Antonin, 22, 161n. 3

Bach, Johann Sebastian, 97
Bacon, Francis, 20, 38–40, 88
Bamberger, Bernard J., 172n. 2
Barthes, Roland, 36, 163–64n. 9
Baudrillard, Jean, 28–29, 33–34, 162–63n. 1
Beaufret, Jean, 143, 150–55, 175n. 12, 175n. 13
Beckett, Samuel: and boring holes in language, 19–20, 75, 131, 171n. 6; and the *espace quelconque*, 127, 135, 137–38, 140; and language I, language II, and language III, 133–35; and the limits of language, 24–25, 131–32, 138; and minor literature, 69; and pure images, 134–35; and sobriety 10, 92; and stuttering in language, 21, 71; and television plays, 5, 13, 16–17, 133–42; works by: *...but the clouds ...*, 135–39; *Dream of Fair to Middling Women*, 131–32; *Eh Joe*, 130; *Ghost Trio*, 127; *Happy Days*, 130, 171n. 5; *Krapp's Last Tape*, 130; *Murphy*, 133; *Not I*, 130; *Nacht und Träume*, 127; *Ohio Impromptu*, 130; *Quad*, 133–34; *Rockaby*, 130; *That Time*, 130; *Watt*, 133
becoming, 67, 72–80, 84, 90–91, 96, 107–08
becoming-imperceptible, 11, 25, 72–74, 107
becoming-metal, 84, 105, 107–08
becoming-other, 2, 4, 22, 72–73
becoming-woman, 4, 11, 72–73, 106–08, 165n. 9
Beethoven, Ludwig von, 75, 132
Benjamin, Walter, 33
Bensmaïa, Réda, 165n. 8
Bentham, Jeremy, 111
Benton, Glen, 103, 168n. 11
Berg, Alban, 34
Berger, Harris M., 166n. 4
Bergson, Henri, 32, 58, 59, 68, 115–17, 167–68n. 10
black metal music, 165–66n. 1
Blair, Linda 169n. 17
Blanchot, Maurice, 13, 56–57
body without organs, 14, 18, 22, 37, 83, 105–06, 108
Boulez, Pierre, 96–98

Braidotti, Rosi, 165n. 9
Bréhier, Émile, 161n. 2
Bresson, Robert, 123
Brujeria, 104–05, 107
Buchanan, Ian, 165n. 9

Cain, 146–48, 174n. 8
catatonia and rushes, 99
Cézanne, Paul, 75, 132
Challenger, Professor, 26
chaosmos, 1, 6
chromaticism, generalized, 91–92
Chronos, 67, 96–97. *See also* Aion
cinematic signs, 5
Colebrook, Claire, 165n. 9
collective assemblage of enunciation, 66, 71
concept, 1–2, 6, 13, 21–25, 64–65, 67, 162n. 6: and movement of concepts, 22, 25; and paradox, 22. *See also* philosophy as the invention of concepts
conceptual characters, 25
constructionism, 64
Couchot, Edmond, 140, 172n. 10
Crisis, Karyn, 169n. 18
cultural studies, 63, 68, 80–81, 165n. 7

death metal music, 4, 83–108: and gender, 106–08, 169n. 16, 169n. 18; and metal, 89–90; lyrics in, 102–05, 108; musical vocabulary of, 93–95; speed in, 98–102; timbre in, 89, 93; volume in, 88–89
Debussy, Claude, 91
Deleuze, Gilles, works by: *Anti-Oedipus*, 13–14, 18, 22, 30, 32, 35, 63, 65, 105, 162–63n. 2, 163n. 5; *Cinema 1*, 39, 65, 109, 114–19, 126, 167–68n. 10; *Cinema 2*, 23, 39, 109, 114, 118–19, 121–26, 140, 172n. 9, 172n. 10; *Dialogues*, 11, 73, 161–62n. 5, 162n. 6; *Difference and Repetition*, 10–11, 14, 19, 23, 31–32, 34–35, 41, 63–64, 109, 155, 163n. 6, 163n. 8, 164n. 4, 164n. 2, 165n. 6, 167–68n. 10, 170n. 7, 175n. 14, 175n. 15; *L'Épuisé*, 13, 15–17, 19, 23–25, 71, 127, 131–35, 172n. 9; *Essays Critical and Clinical*, 17–18, 20–23, 70–72, 74–79, 109, 138, 154–60, 161n. 3, 175–76n. 16; *The Fold*, 19; *Foucault*, 20–21, 24, 48–49, 51–53, 55–60, 109, 111–13, 126, 163n. 7, 165n. 4, 169–70n. 3, 170n. 4; *Francis Bacon*, 18–20, 23, 38–39, 170n. 8; *Kafka: Toward a Minor Literature*, 10, 37–38, 68, 80, 92, 170n. 9; *The Logic of Sense*, 10, 18, 22, 27, 63, 65, 163n. 8, 164n. 2, 165n. 6, 171–72n. 8; *Negotiations*, 11–15, 18–20, 22, 24, 26, 30, 64–65, 67, 161n. 4, 162n. 6, 165n. 4; *Nietzsche and Philosophy*, 30, 109, 163n. 4, 164n. 4; *Proust and Signs*, 13, 22, 37, 65; *Spinoza: Practical Philosophy*, 165n. 4; *A Thousand Plateaus*, 11, 14, 18, 23, 31–33, 35, 40, 63, 65–67, 70, 73–75, 83, 90–92, 95–96, 99, 106–11, 113, 143–44, 148–50, 162–63n. 2, 163n. 5, 163n. 7, 165n. 4, 165n. 6, 167–68n. 10; *What Is Philosophy?*, 13, 21–22, 24–26, 58, 63, 75–76, 165n. 6

Derrida, Jacques, 64, 163n. 8, 164n. 1, 164n. 2
Descombes, Vincent, 163n. 4
desire, 32–33
despotic, signifying regime of signs, 143, 147. *See also* regime of signs
deterritorialization of the refrain, music as, 90–91
difference, 31–32
DiLeo, Jeffrey R., 164n. 1, 165n. 5
disjunctive synthesis, 22
disjunctive use of the faculties, 23, 31
Duras, Marguerite, 39, 124, 126

effects, 11–12, 22, 25
egg, page as, 14–16, 25
énonçable, and *visible*, 109–10, 112–13, 121, 124–26. *See also* statable and visible in Foucault
espace quelconque, 127, 135, 137–38, 140
Eternal Return, 59, 164n. 4
event, 6, 9–11, 25, 58, 74–75, 77–78, 96
Exorcist, The, 169n. 17

fabulation, 74, 78–80
fanzines, 86–87

Flaubert, Gustave, 123
fold, 3, 20–21, 51–52, 55, 57–58, 60
forces, 49–52
Forster, E. M., 77–78
Foucault, Michel, 3, 5, 20, 28, 31–32, 43–60, 64–65, 67, 109, 111–13, 163n. 3, 163n. 7, 164n. 2, 164n. 3, 164n. 1, 165n. 4, 169–70n. 3: works by: *The Archaeology of Knowledge*, 31, 44; *The Birth of the Clinic*, 112–13; *Death and the Labyrinth*, 55–56; *Discipline and Punish*, 5, 31, 48, 50, 53, 111; *The History of Sexuality, Vol. 1*, 44, 48, 112, 163n. 7; *The History of Sexuality, Vol. 2 (The Use of Pleasure)*, 43–48, 53–55; *Madness and Civilization*, 49, 56–57, 112; *The Order of Things*, 113
free indirect speech, 123
functionalists, Deleuze and Guattari as, 64, 164–65n. 3

gender and death metal music, 106–08, 169n. 16, 169n. 18
Genet, Jacqueline, 171n. 4
Glass, Philip, 97
Godard, Jean-Luc, 39, 139
Grand Theory, 63, 81, 164n. 1
Griggers, Camilla, 165n. 9
Grosz, Elizabeth, 165n. 9
Guattari, Félix, 161n.1, 163n. 2

Hale, Mark, 165–66n. 1
Hardt, Michael, 163n. 5
Harrell, Jack, 166n. 4
Headbanger's Ball, 85–86
Hegel, Georg Wilhelm Friedrich, 30
Heidegger, Martin, 28, 30, 56, 60, 64, 150
Hicks, D. Emily, 165n. 7
Hjelmslev, Louis, 110, 169n. 2
hodological space, 119
Hölderlin, Friedrich, 6, 150–56, 158, 160, 175n. 11, 175n. 12, 175n. 13, 175n. 14
Holland, Eugene, 32–33
Homan, Sidney, 171n. 7
Houdini, Harry, 15, 25
Hoy, David Couzens, 31, 163n. 3
Hume, David, 19, 59, 68

Hutcheon, Linda, 28
Huyssen, Andreas, 36, 38

image, 5, 134–42
immedia, 140
immobile cut, 115, 120
impulse-image, 118
incorporeal transformation, 66, 110–11, 171–72n. 8
indefinite postponement, 156–58
insomnia, 13–14, 22–23, 161n. 3
intensities, 34–36

Jameson, Fredric, 28–29, 33, 35–36, 40, 162–63n. 1
Je fêlé (split I/Self), 155, 159–60
Jewett, Sarah Orne, 69
Jonah, 6, 144–49, 154, 159–60, 172–73n. 3, 173n. 4, 173n. 5, 173–74n. 6, 174n. 7, 174n. 8, 174n. 9
joy, 9–10
Joyce, James, 1, 69
judgment, 156–60, 175–76n. 16

Kafka, Franz, 10–11, 13, 15, 37–40, 68–70, 74–75, 92, 152, 156–57, 161n. 3
Kant, Immanuel, 6, 19–20, 153–56, 158–59, 163n. 6
Kaplan, Caren 70
Kleist, Heinrich von, 22, 99
Kristeva, Julia, 66

LaVey, Anton Szandor, 103, 168n. 12, 168n. 13
law, in Kant and Kafka, 156–58
Lawrence, D. H., 161n. 3, 175–76n. 16
Lawrence, T. E., 77–79, 172n. 1
Leibniz, Gottfried Wilhelm von, 59, 120
Leiris, Michel, 20, 55–56
lekton, 171–72n. 8
Lewin, Kurt, 119
Lindon, Jérôme, 143–49, 154, 156, 159–60, 172–73n. 3, 173n. 5, 174n. 7, 174n. 9
line of flight, 15–17, 25
lines of continuous variation, 71–73, 75

Lloyd, David, 165n. 7, 165n. 8
Luca, Gherasim, 21, 71
Lyotard, Jean-François, 28–30, 39, 162–63n. 1, 169n. 1

machinic assemblages (social technological machines), 66, 71–73
McClary, Susan, 106
Megill, Allan, 64
Melville, Herman, 74
memory and forgetting, 56–59
Messiaen, Olivier, 90–91, 96–97, 167n. 8
meter. *See* rhythm and meter
Metz, Christian, 114
Miller, Henry, 11
mimesis, 43–44, 47, 60, 164n. 1
minor literature, 3–4, 37–38, 68–76, 80, 165n. 7, 170n. 9
minor writing, 76–80
minorization of language, 21–22, 69
mobile cut, 115–16, 122
Moraru, Christian, 164n. 1, 165n. 5
mot d'ordre, 169–70n. 3
movement. *See* speed, movement and movement-image, 116–23
Moynihan, Michael, 165–66n. 1
Mozart, Wolfgang Amadeus, 89, 97

Negri, Antonio, 163n. 5
Nietzsche, Friedrich, 2, 28, 30–31, 41, 44, 48, 59–60, 64, 67–68, 77, 156–57, 161n. 3, 164n. 2, 175n. 12, 175–76n. 16. *See also* Eternal Return; judgment; untimely, the
Noah, 145, 147–48, 172–73n. 3
Noh drama, 5, 127–31, 137, 141–42, 171n. 2, 171n. 3, 171n. 4
nomadic, countersignifying regime of signs, 172n. 1. *See also* regime of signs
nonorganic life, 9
nonpulsed time, 96

Oedipus, 149–54, 156, 158, 160, 175n. 14
open whole, 65, 115, 120. *See also* Whole
opsign, 5, 119–20
Outside, 3, 6, 23, 51–52, 55–60

Paik, Nam June, 139, 172n. 10
Panopticon, 5, 51, 111–12
passional, postsignifying regime of signs, 143, 149, 156, 159. *See also* regime of signs
Paxson, James, 164n. 1
peaks of the present, 120
perception-image, 117–18, 120
percepts, 1–2, 24–25, 76–80
philosophy as the invention of concepts, 1, 6, 64–65, 67, 162n. 6, 162n. 7
plane of consistency, 66, 76, 95–96
Plato, 34
postmodernism, 2–3, 27–41, 162–63n. 1, 163n. 2, 163n. 3, 163–64n. 9: and metanarratives, 29–30; and poststructuralism, 36; and schizophrenia, 35–36; and simulation, 33–34; and the unthought, 30–33
poststructuralism, 36, 63–64, 66, 68, 164n. 2
Pound, Ezra, 128, 171n. 1
power of the false, 120
problem, concept of, 162n. 6, 165n. 6. *See also* philosophy as the invention of concepts
Prokofiev, Sergei, 97
Proust, Marcel, 13, 17–18, 22, 32, 37, 39–40

qîqayôn plant, 146, 174n. 8

Rabinow, Paul, 169–70n. 3
race and death metal music, 168n. 14
Rajchman, John, 113
reflection-image, 118
refrain, 14–15, 90–91, 165n. 4
regime of light, 113, 125–26
regime of signs, 5, 66, 71–73, 111–12, 125–26, 143, 147–49, 156, 159–60. *See also* despotic, signifying regime of signs; nomadic, countersignifying regime of signs; passional, postsignifying regime of signs
Reizbaum, Marilyn, 165n. 7, 165n. 9
relation-image, 118
Rembrandt, Harmensz van Rijn, 75, 132

Renza, Louis A., 69–70
resistance and power, 53–54, 59–60
Resnais, Alain, 119
rhythm, and meter, 96–98
Ricoeur, Paul, 66
Robbe-Grillet, Alain, 119
Robinson, Bernard P., 174n. 8
Rohmer, Eric, 123
Rorty, Richard, 65
Rossellini, Roberto, 126
Rosset, Clément, 10, 12
Roussel, Raymond, 55–56

Sacher-Masoch, Leopold von, 18
Sasson, Jack M., 173n. 4, 173n.5, 173–74n. 6, 174n. 7
Satanism, 103, 105, 108, 165–66n. 1, 168n. 11, 168n. 12, 168n. 13, 169n. 17
scapegoat, 144, 147–50
schizophrenia, 35–36
Schubert, Franz, 75, 132
Schumann, Robert, 91
Self: as fold, 3, 6; in ancient Greece, 44–47, 52
semiosis, 4, 109–26
sensation, 75–76
sense, 171–72n. 8
sensorimotor schema, 119–20, 126
Sepultura, 103–04, 107
set, 115–16
Shapiro, Marc, 166n. 4
Shaw, George Bernard, 130
sheets of the past, 120
signs, 65, 114–20, 170n. 5
simulacra and simulation, 33–34, 163n. 8
singular points, 50, 55
Sinister, "Sadistic Intention," 100–02
Skinner, Quentin, 164n. 1
Slayer, 167n. 9
Søderlind, Didrik, 165–66n. 1
Sophocles, 6, 149–54
sound image, 170n. 6
Spariosu, Mihai, 164n. 1
speed: movement and, 167–68n. 10; quantitative and qualitative, 84, 95–96, 99
Spinoza, Baruch, 16–20, 59, 68, 165n. 4

statable and visible in Foucault, 48–49, 54–55. *See also énonçable* and *visible*
statement, 110, 112, 169–70n. 3
Stoics, 19, 26, 68, 171–72n. 8
Straub, Jean-Marie, and Danièle Huillet, 39, 124, 126
Straus, Erwin, 76
style, 9–26: and Deleuze's vocabulary, 12; and sobriety, 10–11; and syntax, 2, 12–13, 23; as stuttering in language, 2, 21–25, 70–72, 74–75; as way of living, 9
Sutherland, Jon, 84, 166n. 4
Syberberg, Hans Jürgen, 126

Takahashi, Yasuanari, 130–31, 137
television, 139–41, 172n. 9
thought and problematizations in Foucault, 54
time: and the "between-time," 3, 6, 58; and the event, 6, 58; pure and empty form of, 153, 158–59. *See also* absolute memory; Aion; Chronos; Eternal Return; event; memory and forgetting; rhythm and meter; time-image; untimely, the
time-image, 119–20
transcendental empiricism, 23, 31, 170n. 7
Tristan and Iseult, 57
truth, 64

untimely, the, 2–3, 41, 67–68, 75, 165n. 6

Van Velde, Bran, 75, 132
Velázquez, Diego Rodriguez de Silva y, 113
Vincent, David, 85, 168n. 13
Visions and Auditions, 4, 23–24, 75–76, 78–80, 138
vitalism, 9

Wagner, Jeremy, 84
Walser, Robert, 83, 85–86, 106, 166n. 3, 166n. 4, 168n. 15
Weinstein, Deena, 94, 102, 166n. 4, 166n. 5, 166–67n. 6
Wenders, Wim, 124

Whole, 115, 123. *See also* open whole
Williams, Jeffrey, 164n. 1
writing, 9

Yeats, William Butler: and *At the Hawk's Well*, 129–31, 142, 171n. 4; and Noh drama, 5, 128–29, 171n. 2, 171n. 3; and "The Tower," 136–39

Yom Kippur, 144–45, 172n. 2, 172–73n. 3

Zappa, Frank, 87–88
Zeami, 141–42

www.ingramcontent.com/pod-product-compliance
Lightning Source LLC
Chambersburg PA
CBHW020737230426
43665CB00009B/467